This enormously helpful book catalogues all the many questions that ordinary people ask about love, marriage, family, and sexuality, providing utterly clear, blessedly brief, right-on-target answers, straight from the documents of the church. If you think making a book like this is easy, you are wrong. If you think it would have to be boring, you are wrong again. Bartel and Grabowski's editorial judgment is pitch-perfect, and the result is a pleasure to read.

—J. Budziszewski, Departments of Government
and Philosophy, University of Texas, author of
On the Meaning of Sex

We are facing a profound crisis in the future of family life. Now is the time for the church to show a better way and not just talk a better game. Rarely do we have such clear moments of conflict in which the Catholic Way is vividly distinct from the way of the world. But we need to beef up our aspirations for a flourishing family life with the practical, solid teaching of the church. Sarah Bartel and John Grabowski do just that. They have composed *A Catechism for Family Life.* "Composed" is the right word because the book is beautifully orchestrated and attention paid to all the flourishes and motifs of the Catholic family. How to choose marriage and a particular spouse? What about my parents' attitude toward my beloved? How to prepare for the wedding day? What do wedding vows mean? How many children? What does the church teach about breastfeeding? How to make ends meet? How to handle physical abuse and infidelity? How does living an authentic Catholic family life contribute to the common good of society? This volume is rich in insight, practical in content, and inspirational in style. I have wanted a work like this since I returned to the Catholic Church and plan to urge its use among my listeners and in all the parishes in which I speak.

—Al Kresta, *Kresta in the Afternoon*, Ave Maria Radio

A Catechism for Family Life will be helpful to students, dating/engaged couples, and married couples, as well as being useful in high school and college courses, from marriage prep to ongoing enrichment and adult faith formation opportunities. It will serve as a handy and trustworthy resource and reference for catechists, teachers, professors, and pastoral leaders in the field of marriage and family ministry.

—Andrew Lichtenwalner, Archdiocese of Atlanta

A Catechism for Family Life is an absolutely essential guide for anyone involved in Catholic teaching on marriage and family. This much-needed resource gathers together what can seem to many of us like daunting information from encyclicals, exhortations, and other church documents into a user-friendly volume. Highly recommended!

—Gregory Popcak, Founder and Director of CatholicCounselors.com

A Catechism for Family Life is the perfect resource for anyone facing tough questions about what the Catholic Church teaches and why. As a mother, a blogger, a public speaker, the leader of a Catholic homeschool group, a parent at a brick and mortar Catholic school, and a person who stands in line at Target surrounded by many small children, I have often been asked to explain or defend the church's position on contraception, sterilization, divorce, pornography, abuse, education, parenting, and/or smart phones.

Sarah Bartel and John S. Grabowski have made answering those questions much more manageable. Quotes from popes, saints, and church documents, primary sources including audiences, encyclicals, exhortations, and the *Catechism of the Catholic Church* will help all of us in the New Evangelization to share with confidence and compassion the Truth and Beauty of our church's positions on modern challenges to family life.

> —Kendra Tierney, mother of nine, author of *The Catholic All Year Compendium: Liturgical Living for Real Life,* and blogger at CatholicAllYear.com

Sarah Bartel and John Grabowski have compiled a valuable treasury of quotes for reflection and discernment on almost every aspect of married life. This book is the perfect resource for couples, clergy, and leaders in marriage and family formation!

> —Mary Rose Verret, Executive Director, Witness to Love

A CATECHISM FOR

Family Life

A CATECHISM FOR
Family Life

INSIGHTS FROM CATHOLIC TEACHING ON LOVE, MARRIAGE, SEX, AND PARENTING

EDITED BY SARAH BARTEL AND
JOHN S. GRABOWSKI

THE CATHOLIC UNIVERSITY OF AMERICA PRESS
Washington, D.C.

The paper used in this publication meets the minimum requirements of American National Standards for Information Science—Permanence of Paper for Printed Library Materials, ANSI Z39.48-1984.

∞

Library of Congress Cataloging-in-Publication Data
Names: Bartel, Sarah Smith, editor.
Title: A catechism for family life : insights from Catholic teaching on love, marriage, sex, and parenting / edited by Sarah Bartel and John S. Grabowski.
Description: Washington, D.C. : The Catholic University of America Press, 2018. | Includes bibliographical references (p.) and index.
Identifiers: LCCN 2018018728 | ISBN 9780813231235 (pbk. : alk. paper)
Subjects: LCSH: Families—Religious aspects—Catholic Church—Miscellanea. | Love—Religious aspects—Catholic Church—Miscellanea. | Sex—Religious aspects—Catholic Church—Miscellanea. | Marriage—Religious aspects—Catholic Church—Miscellanea. | Parenting—Religious aspects—Catholic Church—Miscellanea. | Catholic Church—Doctrines—Miscellanea.
Classification: LCC BX2351 .C276 2018 | DDC 261.8/35088282—dc23
LC record available at https://lccn.loc.gov/2018018728

We dedicate this book to St. Joseph
and the Holy Family

Contents

2. Finding Mr. or Mrs. Right: Marriage as Vocational Discernment 33

3. Tying the Knot: Engagement, Marriage Prep, and the Wedding 59

4. Then Come Kids: Having and Raising Children 91

5. Making "Ends" Meet: Balancing Work, Family, and Finances   141

FAMILY AND WORK ROLES

WEALTH AND FAMILY HEALTH

6. When the Going Gets Tough: Difficult Situations and Hard Questions 175

8. The Good News about the Family 237

Resources for Further Reading 251

Index 259

Introduction

Marriage and family life are facing what Pope Francis calls a "profound cultural crisis."[1] Unfortunately, many Catholics are unclear about church teaching in this area. Even if they confidently understand it themselves, or at least have a sense of it, they may not know how to articulate it to others or how to apply it to specific real-life situations. The great renaissance in the theology of marriage and family that has been blossoming in the church over the last century remains largely a buried treasure for many, hidden in lengthy church documents that can seem intimidating. However, these beautiful teachings were not meant to remain hidden; they have the power to change the world and heal the heart of the human person. This book gathers together pearls of church teaching on marriage, sexuality, and family life, as well as related Catholic social teaching, and places them in your hands in one convenient, organized, and user-friendly volume.

Mainstream media coverage of church events and church teaching can lead to confusing misunderstandings about Catholic ethics. The Catholic Church proposes a rich, detailed, coherent, and positive vision of the meaning of marriage, family, and sexuality, one that is integrated, comprehensive, and uplifting. But digging for the relevant teaching to address specific questions in this area is not always an easy

1. Pope Francis, *Evangelii gaudium*, 66.

task. We have simplified this task for you by organizing relevant teachings by topic in a question-and-answer format.

Whether you are a priest, parent, or professor, a nun, brother, or mother, whether you prepare couples for marriage at your parish or direct a diocesan family life office, you have faced real-life questions about what the church teaches about sex, marriage, and family. Questions about marriage are important for women and men called to marriage at every stage as well, whether you are single, engaged, a newlywed, or a seasoned spouse. This work will assist Catholics (and those who love them!) in finding relevant teaching to address the challenging ethical, religious, and moral questions they face.

Questions such as:

"Can we get married on the beach?"

"How do I choose a husband or wife?"

"How do I know when my significant other and I are ready to get married?"

"What is the problem with living together without being married?"

"What should I do if my child or family member says he or she is same-sex attracted?"

"Aren't natural family planning and contraception basically the same?"

"Should we pray together as a family? How? What if my kids are crazy, wild toddlers, disaffected teens, or away at sports and activities all the time?"

"Should we get rid of our TV?"

"What is my place in the church now that I am a widow?"

Following each question, we have provided pertinent excerpts from church statements. In some cases, the citations answer the question directly. In other cases, they provide the principles that you can use as you discern the best way to answer the question. Where the church has offered precise answers, we have provided them. Where the church has left questions open, we have endeavored to show that as well. As much as possible, we have simply let the documents speak for themselves, quoting directly from them without adding our own interpretation. In a few rare cases we have added a brief editorial comment for clarification. This way, we allow the fullness of the church's teaching to take center stage, unfiltered by any personal bias on our part. We recognize that biases may have crept in despite our efforts, whether in the choice and wording of questions or in the selection of responses. We welcome reader feedback.

After each question, the quotations that follow are arranged in reverse chronological order (newest first), with exceptions when a particularly powerful or relevant older quote seemed worthy of priority placement, as in the case of relevant biblical texts. Some quotations were relevant to more than one question; we repeated them where it made sense to do so.

A young man or woman growing up and thinking about marriage will face many obstacles, whether he or she realizes it or not. From cultural challenges to the value and meaning of marriage to common attitudes that discourage or relativize commitment to the practical difficulties of choosing a spouse or feeling adequately prepared, these topics form the beginning chapters of the book. The organization of topics continues this lifespan-inspired trajectory with practical and spiritual questions about engagement and the wedding. Having children, work-life balance, and special challenges form the following chapters. We conclude by looking more in-depth at the nature of marriage and at praying together in the domestic church and outward at the mission of marriage and family to the world.

HOW TO USE THIS BOOK IN A PROCESS OF MORAL DECISION-MAKING

When facing a difficult question in marriage and family life, we recommend using this book as part of a process of moral discernment by following these five steps:

1. First, pray for guidance and the light of the Holy Spirit. Ask for help to see the goods and values at work in the situation you're facing, and to recognize which virtues are required of you to ask in the most Christ-like manner.

2. Next, locate the question that matches your situation most closely.

3. Read the quotations and meditate on them.

4. If necessary, research further by reading more of the documents that contain the quotations.

5. If you are still uncertain, keep praying and studying and seek the counsel of a trusted pastor or spiritual director. Don't make a decision and act if you are uncertain, unless you have to do so.

6. Apply the principles or answers to your dilemma. Pray and draw on the sacraments to seek grace to help you act virtuously as you carry out your decision.

Facing the difficult questions of marriage and family life in the light of our Catholic faith can open an opportunity for ongoing spiritual growth in holiness and discipleship. It can also draw you closer to your spouse and other members of your family as you seek God's will together. Rather than just following these steps as a wooden exercise, the process of prayer and reflection can invite you to internalize the wisdom of the church's teaching and personally integrate it into your own life.

WHY LISTEN TO WHAT THE CHURCH SAYS? (OR: WHAT
IS THE CHURCH DOING IN THE BEDROOM?)

Grappling with ethical questions in the light of our faith helps us form good consciences. We're human: we're tempted to sin, to follow negative influences, and to prefer our own judgements and reject authoritative teaching (concupiscence, anyone?).

Learning what the church teachings are about particular issues and in specific situations is a great help for correct conscience formation. As St. John Paul II wrote in *Veritatis splendor*, para. 64:

> In forming their consciences the Christian faithful must give careful attention to the sacred and certain teaching of the Church. For the Catholic Church is by the will of Christ the teacher of truth. Her charge is to announce and teach authentically that truth which is Christ, and at the same time with her authority to declare and confirm the principles of the moral order which derive from the human nature itself.

Yet, to know "what is the will of God, what is good and acceptable and perfect," in marriage and family life, as well as in every area of life, we must "be transformed by the renewal of our mind," as St. Paul reminds us in Romans 12:12. We must learn God's law, appreciate the good in it, and make it second nature in ourselves through developing virtue. The church is at the service of conscience. Rather than imposing ethical judgments and onerous burdens, obligations, or restrictions, the moral teachings of the church actually free us for the truth. They free us to live in the truth about the good of the human person and to enjoy the happiness that God desires for us his beloved children.

Like the structure of a sonnet, which defines certain parameters within which the poet's creativity organizes an orderly beauty, the parameters of the church's teachings about sexuality, marriage, family life, and social justice designate and protect the dignity of authentic human love. This frees love to flourish in all the true beauty intended for it by the Creator. So why is "the church in the bedroom"? Because the bedroom is a sanctuary: a protected, sacred space dedicated for a noble and holy purpose. Authentic love requires nothing less than total integrity, which these moral teachings protect. The goal of the moral and spiritual life is to form ourselves for beatitude, for the happiness that corresponds with living well and living in friendship with God.

HOW TO USE THIS BOOK

You can use this book in a variety of ways. You can look up a specific question, read entire chapters individually, or read it straight through. (If you've been assigned it in a course, read whatever your instructor requires, of course.) As we mention in the previous description of the process of discernment, some of the quotations may spark your interest in reading more of the documents excerpted.

We gathered the questions through a process of consultation with Dr. Andrew Lichtenwalner, executive director of the Secretariat for Laity, Marriage, Family Life, and Youth at the United States Conference of Catholic Bishops; John Martino, acquisitions editor at the Catholic University of America Press; and from our own experience teaching university students and other adult learners, working with engaged couples, teaching deacons and their wives, and serving parish and diocesan marriage and family life programs. And we drew from our own experience as married laypeople, spouses, and parents. We recalled questions from our own family members and friends and the audiences to whom we have spoken. Dr. John Grabowski was invited to Rome by Pope Francis for the 2015 Synod on the Family and brought questions that were discussed at that historic meeting. Dr. Sarah Bartel works from home as a consultant for marriage and family life for the Archdiocese of Seattle, while raising her four children. In this way she is privileged to hear questions from the trenches, both through mom's groups and park playdates and through queries from pastoral associates and individuals who contact the chancery.

BACKGROUND, ACKNOWLEDGMENTS, AND TRANSLATION

Having compiled these questions, the authors found passages relevant to these questions by researching church documents on marriage and family, primarily from the past one hundred years. These sources include sacred scripture, papal audiences, encyclicals, apostolic exhortations, homilies and addresses, Vatican II documents, and the *Catechism of the Catholic Church*. We've even included some papal interviews and homilies, statements by dicasteries and curial bodies such as the Pontifical Council for the Family, and statements from the United States Conference of Catholic Bishops. While these do not have the same weight as more formal documents of the magisterium, they still give insight into the mind of the church on the questions at hand.

The inspiration from this book came from *A Catechesis for Business: Tough Ethical Questions and Insights from Catholic Teaching*, edited by Andrew V. Abela and Joseph E. Capizzi (now in its second edition). The question-and-answer approach they developed struck a chord with business leaders and others interested in addressing issues in business ethics in the light of the wisdom of the church. We have followed the format and style of that book in this present work, hoping to offer the same ease of access to church teaching in the challenging questions of marriage and family life. We hope that, like that book, this one will find its way into courses. In marriage and family, it's easier to look ahead and start off with a good plan for one's life than to try to pick up the pieces later on.

Translations from most papal and conciliar documents are the Vatican's official translations, which can be found at www.vatican.va. Where noted, translations from St. John Paul II's catechesis on Genesis, now commonly referred to as the theology of the body, are taken from Michael Waldstein's critical edition of *Man and Woman He Created Them: A Theology of the Body*. We thank Pauline Books and Media for their kind permission. Quotations are identified by document and paragraph number. We used the official English translation of the *Catechism of the Catholic Church*'s second edition, known as the *Editio typica*. Biblical citations are taken from NABRE.

The authors wish to thank John Martino at CUA Press for his inspiration and guidance with this project. We also offer heartfelt thanks to our patient and loving spouses. Nathan Bartel did much more than his fair share of the dishes while Sarah worked on this project. Claire Grabowski exercised patience bordering on heroic when faced with the claims this project made on John's time. We give many thanks to our precious children and grandchildren, who brighten our lives with the joy of family life every day. And, always and everywhere, we give thanks and praise to Jesus Christ, to the Holy Spirit, and to God the Father, "from whom every family in heaven and on earth is named" (Eph 3:15).

A CATECHISM FOR

Family Life

CHAPTER 1

Current Challenges and Timeless Truths

The questions in this chapter deal with the Gospel of the Family (what is it?), the challenges facing marriage and family life in society today from consumerism, individualism, and gender ideology, and the basic truths of church teaching on marriage as instituted by God between man and woman to sacramentally manifest Christ's spousal union with his bride, the church.

LIGHTS AND SHADOWS

———— 1 ————

What are some of the key challenges facing marriage and family today?

It is a fact that progressively fewer people are getting married; this is a fact: young people don't want to get married. In many countries the number of separations is instead increasing while the number of children decreases. The difficulty of staying together—both as a couple and as a family—leads to bonds being broken with ever increasing frequency and swiftness, and the children themselves are the first to suffer the consequences. Let us consider that the first victims, the most important victims, the victims who suffer the most in a separation are the children.

—Francis, General Audience, April 29, 2015

The family is experiencing a profound cultural crisis, as are all communities and social bonds. In the case of the family, the weakening of these bonds is particularly serious because the family is the fundamental cell of society, where we learn to live with others despite our differences and to belong to one another; it is also the place where parents pass on the faith to their children. Marriage now tends to be viewed as a form of mere emotional satisfaction that can be constructed in any way or modified at will. But the indispensable contribution of marriage to society transcends the feelings and momentary needs of the couple. As the French bishops have taught, it is not born "of loving sentiment, ephemeral by definition, but from the depth of the obligation assumed by the spouses who accept to enter a total communion of life."

—Francis, *Evangelii gaudium*, 66 (quoting the French Bishops' Conference, Conseil Famille et Société, *Élargir le mariage aux personnes de même sexe? Ouvrons le débat!*, 2012)

Signs are not lacking of a disturbing degradation of some fundamental values: a mistaken theoretical and practical concept of the independence of the spouses in relation to each other; serious misconceptions regarding the relationship of authority between parents and children; the concrete difficulties that the family itself experiences in the transmission of values; the growing number of divorces; the scourge of abortion; the ever more frequent recourse to sterilization; the appearance of a truly contraceptive mentality ... in the countries of the so-called Third World, families often lack both the means necessary for survival, such as food, work, housing, and medicine, and the most elementary freedoms.

—John Paul II, *Familiaris consortio,* 6

Yet not only do We, looking with paternal eye on the universal world from this Apostolic See as from a watch-tower, but you, also, Venerable Brethren, see, and seeing deeply grieve with Us that a great number of men, forgetful of that divine work of redemption, either entirely ignore or shamelessly deny the great sanctity of Christian wedlock, or relying on the false principles of a new and utterly perverse morality, too often trample it under foot.

—Pius XI, *Casti connubii,* 3

For now, alas, not secretly nor under cover, but openly, with all sense of shame put aside, ... the sanctity of marriage is trampled upon and derided; divorce, adultery, all the basest vices either are extolled or at least are depicted in such colors as to appear to be free of all reproach and infamy.

—Pius XI, *Casti connubii,* 45

————— 2 —————

What currents of modern society are driving this "breakdown" of marriage and the family?

Should you feel from childhood that marriage is a "temporary" bond, unconsciously it will be so for you. In fact, many young people are led to reject the very plan of an irrevocable bond and of a lasting family. I believe that we must reflect very seriously on why so many young people "don't feel like" getting married. There is a culture of the provisional … everything is provisional, it seems there is nothing definitive.

This matter of young people not wanting to marry is one of the emerging concerns of today: why aren't young people getting married? Why is it that they frequently prefer cohabitation and "limited responsibility"? Why is that many—even among the baptized—have little trust in marriage and in the family? If we want young people to be able to find the right road to follow, it is important to try to understand this. Why do they have no trust in the family?

—Francis, General Audience, April 29, 2015

On the other hand, "equal consideration needs to be given to the growing danger represented by an extreme individualism which weakens family bonds and ends up considering each member of the family as an isolated unit, leading in some cases to the idea that one's personality is shaped by his or her desires, which are considered absolute." "The tensions created by an overly individualistic culture, caught up with possessions and pleasures, leads to intolerance and hostility in families." Here I would also include today's fast pace of life, stress and the organization of society and labor, since all these are cultural factors which militate against permanent decisions. We also encounter widespread uncertainty and ambiguity. For example, we rightly value a personalism that opts for authenticity as opposed to mere conformity. While this can favor spontaneity and a better use of people's talents, if misdirected it can foster attitudes of constant suspicion, fear of commitment, self-centeredness and arrogance. Freedom of choice makes it possible to plan our lives and to make the most of ourselves. Yet if this freedom lacks noble goals or personal discipline, it degenerates into an inability to give oneself generously to others. Indeed, in many countries where the number of marriages is decreasing, more and more people are choosing to live alone or simply to spend time together without cohabiting. We can also point to a praiseworthy concern for justice; but if misunderstood, this can turn citizens into clients interested solely in the provision of services.

—Francis, *Amoris laetitia*, 33 (quoting the *Relatio synodi* of the 2014 Synod on the Family, 5; and the Final Report of the 2015 Synod on the Family, 8)

The individualism of our postmodern and globalized era favors a lifestyle which weakens the development and stability of personal relationships and distorts family bonds. Pastoral activity needs to bring out more clearly the fact that our relationship with the Father demands and encourages a communion which heals, promotes and reinforces interpersonal bonds. In our world, especially in some countries, different forms of war and conflict are re-emerging, yet we Christians remain steadfast in our intention to respect others, to heal wounds, to build bridges, to strengthen relationships and to "bear one another's burdens" (Gal 6:2). Today too, various associations for the defense of rights and the pursuit of noble goals are being founded. This is a sign of the desire of many people to contribute to social and cultural progress.

—Francis, *Evangelii gaudium*, 67

It is important to ask the deep reasons why contemporary culture is witnessing a crisis in marriage, both in its religious and civil dimensions, and the attempt to gain recognition and equivalency for *de facto* unions. In this way, unstable situations, which are defined more by their negative aspect (the omission of marriage) than by their positive characteristics, seem to be on a level similar to marriage. In fact, all these situations are consolidated in different kinds of relations, but all are in contrast with a real and full reciprocal self-giving that is stable and recognized socially. In a context of privatization of love and the elimination of the institutional character of marriage, the complexity of the economic, sociological and psychological reasons suggests the need to delve into the ideological and cultural background on which the phenomenon of *de facto* unions, as we know it today, has been progressively growing and becoming affirmed.

The progressive decrease in the number of marriages and families recognized as such by the laws of different States, and the increase in some countries in the number of unmarried couples who are living together cannot be explained adequately as an isolated and spontaneous cultural movement. It seems to be a response to the historical changes in societies in the contemporary cultural moment that some authors describe as "post-modernism."

—Pontifical Council for the Family, *Family, Marriage, and "De Facto" Unions*, 7

In the richer countries, on the contrary, excessive prosperity and the consumer mentality, paradoxically joined to a certain anguish and uncertainty about the future, deprive married couples of the generosity and courage needed for raising up new human life: thus life is often perceived not as a blessing, but as a danger from which to defend oneself.

—John Paul II, *Familiaris consortio*, 6

—— 3 ——

Isn't cost also a big factor? I know people who
say they would marry, but it's either too expensive or
financially disadvantageous.

In some countries, many young persons "postpone a wedding for economic reasons, work or study. Some do so for other reasons, such as
the influence of ideologies which devalue marriage and family, the desire to avoid the failures of other couples, the fear of something they
consider too important and sacred, the social opportunities and economic benefits associated with simply living together, a purely emotional and romantic conception of love, the fear of losing their freedom
and independence, and the rejection of something conceived as purely
institutional and bureaucratic."

—Francis, *Amoris laetitia*, 40 (citing the Final Report of the 2015
Synod on the Family, 29)

"Simply to live together is often a choice based on a general attitude opposed to anything institutional or definitive; it can also be done while
awaiting more security in life (a steady job and steady income). In some
countries, *de facto* unions are very numerous, not only because of a rejection of values concerning the family and matrimony, but primarily
because celebrating a marriage is considered too expensive in the social
circumstances. As a result, material poverty drives people into *de facto*
unions." Whatever the case, "all these situations require a constructive
response seeking to transform them into opportunities that can lead to
the full reality of marriage and family in conformity with the Gospel.
These couples need to be welcomed and guided patiently and discreetly." That is how Jesus treated the Samaritan woman (cf. Jn 4:1–26): he
addressed her desire for true love, in order to free her from the darkness
in her life and to bring her to the full joy of the Gospel.

—Francis, *Amoris laetitia*, 294 (citing the *Relatio synodi* of the 2014
Synod on the Family, 42)

—— 4 ——

What contemporary ideologies are exacerbating these problems?

In Europe, America, Latin America, Africa, and in some countries of Asia, there are genuine forms of ideological colonization taking place. And one of these—I will call it clearly by its name—is [the ideology of] "gender." Today children—children!—are taught in school that everyone can choose his or her sex. Why are they teaching this? Because the books are provided by the persons and institutions that give you money. These forms of ideological colonization are also supported by influential countries. And this is terrible!

—Francis, Address to Polish Bishops in Krakow, July 27, 2016

The angel of the Lord revealed to Joseph the dangers which threatened Jesus and Mary, forcing them to flee to Egypt and then to settle in Nazareth. So too, in our time, God calls upon us to recognize the dangers threatening our own families and to protect them from harm. Let us be on guard against colonization by new ideologies. There are forms of ideological colonization which are out to destroy the family.

—Francis, Address to Meeting with Families in Manila, January 16, 2016

Yet another challenge is posed by the various forms of an ideology of gender that "denies the difference and reciprocity in nature of a man and a woman and envisages a society without sexual differences, thereby eliminating the anthropological basis of the family. This ideology leads to educational programs and legislative enactments that promote a personal identity and emotional intimacy radically separated from the biological difference between male and female. Consequently, human identity becomes the choice of the individual, one which can also change over time." It is a source of concern that some ideologies of this sort, which seek to respond to what are at times understandable aspirations, manage to assert themselves as absolute and unquestionable, even dictating how children should be raised. It needs to be emphasized that "biological sex and the socio-cultural role of sex (gender) can be distinguished but not separated."

—Francis, *Amoris laetitia*, 56 (citing the Final Report of the 2015 Synod on the Family, 8 and 58)

The Chief Rabbi of France, Gilles Bernheim, has shown in a very detailed and profoundly moving study that the attack we are currently experiencing on the true structure of the family, made up of father, mother, and child, goes much deeper. While up to now we regarded a false understanding of the nature of human freedom as one cause of the crisis of the family, it is now becoming clear that the very notion of being—of what being human really means—is being called into question. He quotes the famous saying of Simone de Beauvoir: "one is not born a woman, one becomes so" (*on ne naît pas femme, on le devient*). These words lay the foundation for what is put forward today under the term "gender" as a new philosophy of sexuality. According to this philosophy, sex is no longer a given element of nature, that man has to accept and personally make sense of: it is a social role that we choose for ourselves, while in the past it was chosen for us by society.... The words of the creation account: "male and female he created them" (Gn 1:27) no longer apply. No, what applies now is this: it was not God who created them male and female—hitherto society did this, now we decide for ourselves. Man and woman as created realities, as the nature of the human being, no longer exist.... But if there is no pre-ordained duality of man and woman in creation, then neither is the family any longer a reality established by creation. Likewise, the child has lost the place he had occupied hitherto and the dignity pertaining to him. Bernheim shows that now, perforce, from being a subject of rights, the child has become an object to which people have a right and which they have a

right to obtain. When the freedom to be creative becomes the freedom
to create oneself, then necessarily the Maker himself is denied and ultimately man too is stripped of his dignity as a creature of God, as the
image of God at the core of his being. The defense of the family is about
man himself. And it becomes clear that when God is denied, human
dignity also disappears. Whoever defends God is defending man.

—Benedict XVI, Christmas Address to the Roman Curia, 2012

Starting from the decade between 1960–1970, some theories (which
today are usually described by experts as "constructionist") hold not
only that generic sexual identity ("gender") is the product of an interaction between the community and the individual, but that this generic identity is independent from personal sexual identity: i.e., that
masculine and feminine genders in society are the exclusive product
of social factors, with no relation to any truth about the sexual dimension of the person. In this way, any sexual attitude can be justified, including homosexuality, and it is society that ought to change in order
to include other genders, together with male and female, in its way of
shaping social life.

The ideology of "gender" found a favorable environment in the in-
dividualist anthropology of radical neo-liberalism. Claiming a similar
status for marriage and *de facto* unions (including homosexual unions)
is usually justified today on the basis of categories and terms that come
from the ideology of "gender." In this way, there is a certain tendency to
give the name "family" to all kinds of consensual unions, thus ignoring
the natural inclination of human freedom to reciprocal self-giving and
its essential characteristics which are the basis of that common good of
humanity, the institution of marriage.

—Pontifical Council for the Family, *Family, Marriage, and "De
Facto" Unions*, 8

At the root of these negative phenomena there frequently lies a corruption of the idea and the experience of freedom, conceived not as a capacity for realizing the truth of God's plan for marriage and the family, but as an autonomous power of self-affirmation, often against others, for one's own selfish well-being.

—John Paul II, *Familiaris consortio*, 6

———— 5 ————

Why does the church teach that marriage has to be between a man and a woman?

Then God said: Let us make human beings in our image, after our
   likeness....
God created mankind in his image;
In the image of God he created them;
male and female he created them.
God blessed them and God said to them: Be fertile and
   multiply...

—Genesis 1:26–27, New American Bible Revised Edition

That is why a man leaves his father and mother and clings to his wife, and the two of them become one body.

—Genesis 2:24, New American Bible Revised Edition

Sexuality, by means of which man and woman give themselves to one another through the acts which are proper and exclusive to spouses, is by no means something purely biological, but concerns the innermost being of the human person as such. It is realized in a truly human way only if it is an integral part of the love by which a man and a woman commit themselves totally to one another until death.

—John Paul II, *Familiaris consortio*, 11

At the center we see the father and mother, a couple with their personal story of love. They embody the primordial divine plan clearly spoken of by Christ himself: "Have you not read that he who made them from the beginning made them male and female?" (Mt 19:4). We hear an echo of the command found in the Book of Genesis: "Therefore a man shall leave his father and mother and cleave to his wife, and they shall become one flesh" (Gn 2:24).

The majestic early chapters of Genesis present the human couple in its deepest reality. Those first pages of the Bible make a number of very clear statements. The first, which Jesus paraphrases, says that "God created man in his own image, in the image of God he created them; male and female he created them" (1:27). It is striking that the "image of God" here refers to the couple, "male and female." Does this mean that sex is a property of God himself, or that God has a divine female companion, as some ancient religions held? Naturally, the answer is no. We know how clearly the Bible rejects as idolatrous such beliefs, found among the Canaanites of the Holy Land. God's transcendence is preserved, yet inasmuch as he is also the Creator, the fruitfulness of the human couple is a living and effective "image," a visible sign of his creative act. The couple that loves and begets life is a true, living icon—not an idol like those of stone or gold prohibited by the Decalogue—capable of revealing God the Creator and Savior. For this reason, fruitful love becomes a symbol of God's inner life (cf. Gn 1:28; 9:7; 17:2–5, 16; 28:3; 35:11; 48:3–4). This is why the Genesis account, following the "priestly tradition," is interwoven with various genealogical accounts (cf. 4:17–22, 25–26; 5; 10; 11:10–32; 25:1–4, 12–17, 19–26; 36). The ability of human couples to beget life is the path along which the history of salvation progresses. Seen this way, the couple's fruitful relationship becomes an image for understanding and describing the mystery of God himself, for in the Christian vision of the Trinity, God is contemplated as Father, Son and Spirit of love. The triune God is a communion of love, and the family is its living reflection.

—Francis, *Amoris laetitia*, 9–11

The Church's teaching on marriage and on the complementarity of the sexes reiterates a truth that is evident to right reason and recognized as such by all the major cultures of the world. Marriage is not just any relationship between human beings. It was established by the Creator with its own nature, essential properties and purpose. No ideology can erase from the human spirit the certainty that marriage exists solely between a man and a woman, who by mutual personal gift, proper and exclusive to themselves, tend toward the communion of their persons. In this way, they mutually perfect each other, in order to cooperate with God in the procreation and upbringing of new human lives.

—Congregation for the Doctrine of the Faith, *Considerations Regarding Proposals to Give Legal Recognition to Unions between Homosexual Persons*, 2

For, God Himself is the author of matrimony, endowed as it is with various benefits and purposes. All of these have a very decisive bearing on the continuation of the human race, on the personal development and eternal destiny of the individual members of a family, and on the dignity, stability, peace and prosperity of the family itself and of human society as a whole. By their very nature, the institution of matrimony itself and conjugal love are ordained for the procreation and education of children, and find in them their ultimate crown. Thus a man and a woman, who by their compact of conjugal love "are no longer two, but one flesh" (Mt 19:ff), render mutual help and service to each other through an intimate union of their persons and of their actions.

—Second Vatican Council, *Gaudium et spes*, 48

The body which expresses femininity "for" masculinity and, vice versa, masculinity "for" femininity manifests the reciprocity and communion of persons. It expresses through gift as the fundamental characteristic of personal existence. This is the body, a witness to creation as a fundamental gift, and therefore a witness to Love as the source from which this same giving springs. Masculinity and femininity—namely, sex—is the original sign of a creative donation and at the same time "the sign of a gift that," man, male-female, becomes aware of as a gift lived in an original way. This is the meaning with which sex enters into the theology of the body.

That beatifying "beginning" of man's being and existing, as male and female, is connected with the revelation and discovery of the meaning of the body that is rightly called "spousal." If we speak of revelation together with discovery, we do so in relation to the specificity of the Yahwist text, in which the theological guiding thread is also anthropological, or better still, appears as a certain reality consciously lived by man. We have already observed that after the words which express the first joy of man's coming to existence as "male and female" (Gn 2:23) there follows the verse that establishes their conjugal unity (cf. Gn 2:24) and then the one that attests the nakedness of both without reciprocal shame (Gn 2:25). That these verses face each other in such a significant way allows us to speak of revelation together with the discovery of the "spousal" meaning of the body in the mystery of creation.

> —John Paul II, General Audience on the Theology of the Body,
> January 14, 1980. The translation is from *Man and Woman He
> Created Them: A Theology of the Body*, translated and edited by
> Michael Waldstein (Boston: Pauline, 2006), 14:4–5, 183–84

EDITORS' NOTE: The spousal" or "nuptial" meaning of the body refers to the body's capacity in its masculinity or femininity to express the person's vocation to make a gift of him or herself in love. Hence it applies to every man and woman in any state of life. See question 11. ✤

——— 6 ———

If the popular view of marriage is changing,
why will the church not change its understanding
of this relationship?

Conjugal love reveals its true nature and nobility when it is considered
in its supreme origin, God, who is love (cf. Jn 4:8), "the Father from
whom every family in heaven and on earth is named" (Eph 3:15.) Marriage is not, then, the effect of chance or the produce of evolution of
unconscious natural forces; it is the wise institution of the Creator to
realize in mankind his design of love.

—Paul VI, *Humanae vitae*, 8

The intimate partnership of married life and love has been established
by the Creator and qualified by His laws, and is rooted in the conjugal
covenant of irrevocable personal consent. Hence by that human act
whereby spouses mutually bestow and accept each other a relationship
arises which by divine will and in the eyes of society too is a lasting
one. For the good of the spouses and their off-springs as well as of society, the existence of the sacred bond no longer depends on human decisions alone. For, God Himself is the author of matrimony, endowed
as it is with various benefits and purposes.

—Second Vatican Council, *Gaudium et spes*, 48

And to begin with that same Encyclical, which is wholly concerned in
vindicating the divine institution of matrimony, its sacramental dignity,
and its perpetual stability, let it be repeated as an immutable and inviolable fundamental doctrine that matrimony was not instituted or restored by man but by God; not by man were the laws made to strength-
en and confirm and elevate it but by God, the Author of nature, and by
Christ Our Lord by Whom nature was redeemed, and hence these laws
cannot be subject to any human decrees or to any contrary pact even

of the spouses themselves. This is the doctrine of Holy Scripture; this is the constant tradition of the Universal Church; this the solemn definition of the sacred Council of Trent, which declares and establishes from the words of Holy Writ itself that God is the Author of the perpetual stability of the marriage bond, its unity and its firmness.

—Pius XI, *Casti connubii*, 5

The true origin of marriage, venerable brothers, is well known to all. Though revilers of the Christian faith refuse to acknowledge the never-interrupted doctrine of the Church on this subject, and have long striven to destroy the testimony of all nations and of all times, they have nevertheless failed not only to quench the powerful light of truth, but even to lessen it. We record what is to all known, and cannot be doubted by any, that God, on the sixth day of creation, having made man from the slime of the earth, and having breathed into his face the breath of life, gave him a companion, whom He miraculously took from the side of Adam when he was locked in sleep. God thus, in His most far-reaching foresight, decreed that this husband and wife should be the natural beginning of the human race, from whom it might be propagated and preserved by an unfailing fruitfulness throughout all futurity of time. And this union of man and woman, that it might answer more fittingly to the infinite wise counsels of God, even from the beginning manifested chiefly two most excellent properties—deeply sealed, as it were, and signed upon it—namely, unity and perpetuity. From the gospel we see clearly that this doctrine was declared and openly confirmed by the divine authority of Jesus Christ. He bore witness to the Jews and to His Apostles that marriage, from its institution, should exist between two only, that is, between one man and one woman; that of two they are made, so to say, one flesh; and that the marriage bond is by the will of God so closely and strongly made fast that no man may dissolve it or render it asunder.

—Leo XIII, *Arcanum*, 5

——— 7 ———

Even if the church views marriage as an
unchanging sacrament, why does it care what the
government says about marriage? Why does it matter
to the church how society defines marriage, or how
non-Catholics marry or cohabit?

It is only right, however, that at all times and in all places, the Church
should have true freedom to preach the faith, to teach her social doctrine, to exercise her role freely among men, and also to pass moral
judgment in those matters which regard public order when the fundamental rights of a person or the salvation of souls require it.

—Second Vatican Council, *Gaudium et spes*, 48

In a so-called *free union*, a man and a woman refuse to give juridical
and public form to a liaison involving sexual intimacy. The expression
"free union" is fallacious: what can "union" mean when the partners
make no commitment to one another, each exhibiting a lack of trust in
the other, in himself, or in the future? The expression covers a number
of different situations: concubinage, rejection of marriage as such, or
inability to make long-term commitments. All these situations offend
against the dignity of marriage; they destroy the very idea of the family;
they weaken the sense of fidelity. They are contrary to the moral law.
The sexual act must take place exclusively within marriage. Outside of
marriage it always constitutes a grave sin and excludes one from sacramental communion.

—*Catechism of the Catholic Church*, 2390

A first example of an irregular situation is provided by what are called
"trial marriages," which many people today would like to justify by attributing a certain value to them. But human reason leads one to see
that they are unacceptable, by showing the unconvincing nature of

carrying out an "experiment" with human beings, whose dignity demands that they should be always and solely the term of a self-giving love without limitations of time or of any other circumstance.

The Church, for her part, cannot admit such a kind of union, for further and original reasons which derive from faith. For, in the first place, the gift of the body in the sexual relationship is a real symbol of the giving of the whole person: such a giving, moreover, in the present state of things cannot take place with full truth without the concourse of the love of charity, given by Christ. In the second place, marriage between two baptized persons is a real symbol of the union of Christ and the Church, which is not a temporary or "trial" union but one which is eternally faithful.

—John Paul II, *Familiaris consortio*, 80

It has always been the duty of Christian married partners but today it is the greatest part of their apostolate to manifest and prove by their own way of life the indissolubility and sacredness of the marriage bond, strenuously to affirm the right and duty of parents and guardians to educate children in a Christian manner, and to defend the dignity and lawful autonomy of the family. They and the rest of the faithful, therefore, should cooperate with men of good will to ensure the preservation of these rights in civil legislation and to make sure that governments give due attention to the needs of the family regarding housing, the education of children, working conditions, social security, and taxes; and that in policy decisions affecting migrants their right to live together as a family should be safeguarded.

—Second Vatican Council, *Apostolicam actuositatem*, 11

From this it is clear that legitimately constituted authority has the right and therefore the duty to restrict, to prevent, and to punish those base unions which are opposed to reason and to nature; but since it is a matter which flows from human nature itself, no less certain is the teaching of Our predecessor, Leo XIII of happy memory: "In choosing a state of life there is no doubt but that it is in the power and discretion of each one to prefer one or the other: either to embrace the counsel of virginity given by Jesus Christ, or to bind himself in the bonds of matrimony. To take away from man the natural and primeval right of marriage, to circumscribe in any way the principal ends of marriage laid down in the beginning by God Himself in the words 'Increase and multiply,' (Gn 1:28) is beyond the power of any human law."

—Pius XI, *Casti connubii*, 8 (quoting Leo XIII, *Rerum novarum*, 12)

—— 8 ——

As opposed to these "shadows," what are some of the hopeful signs or "lights" for marriage and the family in the world today?

We must be grateful that most people do value family relationships that are permanent and marked by mutual respect. They appreciate the Church's efforts to offer guidance and counseling in areas related to growth in love, overcoming conflict and raising children. Many are touched by the power of grace experienced in sacramental Reconciliation and in the Eucharist, grace that helps them face the challenges of marriage and the family. In some countries, especially in various parts of Africa, secularism has not weakened certain traditional values, and marriages forge a strong bond between two wider families, with clearly defined structures for dealing with problems and conflicts. Nowadays we are grateful too for the witness of marriages that have not only proved lasting, but also fruitful and loving. All these factors can inspire a positive and welcoming pastoral approach capable of helping couples to grow in appreciation of the demands of the Gospel.

—Francis, *Amoris laetitia*, 38

Most families have great respect for the elderly, surrounding them with affection and considering them a blessing. A special word of appreciation is due to those associations and family movements committed to serving the elderly, both spiritually and socially....

> —Francis, *Amoris laetitia*, 48 (citing the Final Report of the 2015 Synod on the Family, 21)

There are still many married couples who, with a generous sense of responsibility, are ready to accept children as "the supreme gift of marriage." Nor is there a lack of families which, over and above their everyday service to life, are willing to accept abandoned children, boys and girls and teenagers in difficulty, handicapped persons, elderly men and women who have been left alone. Many centers in support of life, or similar institutions, are sponsored by individuals and groups which, with admirable dedication and sacrifice, offer moral and material support to mothers who are in difficulty and are tempted to have recourse to abortion. Increasingly, there are appearing in many places groups of volunteers prepared to offer hospitality to persons without a family, who find themselves in conditions of particular distress or who need a supportive environment to help them to overcome destructive habits and discover anew the meaning of life.

> —John Paul II, *Evangelium vitae*, 26 (citing the Second Vatican Council, *Gaudium et spes*, 50)

There is a more lively awareness of personal freedom and greater attention to the quality of interpersonal relationships in marriage, to promoting the dignity of women, to responsible procreation, to the education of children. There is also an awareness of the need for the development of interfamily relationships, for reciprocal spiritual and material assistance, the rediscovery of the ecclesial mission proper to the family and its responsibility for the building of a more just society.

> John Paul II, *Familiaris consortio*, 6

THE SACRAMENT
OF MARRIAGE IN THE
CATHOLIC CHURCH

—— 9 ——

What is the difference in the church's eyes
between a valid marriage, a legitimate marriage, a
sacramental marriage, and a civil marriage?

EDITORS' NOTE: A true marriage in which one or both parties is not
baptized is a legitimate, natural marriage. A true marriage between baptized persons is a valid, sacramental marriage. ✢

In the Church's Latin tradition, the ministers of the sacrament of marriage are the man and the woman who marry; by manifesting their consent and expressing it physically, they receive a great gift. Their consent
and their bodily union are the divinely appointed means whereby they
become "one flesh." By their baptismal consecration, they were enabled
to join in marriage as the Lord's ministers and thus to respond to God's
call. Hence, when two non-Christian spouses receive baptism, they
need not renew their marriage vows; they need simply not reject them,
since by the reception of baptism their union automatically becomes
sacramental. Canon Law also recognizes the validity of certain unions
celebrated without the presence of an ordained minister. The natural
order has been so imbued with the redemptive grace of Jesus that "a
valid matrimonial contract cannot exist between the baptized without
it being by that fact a sacrament." The Church can require that the wedding be celebrated publicly, with the presence of witnesses and other
conditions that have varied over the course of time, but this does not
detract from the fact that the couple who marry are the ministers of the

sacrament. Nor does it affect the centrality of the consent given by the man and the woman, which of itself establishes the sacramental bond.

—Francis, *Amoris laetitia*, 75 (citing the *Code of Canon Law*, c. 1116)

There are increasing cases of Catholics who for ideological or practical reasons, prefer to contract a merely civil marriage, and who reject or at least defer religious marriage. Their situation cannot of course be likened to that of people simply living together without any bond at all, because in the present case there is at least a certain commitment to a properly defined and probably stable state of life, even though the possibility of a future divorce is often present in the minds of those entering a civil marriage. By seeking public recognition of their bond on the part of the State, such couples show that they are ready to accept not only its advantages but also its obligations. Nevertheless, not even this situation is acceptable to the Church.

—John Paul II, *Familiaris consortio*, 82

———— 10 ————

What does it mean that a
Christian couple receives grace through
the sacrament of matrimony?
What does this grace help them do?
What do they need
to do in order to receive and nurture
this grace?

The sacrament is not a "thing" or a "power," for in it Christ himself "now encounters Christian spouses.... He dwells with them, gives them the strength to take up their crosses and so follow him, to rise again after they have fallen, to forgive one another, to bear one another's burdens." Christian marriage is a sign of how much Christ loved his Church in the covenant sealed on the cross, yet it also makes that love present in the communion of the spouses. By becoming one flesh, they embody the espousal of our human nature by the Son of God. That is why "in the joys of their love and family life, he gives them here on earth a foretaste of the wedding feast of the Lamb."

> —Francis, *Amoris laetitia,* 73 (citing the *Catechism of the Catholic Church,* 1642)

The entire Christian life bears the mark of the spousal love of Christ and the Church. Already Baptism, the entry into the People of God, is a nuptial mystery; it is so to speak the nuptial bath which precedes the wedding feast, the Eucharist. Christian marriage in its turn becomes an efficacious sign, the sacrament of the covenant of Christ and the Church. Since it signifies and communicates grace, marriage between baptized persons is a true sacrament of the New Covenant.

> —*Catechism of the Catholic Church,* 1617

The gift of the Spirit is a commandment of life for Christian spouses and at the same time a stimulating impulse so that every day they may progress towards an ever richer union with each other on all levels—of the body, of the character, of the heart, of the intelligence and will, of the soul—revealing in this way to the Church and to the world the new communion of love, given by the grace of Christ.

> —John Paul II, *Familiaris consortio,* 19

By coming to restore the original order of creation disturbed by sin, he himself gives the strength and grace to live marriage in the new dimension of the Reign of God. It is by following Christ, renouncing themselves, and taking up their crosses that spouses will be able to "receive" the original meaning of marriage and live it with the help of Christ. This grace of Christian marriage is a fruit of Christ's cross, the source of all Christian life.

> —John Paul II, *Familiaris consortio,* 33

The sacrament of Matrimony signifies the union of Christ and the Church. It gives spouses the grace to love each other with the love with which Christ has loved his Church; the grace of the sacrament thus perfects the human love of the spouses, strengthens their indissoluble unity, and sanctifies them on the way to eternal life (cf. Council of Trent: DS 1799).

> —*Catechism of the Catholic Church*, 1661

This grace proper to the sacrament of Matrimony is intended to perfect the couple's love and to strengthen their indissoluble unity. By this grace they "help one another to attain holiness in their married life and in welcoming and educating their children."

> —*Catechism of the Catholic Church*, 1641 (citing the Second Vatican Council, *Lumen gentium*, 11)

Spouses are therefore the permanent reminder to the Church of what happened on the Cross; they are for one another and for the children witnesses to the salvation in which the sacrament makes them sharers. Of this salvation event marriage, like every sacrament, is a memorial, actuation and prophecy: "As a memorial, the sacrament gives them the grace and duty of commemorating the great works of God and of bearing witness to them before their children. As actuation, it gives them the grace and duty of putting into practice in the present, towards each other and their children, the demands of a love which forgives and redeems. As prophecy, it gives them the grace and duty of living and bearing witness to the hope of the future encounter with Christ."

> —John Paul II, *Familiaris consortio*, 13 (quoting his own Address to the Delegates of the Centre de Liason des Équipes de Recherche [November 3, 1979], 3)

The social and political role is included in the kingly mission of service in which Christian couples share by virtue of the sacrament of marriage, and they receive both a command which they cannot ignore and a grace which sustains and stimulates them.

The Christian family is thus called upon to offer everyone a witness of generous and disinterested dedication to social matters, through a "preferential option" for the poor and disadvantaged. Therefore, advancing in its following of the Lord by special love for all the poor, it must have special concern for the hungry, the poor, the old, the sick, drug victims and those who have no family.

—John Paul II, *Familiaris consortio*, 47

Just as husbands and wives receive from the sacrament the gift and responsibility of translating into daily living the sanctification bestowed on them, so the same sacrament confers on them the grace and moral obligation of transforming their whole lives into a "spiritual sacrifice."

—John Paul II, *Familiaris consortio*, 56 (citing Eph 2:4)

By the very fact, therefore, that the faithful with sincere mind give such consent, they open up for themselves a treasure of sacramental grace from which they draw supernatural power for the fulfilling of their rights and duties faithfully, holily, perseveringly even unto death. Hence this sacrament not only increases sanctifying grace, the permanent principle of the supernatural life, in those who, as the expression is, place no obstacle (*obex*) in its way, but also adds particular gifts, dispositions, seeds of grace, by elevating and perfecting the natural powers. By these gifts the parties are assisted not only in understanding, but in knowing intimately, in adhering to firmly, in willing effectively, and in successfully putting into practice, those things which pertain to the marriage state, its aims and duties, giving them in fine right to the actual assistance of grace, whensoever they need it for fulfilling the duties of their state.

Nevertheless, since it is a law of divine Providence in the supernatural order that men do not reap the full fruit of the Sacraments which they receive after acquiring the use of reason unless they cooperate with grace, the grace of matrimony will remain for the most part an unused talent hidden in the field unless the parties exercise these supernatural powers and cultivate and develop the seeds of grace they have received. If, however, doing all that lies with their power, they cooperate diligently, they will be able with ease to bear the burdens of their state and to fulfill their duties. By such a sacrament they will be strengthened, sanctified and in a manner consecrated.

—Pius XI, *Casti connubii*, 40–41

——— 11 ———

How does the sacramentally
married couple manifest the love of Christ, the
bridegroom, and his bride,
the church?

Be subordinate to one another out of reverence for Christ. Wives should be subordinate to their husbands as to the Lord. For the husband is head of his wife just as Christ is head of the church, he himself the savior of the body. As the church is subordinate to Christ, so wives should be subordinate to their husbands in everything. Husbands, love your wives, even as Christ loved the church and handed himself over for her to sanctify her, cleansing her by the bath of water with the word, that he might present to himself the church in splendor, without spot or wrinkle or any such thing, that she might be holy and without blemish. So [also] husbands should love their wives as their own bodies. He who loves his wife loves himself. For no one hates his own flesh but rather nourishes and cherishes it, even as Christ does the church, because we are members of his body. "For this reason a man shall leave [his] father and [his] mother and be joined to his wife, and the two shall become one flesh." This is a great mystery, but I speak in reference to Christ and the church. In any case, each one of you should love his wife as himself, and the wife should respect her husband.

> —Ephesians 5:21–33, New American Bible Revised Edition (citing Genesis 2:24)

EDITORS' NOTE: Modern church teaching reads this text in light of verse 21: "Be subordinate to one another out of reverence for Christ." Therefore, Ephesians calls husbands and wives to mutual submission to one another in light of their common commitment to Christ. See question 69. ⤳

For baptized persons, moreover, marriage invests the dignity of a sacramental sign of grace, inasmuch as it represents the union of Christ and of the Church.

> —Paul VI, *Humanae vitae*, 8

Christ the Lord abundantly blessed this many-faceted love, welling up as it does from the fountain of divine love and structured as it is on the model of His union with His Church. For as God of old made Himself present to His people through a covenant of love and fidelity, so now the Savior of men and the Spouse of the Church comes into the lives of married Christians through the sacrament of matrimony. He abides with them thereafter so that just as He loved the Church and handed Himself over on her behalf, the spouses may love each other with perpetual fidelity through mutual self-bestowal.

Authentic married love is caught up into divine love and is governed and enriched by Christ's redeeming power and the saving activity of the Church, so that this love may lead the spouses to God with powerful effect and may aid and strengthen them in sublime office of being a father or a mother. For this reason Christian spouses have a special sacrament by which they are fortified and receive a kind of consecration in the duties and dignity of their state. By virtue of this sacrament, as spouses fulfil their conjugal and family obligation, they are penetrated with the spirit of Christ, which suffuses their whole lives with faith, hope and charity. Thus they increasingly advance the perfection of their own personalities, as well as their mutual sanctification, and hence contribute jointly to the glory of God.

—Second Vatican Council, *Gaudium et spes*, 48

For matrimonial faith demands that husband and wife be joined in an especially holy and pure love, not as adulterers love each other, but as Christ loved the Church. This precept the Apostle laid down when he said: "Husbands, love your wives as Christ also loved the Church," that Church which of a truth He embraced with a boundless love not for the sake of His own advantage, but seeking only the good of His Spouse. The love, then, of which We are speaking is not that based on the passing lust of the moment nor does it consist in pleasing words only, but in the deep attachment of the heart which is expressed in action, since love is proved by deeds. This outward expression of love in the home demands not only mutual help but must go further; must have as its primary purpose that man and wife help each other day by day in forming and perfecting themselves in the interior life, so that through their partnership in life they may advance ever more and more in virtue, and above all that they may grow in true love toward God and their neighbor, on which indeed "dependeth the whole Law and the Prophets." For all men of every condition, in whatever honorable walk of life they may be, can and ought to imitate that most perfect example of holiness placed before man by God, namely Christ Our Lord, and by God's grace to arrive at the summit of perfection, as is proved by the example set us of many saints.

—Pius XI, *Casti connubii*, 23

Marriage, moreover, is a sacrament, because it is a holy sign which gives grace, showing forth an image of the mystical nuptials of Christ with the Church. But the form and image of these nuptials is shown precisely by the very bond of that most close union in which man and woman are bound together in one; which bond is nothing else but the marriage itself.

—Leo XIII, *Arcanum*, 24

———— 12 ————

Why is marriage one of the sacraments in service of Communion, like Holy Orders (i.e., the ordination of deacons, priests, and bishops)?

Man's need for truth and love opens him both to God and to creatures: it opens him to other people, to life "in communion," and in particular to marriage and to the family. In the words of the Council, the "communion" of persons is drawn in a certain sense from the mystery of the Trinitarian "We," and therefore "conjugal communion," also refers to this mystery. The family, which originates in the love of man and woman, ultimately derives from the mystery of God. This conforms to the innermost being of man and woman, to their innate and authentic dignity as persons.

In marriage man and woman are so firmly united as to become—to use the words of the Book of Genesis—"one flesh" (Gn 2:24). Male and female in their physical constitution, the two human subjects, even though physically different, share equally in the capacity to live "in truth and love." This capacity, characteristic of the human being as a person, has at the same time both a spiritual and a bodily dimension. It is also through the body that man and woman are predisposed to form a "communion of persons" in marriage. When they are united by the conjugal covenant in such a way as to become "one flesh" (Gn 2:24), their *union* ought to take place "in truth and love," and thus express the maturity proper to persons created in the image and likeness of God.

The family which results from this union draws its inner solidity from the covenant between the spouses, which Christ raised to a Sacrament. The family draws its proper character as a community, its traits of "communion," from that fundamental communion of the spouses which is prolonged in their children. "Will you accept children lovingly from God, and bring them up according to the law of Christ and his Church?," the celebrant asks during the Rite of Marriage. The answer given by the spouses reflects the most profound truth of the love which unites them. Their unity, however, rather than closing them up in themselves, opens them towards a new life, towards a new person. As parents, they will be capable of giving life to a being like themselves, not only bone of their bones and flesh of their flesh (cf. Gn 2:23), but an image and likeness of God—a person.

—John Paul II, Letter to Families *Gratissimam sane*, 8

If, vice versa, we wish to draw also from the narrative of the Yahwist text the concept of "image of God," we can then deduce that man became the "image and likeness" of God not only through his own humanity, but also through the communion of persons which man and woman form right from the beginning. The function of the image is to reflect the one who is the model, to reproduce its own prototype. Man becomes the image of God not so much in the moment of solitude as in the moment of communion. Right "from the beginning," he is not only an image in which the solitude of a person who rules the world is reflected, but also, and essentially, an image of an inscrutable divine communion of persons.

—John Paul II, General Audience on the Theology of the Body, November 19, 1979

—— 13 ——

Is marriage another form of consecration, like the vows that religious brothers and sisters take?

Marriage responds to a specific vocation and must be considered as a consecration. The man and woman consecrate themselves in their love. Married couples, thanks to the Sacrament, are invested with a genuine mission, that of making visible, starting with simple and ordinary things, the love Christ has for His Church.

—Francis, General Audience, April 2, 2014

The sacrament of marriage is the specific source and original means of sanctification for Christian married couples and families. It takes up again and makes specific the sanctifying grace of Baptism. By virtue of the mystery of the death and Resurrection of Christ, of which the spouses are made part in a new way by marriage, conjugal love is purified and made holy: "This love the Lord has judged worthy of special gifts, healing, perfecting and exalting gifts of grace and of charity."

—John Paul II, *Familiaris consortio,* 56 (quoting Second Vatican Council, *Gaudium et spes,* 49)

CHAPTER 2

Finding Mr. or Mrs. Right

Marriage as Vocational Discernment

Questions in this chapter concern whether one has the vocation to marriage, issues surrounding courtship, choosing a spouse, and marrying a particular person under particular circumstances (e.g., Can I marry someone my parents disapprove of? If my fiancé and I haven't had a good example of married life growing up, will we still be able to have a good marriage?).

————— 14 —————

Is marriage a vocation, like priesthood or religious life? Is it better to be a member of the clergy or a consecrated religious?

The value of virginity lies in its symbolizing a love that has no need to possess the other; in this way it reflects the freedom of the Kingdom of Heaven. Virginity encourages married couples to live their own conjugal love against the backdrop of Christ's definitive love, journeying together towards the fullness of the Kingdom. For its part, conjugal love symbolizes other values. On the one hand, it is a particular reflection of that full unity in distinction found in the Trinity. The family is also a sign of Christ. It manifests the closeness of God who is a part of every human life, since he became one with us through his incarnation, death and resurrection. Each spouse becomes "one flesh" with the other as a sign of willingness to share everything with him or her until death. Whereas virginity is an "eschatological" sign of the risen Christ, marriage is a "historical" sign for us living in this world, a sign of the earthly Christ who chose to become one with us and gave himself up for us even to shedding his blood. Virginity and marriage are, and must be, different ways of loving. For "man cannot live without love."

—Francis, *Amoris laetitia*, 161 (citing John Paul II, *Redemptor hominis*, 10)

Rather than speak absolutely of the superiority of virginity, it should be enough to point out that the different states of life complement one another, and consequently that some can be more perfect in one way and others in another. Alexander of Hales, for example, stated that in one sense marriage may be considered superior to the other sacraments, inasmuch as it symbolizes the great reality of "Christ's union with the Church, or the union of his divine and human natures."

Consequently, "it is not a matter of diminishing the value of matrimony in favor of continence." "There is no basis for playing one off against the other.... If, following a certain theological tradition, one speaks of a 'state of perfection' (*status perfectionis*), this has to do not with continence in itself, but with the entirety of a life based on the evangelical counsel." A married person can experience the highest degree of charity and thus "reach the perfection which flows from charity, through fidelity to the spirit of those counsels. Such perfection is possible and accessible to every man and woman."

> —Francis, *Amoris laetitia*, 159–60 (citing John Paul II, General
> Audience on the Theology of the Body, April 14, 1982; Alexander
> of Hales, *Glossa in quatuor libros sententiarum Petri Lombardi*, IV,
> XXVI, 2; and John Paul II, Catechesis, April 7, 1982)

The period of engagement, very necessary in order to form a couple, is a time of expectation and preparation that needs to be lived in purity of gesture and words. It allows you to mature in love, in concern and in attention for each other; it helps you to practice self-control and to develop your respect for each other. These are the characteristics of true love that does not place emphasis on seeking its own satisfaction or its own welfare. In your prayer together, ask the Lord to watch over and increase your love and to purify it of all selfishness. Do not hesitate to respond generously to the Lord's call, for Christian matrimony is truly and wholly a vocation in the Church.

> —Benedict XVI, Message for World Youth Day,
> January 27, 2007

"The intimate community of life and love which constitutes the married state has been established by the Creator and endowed by him with its own proper laws.... God himself is the author of marriage." The

vocation to marriage is written in the very nature of man and woman as
they came from the hand of the Creator.

—*Catechism of the Catholic Church*, 1603 (citing the Second Vatican
    Council, *Gaudium et spes*, 48)

In his pronouncement, did Christ perhaps suggest the superiority of
continence for the kingdom of heaven to matrimony? Certainly, he said
that this is an exceptional vocation, not a common one. In addition, he
affirmed that it is especially important and necessary to the kingdom
of heaven. If we understand superiority to matrimony in this sense, we
must admit that Christ set it out implicitly. However, he did not express
it directly. Only Paul will say of those who choose matrimony that they
do "well." About those who are willing to live in voluntary continence,
he will say that they do "better" (1 Cor 7:38).

That is also the opinion of the whole of Tradition, both doctrinal
and pastoral. The "superiority" of continence to matrimony in the authentic Tradition of the Church never means disparagement of matrimony or belittlement of its essential value. It does not even mean a
shift, even implicit, on the Manichean positions, or a support of ways
of evaluating or acting based on the Manichean understanding of the
body and sexuality, matrimony and procreation. The evangelical and
authentically Christian superiority of virginity and continence is dictat-
ed by the motive of the kingdom of heaven. In Christ's words recorded
in Matthew (Mt 19:11–12) we find a solid basis for admitting only this
superiority, while we do not find any basis whatever for any disparagement of matrimony which, however, could have been present in the
recognition of that superiority.

—John Paul II, General Audience on the Theology of the Body,
    April 19, 1982

EDITORS' NOTE: Manicheanism is a dualistic heresy that sees materi-
ality, the body, marriage, and procreation as the work of an evil god. ❧

——— 15 ———

What does the vocation to marriage entail? What types of activities are involved, and what is its mission?

Sexual union, lovingly experienced and sanctified by the sacrament, is in turn a path of growth in the life of grace for the couple. It is the "nuptial mystery." … More generally, the common life of husband and wife, the entire network of relations that they build with their children and the world around them, will be steeped in and strengthened by the grace of the sacrament.

—Francis, *Amoris laetitia*, 74

Since the Creator of all things has established conjugal society as the beginning and basis of human society and, by His grace, has made it a great mystery in Christ and the Church (cf. Eph. 5:32), the apostolate of married persons and families is of unique importance for the Church and civil society.

Christian husbands and wives are cooperators in grace and witnesses of faith for each other, their children, and all others in their household. They are the first to communicate the faith to their children and to educate them by word and example for the Christian and apostolic life. They prudently help them in the choice of their vocation and carefully promote any sacred vocation which they may discern in them.

It has always been the duty of Christian married partners but today it is the greatest part of their apostolate to manifest and prove by their own way of life the indissolubility and sacredness of the marriage bond, strenuously to affirm the right and duty of parents and guardians to educate children in a Christian manner, and to defend the dignity and lawful autonomy of the family. They and the rest of the faithful, therefore, should cooperate with men of good will to ensure the preservation of these rights in civil legislation and to make sure that governments give due attention to the needs of the family regarding housing, the education of children, working conditions, social security, and taxes; and that in policy decisions affecting migrants their right to live together as a family should be safeguarded.

This mission—to be the first and vital cell of society—the family has received from God. It will fulfill this mission if it appears as the domestic sanctuary of the Church by reason of the mutual affection of its members and the prayer that they offer to God in common, if the whole family makes itself a part of the liturgical worship of the Church, and if it provides active hospitality and promotes justice and other good works for the service of all the brethren in need. Among the various activities of the family apostolate may be enumerated the following: the adoption of abandoned infants, hospitality to strangers, assistance in the operation of schools, helpful advice and material assistance for adolescents, help to engaged couples in preparing themselves better for marriage, catechetical work, support of married couples and families involved in material and moral crises, help for the aged not only by providing them with the necessities of life but also by obtaining for them a fair share of the benefits of an expanding economy.

At all times and places but particularly in areas where the first seeds of the Gospel are being sown, or where the Church is just beginning, or is involved in some serious difficulty, Christian families can give effective testimony to Christ before the world by remaining faithful to the Gospel and by providing a model of Christian marriage through their whole way of life.

—Second Vatican Council, *Lumen gentium*, 11

—— 16 ——

How do I know if I am called to marriage?

All Christians in whatever state or walk of life are called to the fullness of Christian life and to the perfection of charity.

—Second Vatican Council, *Lumen gentium*, 4

Engagement—one hears it in the word—has to do with trust, confidence, reliability. Confidence in the vocation that God gives, since marriage is first and foremost the discovery of a call from God. Certainly it is a beautiful thing that young people today can choose to marry on the basis of mutual love. But the very freedom of the bond requires a conscious harmony in the decision, not just a simple understanding of the attraction or feeling, for a moment, for a short time … it calls for a journey. Engagement, in other words, is the time when the two are called to perform a real labor of love, an involved and shared work that delves deep. Here they discover one another little by little, i.e., the man "learns" about woman by learning about this woman, his fiancée; and the woman "learns" about man by learning about this man, her fiancé.

—Francis, General Audience, May 27, 2015

The young people should have already been helped to discern their vocation through their own personal efforts and with the aid of the community, and above all the pastors. This discernment must take place before any commitment is made to get engaged.

—Pontifical Council for the Family, *Preparation for the Sacrament of Marriage*, 33

By the fact that it is a vocation, marriage must involve a carefully considered choice, a mutual commitment before God and the constant seeking of his help in prayer.

—Pontifical Council for the Family, *The Truth and Meaning of Human Sexuality*, 27

The very preparation for Christian marriage is itself a journey of faith. It is a special opportunity for the engaged to rediscover and deepen the faith received in Baptism and nourished by their Christian upbringing. In this way they come to recognize and freely accept their vocation to follow Christ and to serve the Kingdom of God in the married state.

—John Paul II, *Familiaris consortio*, 51

—— 17 ——

I have discerned that I have a vocation to marriage. How can I prepare for marriage before meeting my future spouse?

Chastity includes an apprenticeship in self-mastery which is a training in human freedom. The alternative is clear: either man governs his passions and finds peace, or he lets himself be dominated by them and becomes unhappy. "Man's dignity therefore requires him to act out of conscious and free choice, as moved and drawn in a personal way from within, and not by blind impulses in himself or by mere external constraint. Man gains such dignity when, ridding himself of all slavery to the passions, he presses forward to his goal by freely choosing what is good and, by his diligence and skill, effectively secures for himself the means suited to this end."

—*Catechism of the Catholic Church*, 2339 (citing the Second Vatican Council, *Gaudium et spes*, 17)

Formation for true love is always the best preparation for the vocation to marriage. In the family, children and young people can learn to live human sexuality within the solid context of Christian life. They can gradually discover that a stable Christian marriage cannot be regarded as a matter of convenience or mere sexual attraction.

—Pontifical Council for the Family, *The Truth and Meaning of Human Sexuality*, 27

Future spouses must know the profound significance of marriage, understood as a union of love for the realization of the couple and for procreation. The stability of marriage and of conjugal love requires as indispensable conditions: chastity and self-control, the formation of character and the spirit of sacrifice. With regard to certain difficulties of married life, rendered more acute by the conditions of our time, chastity during one's youth as an adequate preparation for marital chastity will be a decisive help to the married. They will need therefore to be informed about the divine law, declared by the ecclesiastical Magisterium, necessary for the formation of their consciences.

> —Sacred Congregation for Catholic Education, *Educational Guidance in Human Love*, 61

Consequently, "it is not a matter of diminishing the value of matrimony in favor of continence." "There is no basis for playing one off against the other.... If, following a certain theological tradition, one speaks of a 'state of perfection' (*status perfectionis*), this has to do not with continence in itself, but with the entirety of a life based on the evangelical counsels." A married person can experience the highest degree of charity and thus "reach the perfection which flows from charity, through fidelity to the spirit of those counsels. Such perfection is possible and accessible to every man and woman."

> —Francis, *Amoris laetitia*, 160 (citing John Paul II, General Audience on the Theology of the Body, April 7, 1982)

This outward expression of love in the home demands not only mutual help but must go further; must have as its primary purpose that man and wife help each other day by day in forming and perfecting themselves in the interior life, so that through their partnership in life they may advance ever more and more in virtue, and above all that they may grow in true love toward God and their neighbor, on which indeed "dependeth the whole Law and the Prophets." For all men of every condition, in whatever honorable walk of life they may be, can and ought to imitate that most perfect example of holiness placed before man by God, namely Christ Our Lord, and by God's grace to arrive at the summit of perfection, as is proved by the example set us of many saints.

This mutual molding of husband and wife, this determined effort to perfect each other, can in a very real sense, as the Roman Catechism teaches, be said to be the chief reason and purpose of matrimony, provided matrimony be looked at not in the restricted sense as instituted for the proper conception and education of the child, but more widely as the blending of life as a whole and the mutual interchange and sharing thereof.

—Pius XI, *Casti connubii*, 23–24 (citing Matthew 22:40)

CHOOSING THIS MAN
OR WOMAN

—— 18 ——

How do I choose a husband or wife?

The LORD God said: It is not good for the man to be alone. I will make a helper suited to him.

—*Genesis* 2:18, New American Bible Revised Edition

Who can find a woman of worth? Far beyond jewels is her value. Her husband trusts her judgment; he does not lack income.... She is clothed with strength and dignity, and laughs at the days to come. She opens her mouth in wisdom; kindly instruction is on her tongue. She watches over the affairs of her household, and does not eat the bread of idleness. Her children rise up and call her blessed; her husband, too, praises her: "Many are the women of proven worth, but you have excelled them all." Charm is deceptive and beauty fleeting; the woman who fears the LORD is to be praised. Acclaim her for the work of her hands, and let her deeds praise her at the city gates.

—Proverbs 31:10–11, 25–31, New American Bible Revised Edition

In their initial enchantment with one another, couples can attempt to conceal or relativize certain things and to avoid disagreements; only later do problems surface. For this reason, they should be strongly encouraged to discuss what each expects from marriage, what they understand by love and commitment, what each wants from the other and what kind of life they would like to build together. Such discussions would help them to see if they in fact have little in common and to realize that mutual attraction alone will not suffice to keep them together. Nothing is more volatile, precarious and unpredictable than desire. The decision to marry should never be encouraged unless the couple has discerned deeper reasons that will ensure a genuine and stable commitment.

In any event, if one partner clearly recognizes the other's weak points, he or she needs to have a realistic trust in the possibility of helping to develop the good points that counterbalance them, and in this way to foster their human growth. This entails a willingness to face eventual sacrifices, problems and situations of conflict; it demands a firm resolve to be ready for this. Couples need to be able to detect danger signals in their relationship and to find, before the wedding, effective ways of responding to them.

—Francis, *Amoris laetitia*, 209–10

Concretely, what does this path of ascent and purification entail? How might love be experienced so that it can fully realize its human and divine promise? Here we can find a first, important indication in the *Song of Songs*, an Old Testament book well known to the mystics. According to the interpretation generally held today, the poems contained in this book were originally love-songs, perhaps intended for a Jewish wedding feast and meant to exalt conjugal love. In this context it is highly instructive to note that in the course of the book two different Hebrew words are used to indicate "love." First there is the word *dodim*, a plural form suggesting a love that is still insecure, indeterminate and searching. This comes to be replaced by the word *ahabà*, which the Greek version of the Old Testament translates with the similar-sounding *agape*, which, as we have seen, becomes the typical expression for the biblical notion of love. By contrast with an indeterminate, "searching" love, this word expresses the experience of a love which involves a real discovery of the other, moving beyond the selfish character that prevailed earlier. Love now becomes concern and care for the other. No longer is it self-seeking, a sinking in the intoxication of happiness; instead it seeks the good of the beloved: it becomes renunciation and it is ready, and even willing, for sacrifice.

—Benedict XVI, *Deus caritas est*, 6

To the proximate preparation of a good married life belongs very specially the care in choosing a partner; on that depends a great deal whether the forthcoming marriage will be happy or not, since one may be to the other either a great help in leading a Christian life, or, a great danger and hindrance. And so that they may not deplore for the rest of their lives the sorrows arising from an indiscreet marriage, those about to enter into wedlock should carefully deliberate in choosing the person with whom henceforward they must live continually: they should, in so deliberating, keep before their minds the thought first of God and of the true religion of Christ, then of themselves, of their partner, of the children to come, as also of human and civil society, for which wedlock is a fountain head. Let them diligently pray for divine help, so that they make their choice in accordance with Christian prudence, not indeed led by the blind and unrestrained impulse of lust, nor by any desire of riches or other base influence, but by a true and noble love and by a sincere affection for the future partner; and then let them strive in their married life for those ends for which the State was constituted by God. Lastly, let them not omit to ask the prudent advice of their parents with regard to the partner, and let them regard this advice in no light manner, in order that by their mature knowledge and experience of human affairs, they may guard against a disastrous choice, and, on the threshold of matrimony, may receive more abundantly the divine blessing of the fourth commandment: "Honor thy father and thy mother (which is the first commandment with a promise) that it may be well with thee and thou mayest be long-lived upon the earth."

—Pius XI, *Casti connubii*, 115

———— 19 ————

What if I or my boyfriend comes from a family marked by divorce or abuse? Our parents were not good examples, and we are suffering serious emotional wounds. Can we still have a good marriage?

Understandably, families often experience problems when one of their members is emotionally immature because he or she still bears the scars of earlier experiences. An unhappy childhood or adolescence can breed personal crises that affect one's marriage. Were everyone mature and normal, crises would be less frequent or less painful. Yet the fact is that only in their forties do some people achieve a maturity that should have come at the end of adolescence. Some love with the selfish, capricious and self-centered love of a child: an insatiable love that screams or cries when it fails to get what it wants. Others love with an adolescent love marked by hostility, bitter criticism and the need to blame others; caught up in their own emotions and fantasies, such persons expect others to fill their emptiness and to satisfy their every desire.

Many people leave childhood without ever having felt uncondi-
tional love. This affects their ability to be trusting and open with others.
A poor relationship with one's parents and siblings, if left unhealed, can
re-emerge and hurt a marriage. Unresolved issues need to be dealt with
and a process of liberation must take place. When problems emerge
in a marriage, before important decisions are made it is important to
ensure that each spouse has come to grips with his or her own history. This involves recognizing a need for healing, insistent prayer for
the grace to forgive and be forgiven, a willingness to accept help, and
the determination not to give up but to keep trying. A sincere self-
examination will make it possible to see how one's own shortcomings
and immaturity affect the relationship. Even if it seems clear that the
other person is at fault, a crisis will never be overcome simply by expecting him or her to change. We also have to ask what in our own life
needs to grow or heal if the conflict is to be resolved.

—Francis, *Amoris laetita,* 239–40

Experience teaches that human love, which naturally tends towards
fatherhood and motherhood, is sometimes affected by a profound *crisis*
and is thus seriously threatened. In such cases, help can be sought at
marriage and family counselling centers, where it is possible, among
other things, to obtain the assistance of specifically trained psycholo-
gists and psychotherapists. At the same time, however, we cannot forget the perennial validity of the words of the Apostle: "I bow my knees
before the Father, from whom every family in heaven and on earth is
named." Marriage, the Sacrament of Matrimony, is a covenant of persons in love. And *love can be deepened and preserved only by Love,* that
Love which is "poured into our hearts through the Holy Spirit which
has been given to us" (Rom 5:5).... Is that not precisely the moment
when there is an indispensable need for the "outpouring of the grace of
the Holy Spirit" invoked in the liturgical celebration of the Sacrament
of Matrimony?

The Apostle, bowing his knees before the Father, asks that the faithful "be strengthened with might through his Spirit in the inner man" (Eph 3:16). This "inner strength" is necessary in all family life, especially at its critical moments, when the love which was expressed in the liturgical rite of marital consent with the words, "I promise to be faithful to you always … all the days of my life," is put to a difficult test.

—John Paul II, Letter to Families *Gratissimam sane*, 7

—— 20 ——

My parents and most of my friends are divorced.
I haven't seen examples of happy, enduring married life,
and I'm not convinced that love can really last for life.
What is the point of marriage, since it's so
unlikely to work out?

Nowadays we are grateful too for the witness of marriages that have not only proved lasting, but also fruitful and loving. All these factors can inspire a positive and welcoming pastoral approach capable of helping couples to grow in appreciation of the demands of the Gospel.

—Francis, *Amoris laetitia*, 38

As the love of God is stable and forever, so too should we want the love on which a family is based to be stable and forever. Please, we mustn't let ourselves be overcome by the "culture of the provisory"! Today this culture invades us all, this culture of the temporary. This is not right!

How, then, does one cure this fear of the "forever"? One cures it day by day, by entrusting oneself to the Lord Jesus in a life that becomes a daily spiritual journey, made in steps—little steps, steps of shared growth—it is accomplished through a commitment to becoming men and women who are mature in faith. For, dear engaged couples, "forever" is not only a question of duration! A marriage is not successful just because it endures; quality is important. To stay together and to know how to love one another forever is the challenge for Christian couples. What comes to mind is the miracle of the multiplication of the loaves: for you too, the Lord can multiply your love and give it to you fresh and good each day. He has an infinite reserve! He gives you the love that stands at the foundation of your union and each day he renews and strengthens it. And he makes it ever greater when the family grows with children. On this journey prayer is important, it is necessary, always: he for her, she for him and both together. Ask Jesus to multiply your love. In the prayer of the *Our Father* we say: "Give us this day our daily bread." Spouses can also learn to pray like this: "Lord, give us this day our daily love" for the daily love of spouses is bread, the true bread of the soul, what sustains them in going forward. And the prayer: can we practice to see if we know how to say it? "Lord give us this day our daily love." All together! [Couples: "Lord give us this day our daily love."] One more time! [Couples: "Lord give us this day our daily love."] This is the prayer for engaged couples and spouses. Teach us to love one another, to will good to the other! The more you trust in him, the more your love will be "forever," able to be renewed, and it will conquer every difficulty.

——Francis, Address to Engaged Couples Preparing for Marriage,
February 14, 2014

In the light of these facts the characteristic features and exigencies of married love are clearly indicated, and it is of the highest importance to evaluate them exactly.

This love is above all fully human, a compound of sense and spirit. It is not, then, merely a question of natural instinct or emotional drive. It is also, and above all, an act of the free will, whose trust is such that it is meant not only to survive the joys and sorrows of daily life, but also to grow, so that husband and wife become in a way one heart and one soul, and together attain their human fulfillment.

It is a love which is total—that very special form of personal friendship in which husband and wife generously share everything, allowing no unreasonable exceptions and not thinking solely of their own convenience. Whoever really loves his partner loves not only for what he receives, but loves that partner for the partner's own sake, content to be able to enrich the other with the gift of himself.

Married love is also faithful and exclusive of all other, and this until death. This is how husband and wife understood it on the day on which, fully aware of what they were doing, they freely vowed themselves to one another in marriage. Though this fidelity of husband and wife sometimes presents difficulties, no one has the right to assert that it is impossible; it is, on the contrary, always honorable and meritorious. The example of countless married couples proves not only that fidelity is in accord with the nature of marriage, but also that it is the source of profound and enduring happiness.

—Paul VI, *Humanae vitae*, 9

——— 21 ———

Can I marry someone my parents don't like? Can they force me to marry someone I don't want to marry? Is this okay with the church?

The parties to a marriage covenant are a baptized man and woman, free to contract marriage, who freely express their consent; "to be free" means:

- not being under constraint;
- not impeded by any natural or ecclesiastical law.

The Church holds the exchange of consent between the spouses to be the indispensable element that "makes the marriage." If consent is lacking there is no marriage.

The consent consists in a "human act by which the partners mutually give themselves to each other": "I take you to be my wife"—"I take you to be my husband." This consent that binds the spouses to each other finds its fulfillment in the two "becoming one flesh."

The consent must be an act of the will of each of the contracting parties, free of coercion or grave external fear. No human power can substitute for this consent. If this freedom is lacking the marriage is invalid.

—*Catechism of the Catholic Church*, 1625–28

When they become adults, children have the right and duty to choose *their profession and state of life*. They should assume their new responsibilities within a trusting relationship with their parents, willingly asking and receiving their advice and counsel. Parents should be careful not to exert pressure on their children either in the choice of a profession or in that of a spouse. This necessary restraint does not prevent them— quite the contrary—from giving their children judicious advice, particularly when they are planning to start a family.

—*Catechism of the Catholic Church*, 2230

In the period leading to *engagement* and the choice of that preferred attachment which can lead to forming a family, the role of parents should not consist merely in prohibitions, much less in imposing the choice of a fiancé or fiancée. On the contrary, they should help their children to define the necessary conditions for a serious, honorable and promising union, and support them on a path of clear and coherent Christian witness in relating with the person of the other sex.

—Pontifical Council for the Family, *The Truth and Meaning of Human Sexuality*, 110

All the Christian faithful have the right to be free from any kind of coercion in choosing a state of life.

—*Code of Canon Law*, c. 219

A marriage is brought into being by the lawfully manifested consent of persons who are legally capable. This consent cannot be supplied by any human power.

Matrimonial consent is an act of will by which a man and a woman by an irrevocable covenant mutually give and accept one another for the purpose of establishing a marriage.

All can contract marriage who are not prohibited by law.

—*Code of Canon Law*, cc. 1057–58

For each individual marriage, inasmuch as it is a conjugal union of a particular man and woman, arises only from the free consent of each of the spouses; and this free act of the will, by which each party hands over and accepts those rights proper to the state of marriage, is so necessary to constitute true marriage that it cannot be supplied by any human power. This freedom, however, regards only the question whether the contracting parties really wish to enter upon matrimony or to marry this particular person; but the nature of matrimony is entirely independent of the free will of man, so that if one has once contracted matrimony he is thereby subject to its divinely made laws and its essential properties.

—Pius XI, *Casti connubii*, 6

––––––– 22 –––––––

Should a Catholic make an effort to marry another Catholic? What special challenges does a Catholic face when marrying a non-Catholic?

Issues involving mixed marriages require particular attention. Marriages between Catholics and other baptized persons "have their own particular nature, but they contain numerous elements that could well be made good use of and developed, both for their intrinsic value and for the contribution that they can make to the ecumenical movement."

Marriages involving disparity of cult represent a privileged place for interreligious dialogue in everyday life.... They involve special difficulties regarding both the Christian identity of the family and the religious upbringing of the children.... Unique challenges face couples and families in which one partner is Catholic and the other is a non-believer. In such cases, bearing witness to the ability of the Gospel to immerse itself in these situations will make possible the upbringing of their children in the Christian faith.... In many countries the situation of a mixed marriage (marriage between a Catholic and a baptized non-Catholic) often arises. It requires particular attention on the part of couples and their pastors. A case of marriage with disparity of cult (between a Catholic and a non-baptized person) requires even greater circumspection.

—Francis, *Amoris laetitia*, 247–24 (citing the Final Report of the
2015 Synod on the Family, 2015, 172–73)

EDITORS' NOTE: The term "disparity of cult" refers to a marriage between a baptized Catholic and an unbaptized person (e.g., an unbeliever, a member of a non-Christian religion, a not yet baptized believer, or someone who belongs to a group whose baptism the Catholic Church regards as invalid). This is an impediment to marriage unless dispensed by the bishop. When such a dispensation is received, the parties can enter a valid natural marriage. Catholics who enter into such a union must promise to do everything in their power to baptize and raise their children in the practice of the Catholic faith. ⚓

Difference of confession between the spouses does not constitute an insurmountable obstacle for marriage, when they succeed in placing in common what they have received from their respective communities, and learn from each other the way in which each lives in fidelity to Christ. But the difficulties of mixed marriages must not be underestimated. They arise from the fact that the separation of Christians has not yet been overcome. The spouses risk experiencing the tragedy of

Christian disunity even in the heart of their own home. Disparity of cult can further aggravate these difficulties. Differences about faith and the very notion of marriage, but also different religious mentalities, can become sources of tension in marriage, especially as regards the education of children. The temptation to religious indifference can then arise.

According to the law in force in the Latin Church, a mixed marriage needs for liceity the *express permission* of ecclesiastical authority. In case of disparity of cult an *express dispensation* from this impediment is required for the validity of the marriage. This permission or dispensation presupposes that both parties know and do not exclude the essential ends and properties of marriage; and furthermore that the Catholic party confirms the obligations, which have been made known to the non-Catholic party, of preserving his or her own faith and ensuring the baptism and education of the children in the Catholic Church.

Through ecumenical dialogue Christian communities in many regions have been able to put into effect a *common pastoral practice for mixed marriages*. Its task is to help such couples live out their particular situation in the light of faith, overcome the tensions between the couple's obligations to each other and towards their ecclesial communities, and encourage the flowering of what is common to them in faith and respect for what separates them.

In marriages with disparity of cult the Catholic spouse has a particular task: "For the unbelieving husband is consecrated through his wife, and the unbelieving wife is consecrated through her husband." It is a great joy for the Christian spouse and for the Church if this "consecration" should lead to the free conversion of the other spouse to the Christian faith. Sincere married love, the humble and patient practice of the family virtues, and perseverance in prayer can prepare the non-believing spouse to accept the grace of conversion.

—*Catechism of the Catholic Church*, 1633–37

Couples living in a mixed marriage have special needs, which can be put under three main headings.

In the first place, attention must be paid to the obligations that faith imposes on the Catholic party with regard to the free exercise of the faith and the consequent obligation to ensure, as far as is possible, the Baptism and upbringing of the children in the Catholic faith. There must be borne in mind the particular difficulties inherent in the relationships between husband and wife with regard to respect for religious freedom: this freedom could be violated either by undue pressure to make the partner change his or her beliefs, or by placing obstacles in the way of the free manifestation of these beliefs by religious practice.

With regard to the liturgical and canonical form of marriage, Ordinaries can make wide use of their faculties to meet various necessities.

In dealing with these special needs, the following points should be kept in mind:

In the appropriate preparation for this type of marriage, every reasonable effort must be made to ensure a proper understanding of Catholic teaching on the qualities and obligations of marriage, and also to ensure that the pressures and obstacles mentioned above will not occur.

- It is of the greatest importance that, through the support of the community, the Catholic party should be strengthened in faith and positively helped to mature in understanding and practicing that faith, so as to become a credible witness within the family through his or her own life and through the quality of love shown to the other spouse and the children.

- Marriages between Catholics and other baptized persons have their own particular nature, but they contain numerous elements that could well be made good use of and developed, both for their intrinsic value and for the contribution that they can make to the ecumenical movement. This is particularly true when both parties are faithful to their religious duties. Their common Baptism and the dynamism of grace provide the spouses in these marriages with the basis and motivation for expressing their unity in the sphere of moral and spiritual values.

—John Paul II, *Familiaris consortio*, 78

----- 23 -----

How do I know when my significant other and I are ready to get married?

Often the engagement period is not long enough, the decision is precipitated for various reasons and, what is even more problematic, the couple themselves are insufficiently mature.

—Francis, *Amoris laetitia*, 217

As engaged couples, you find yourselves living a unique season that opens you to the wonder of the encounter and enables you to discover the beauty of existence and of being precious to someone, of being able to say to each other: you are important to me. Live this journey intensely, gradually and truthfully. Do not give up following a high ideal of love, a reflection and testimony of God's love! But how should you live this stage of your life and bear witness to love in the community? I would like to tell you first of all to avoid shutting yourselves into intimism, falsely reassuring relationships; rather, endeavor to make your relationship become a leaven of active and responsible presence in the community.

Then do not forget that if it is to be genuine, love too requires a process of maturation: from the initial attraction and from that "feeling good" with the other, learn to "love" the other and "to want the best" for the other. Love lives by giving freely, by self-sacrifice, by forgiveness and by respect for the other.…

Prepare yourselves to choose with conviction the "forever" which connotes love; indissolubility, before being a condition, is a gift to be desired, asked for and lived out, over and above any other changeable human situation. And do not imagine, in accordance with a widespread idea, that coexistence is a guarantee for the future....

Be grateful to those who guide you in your formation with commitment, competence and availability: they are a sign of the Christian community's attention and care for you. You are not alone: be the first to seek and welcome the Church's company!

I would like to go back over an essential point: the experience of love contains the quest for God. True love promises the Infinite! Therefore make this period of your preparation for marriage an itinerary of faith: rediscover for your life as a couple the centrality of Jesus Christ and of walking with the Church.

—Benedict XVI, Meeting with Young Couples, September 11, 2011

Yet *eros* and *agape*—ascending love and descending love—can never be completely separated. The more the two, in their different aspects, find a proper unity in the one reality of love, the more the true nature of love in general is realized. Even if *eros* is at first mainly covetous and ascending, a fascination for the great promise of happiness, in drawing near to the other, it is less and less concerned with itself, increasingly seeks the happiness of the other, is concerned more and more with the beloved, bestows itself and wants to "be there for the other." The element of *agape* thus enters into this love, for otherwise *eros* is impoverished and even loses its own nature. On the other hand, man cannot live by oblative, descending love alone. He cannot always give, he must also receive. Anyone who wishes to give love must also receive love as a gift. Certainly, as the Lord tells us, one can become a source from which rivers of living water flow (cf. Jn 7:37–38). Yet to become such a source, one must constantly drink anew from the original source, which is Jesus Christ, from whose pierced heart flows the love of God (cf. Jn 19:34).

—Benedict XVI, *Deus caritas est*, 7

EDITORS' NOTE: *Eros* is the Greek word for a love that indicates a passionate desire for union with another. *Agape* is the Greek term for a sacrificial love that seeks the good of the other, regardless of cost. Pope Benedict XVI taught that these two loves are dimensions of all authentic love—both divine and human. ⚓

A man before he has completed his sixteenth year of age and a woman before she has completed her fourteenth year of age cannot enter into a valid marriage. The conference of bishops is free to establish a higher age for the licit celebration of marriage.

—*Code of Canon Law*, c. 1083

EDITORS' NOTE: Some national conferences of bishops have raised the minimum age to enter marriage. The bishops of the United States have not done so, but it should be noted that bishops would not permit fourteen-year-old girls or sixteen-year-old boys to marry. ⚓

This perspective is deeply rooted in the consciousness of humanity (cf. Gn 2:23) and also in the particular consciousness of the nuptial meaning of the body (Gn 2:25). Before becoming husband and wife (later Gn 4:1 speaks of this in the concrete), the man and the woman emerge from the mystery of creation in the first place as brother and sister in the same humanity. Understanding the nuptial meaning of the body in its masculinity and femininity reveals the depths of their freedom, which is freedom of giving.

From here that communion of persons begins, in which both meet and give themselves to each other in the fullness of their subjectivity. Thus both grow as persons-subjects.... At the same time, this solitude becomes in a marvelous way permeated and broadened by the gift of the "other."

—John Paul II, General Audience on the Theology of the Body, February 13, 1980

CHAPTER 3

Tying the Knot

Engagement, Marriage Prep, and the Wedding

What are the stages of marriage preparation? What should an engaged couple expect in a good marriage preparation program? Why does the church say an engaged couple shouldn't live together before marriage when everyone else thinks it's okay? How can we plan the wedding liturgy and attendant festivities with an eye to keeping them simple, joyful, holy, and spiritual? These are the types of questions covered in this chapter.

—— 24 ——

When does preparation for marriage begin and what are its stages?

Both short-term and long-term marriage preparation should ensure that the couple do not view the wedding ceremony as the end of the road, but instead embark upon marriage as a lifelong calling based on a firm and realistic decision to face all trials and difficult moments together. The pastoral care of engaged and married couples should be centered on the marriage bond, assisting couples not only to deepen their love but also to overcome problems and difficulties. This involves not only helping them to accept the Church's teaching and to have recourse to her valuable resources, but also offering practical programs, sound advice, proven strategies and psychological guidance. All this calls for a pedagogy of love, attuned to the feelings and needs of young people and capable of helping them to grow interiorly. Marriage preparation should also provide couples with the names of places, people and services to which they can turn for help when problems arise. It is also important to remind them of the availability of the sacrament of Reconciliation, which allows them to bring their sins and past mistakes, and their relationship itself, before God, and to receive in turn his merciful forgiveness and healing strength.

—Francis, *Amoris laetitia*, 211

Formation for true love is always the best preparation for the vocation to marriage. In the family, children and young people can learn to live human sexuality within the solid context of Christian life. They can gradually discover that a stable Christian marriage cannot be regarded as a matter of convenience or mere sexual attraction. By the fact that it is a vocation, marriage must involve a carefully considered choice, a mutual commitment before God and the constant seeking of his help in prayer.

—Pontifical Council for the Family, *The Truth and Meaning of Human Sexuality*, 27

Marriage preparation has to be seen and put into practice as a gradual and continuous process. It includes three main stages: remote, proximate and immediate preparation.

Remote preparation begins in early childhood, in that wise family training which leads children to discover themselves as being endowed with a rich and complex psychology and with a particular personality with its own strengths and weaknesses. It is the period when esteem for all authentic human values is instilled, both in interpersonal and in social relationships, with all that this signifies for the formation of character, for the control and right use of one's inclinations, for the manner of regarding and meeting people of the opposite sex, and so on. Also necessary, especially for Christians, is solid spiritual and catechetical formation that will show that marriage is a true vocation and mission, without excluding the possibility of the total gift of self to God in the vocation to the priestly or religious life.

Upon this basis there will subsequently and gradually be built up the proximate preparation, which—from the suitable age and with adequate catechesis, as in a catechumenal process—involves a more specific preparation for the sacraments, as it were, a rediscovery of them.... The religious formation of young people should be integrated, at the right moment and in accordance with the various concrete requirements, with a preparation for life as a couple. This preparation will present marriage as an interpersonal relationship of a man and a woman that has to be continually developed, and it will encourage those concerned to study the nature of conjugal sexuality and responsible parenthood, with the essential medical and biological knowledge connected with it....

The immediate preparation for the celebration of the sacrament of Matrimony should take place in the months and weeks immediately preceding the wedding, so as to give a new meaning, content and form to the so-called premarital enquiry required by Canon Law. This preparation is not only necessary in every case, but is also more urgently needed for engaged couples that still manifest shortcomings or difficulties in Christian doctrine and practice.

Among the elements to be instilled in this journey of faith, which is similar to the catechumenate, there must also be a deeper knowledge of the mystery of Christ and the Church, of the meaning of grace and of the responsibility of Christian marriage, as well as preparation for taking an active and conscious part in the rites of the marriage liturgy.

—John Paul II, *Familiaris consortio*, 66

―――― 25 ――――

Is there an ideal amount of time an engagement period should last?

Engagement is a path of life that has to ripen like fruit; it is a way of maturing in love, until the moment it becomes marriage....

Therefore engagement needs to be re-evaluated as a time of getting to know one another and sharing a plan. The path of preparation for marriage should be implemented from this perspective, also with the benefit of the simple but intense witness of Christian spouses. And also by focusing on the essentials: the Bible, by consciously rediscovering it together; prayer, in its liturgical dimension, but also in "domestic prayer" to live out in the home, the Sacraments, the Sacramental life, Confession, ... where the Lord comes to abide in the engaged couple and prepare them truly to receive one another "with the grace of Christ"; and fraternity with the poor and those in need, who lead us to live soberly and to share.

Engaged couples who commit themselves to this path both grow, and all of this leads to preparing for a beautiful celebration of Marriage in a different way, not in a worldly way, but in a Christian way! Let us consider these words of God we have heard, when he speaks to his people as bridegroom to his future bride: "I will betroth you to me forever; I will betroth you to me in righteousness and in justice, in steadfast love, and in mercy. I will betroth you to me in faithfulness; and you shall know the Lord" (Hos 2:19–20). May every engaged couple think of this and say to one another: "I will take you as my bride, I will take you as my bridegroom." Wait for that moment. It is a moment, it is a path that goes slowly ahead, but it is a path of maturation. The steps of the journey should not be rushed. This is how we mature, step by step.

The time of betrothal can truly become a time of initiation, into what? Into surprise. Into the surprise of the spiritual gifts with which the Lord, through the Church, enriches the horizon of the new family that stands ready to live in his blessing.

—Francis, General Audience, May 27, 2015

If you are engaged to be married, God has a project of love for your future as a couple and as a family. Therefore, it is essential that you discover it with the help of the Church, free from the common prejudice that says that Christianity with its commandments and prohibitions places obstacles to the joy of love and impedes you from fully enjoying the happiness that a man and woman seek in their reciprocal love. The love of a man and woman is at the origin of the human family and the couple formed by a man and a woman has its foundation in God's original plan (cf. Gn 2:18–25). Learning to love each other as a couple is a wonderful journey, yet it requires a demanding "apprenticeship."

—Benedict XVI, Message for World Youth Day, January 27, 2007

A promise of marriage, whether unilateral or bilateral, which is called an engagement, is governed by the particular law established by the conference of bishops, after he has considered any existing customs and civil laws. A promise to marry does not give rise to an action to seek the celebration of marriage; an action to repair damages, however, does arise if warranted.

—*Code of Canon Law*, c. 1062

———— 26 ————

What kind of marriage preparation does the church require? What should I look for in a good marriage prep program?

The complexity of today's society and the challenges faced by the family require a greater effort on the part of the whole Christian community in preparing those who are about to be married. The importance of the virtues needs to be included. Among these, chastity proves invaluable for the genuine growth of love between persons. In this regard, the Synod Fathers agreed on the need to involve the entire community more extensively by stressing the witness of families themselves and by grounding marriage preparation in the process of Christian initiation by bringing out the connection between marriage, baptism and the other sacraments. The Fathers also spoke of the need for specific programs of marriage preparation aimed at giving couples a genuine experience of participation in ecclesial life and a complete introduction to various aspects of family life.

—Francis, *Amoris laetitia*, 206 (citing the *Relatio synodi* of the 2014 Synod on the Family, 39)

Marriage preparation must be set within the urgent need to evangelize culture—by permeating it to its roots (cf. Apostolic Exhortation *Evangelii Nuntiandi*, 19)—in everything that concerns the institution of marriage: making the Christian spirit penetrate minds and behavior, as well as the laws and structures of the community where Christians live (cf. *Catechism of the Catholic Church*, n. 2105). This preparation, both implicitly and explicitly, constitutes one aspect of evangelization, so much so that it can deepen the strength of the Holy Father's affirmation: "The family is the heart of the New Evangelization." The preparation itself "is a responsibility which first concerns married couples, called to be givers of life, on the basis of an ever greater awareness of the meaning of procreation as a unique event which clearly reveals that human life is a gift received in order then to be given as a gift."

—Pontifical Council for the Family, *Preparation for the Sacrament of Marriage*, 20 (quoting John Paul II, *Evangelium vitae*, 92)

This religious character of marriage, its sublime signification of grace and the union between Christ and the Church, evidently requires that those about to marry should show a holy reverence towards it, and zealously endeavor to make their marriage approach as nearly as possible to the archetype of Christ and the Church.

—Pius XI, *Casti connubii*, 81

—— 27 ——

My fiancée was raised Protestant, but she has been agnostic for a number of years. As we prepare for marriage, she is reexamining her beliefs. How appropriate is it for me to invite her to consider becoming Catholic?

In marriages with disparity of cult the Catholic spouse has a particular task: "For the unbelieving husband is consecrated through his wife, and the unbelieving wife is consecrated through her husband" (1 Cor 7:16). It is a great joy for the Christian spouse and for the Church if this "consecration" should lead to the free conversion of the other spouse to the Christian faith. Sincere married love, the humble and patient practice of the family virtues, and perseverance in prayer can prepare the non-believing spouse to accept the grace of conversion.

—*Catechism of the Catholic Church*, 1637

—— 28 ——

What is the problem with living together without
being married? How are cohabitation and marriage
morally and spiritually different? What do I tell my
adult children who want to live together?

"At the risk of oversimplifying, we might say that we live in a culture
which pressures young people not to start a family, because they lack
possibilities for the future. Yet this same culture presents others with
so many options that they too are dissuaded from starting a family."
In some countries, many young persons "postpone a wedding for economic reasons, work or study. Some do so for other reasons, such as
the influence of ideologies which devalue marriage and family, the desire to avoid the failures of other couples, the fear of something they
consider too important and sacred, the social opportunities and economic benefits associated with simply living together, a purely emotional and romantic conception of love, the fear of losing their freedom
and independence, and the rejection of something conceived as purely institutional and bureaucratic." We need to find the right language,
arguments and forms of witness that can help us reach the hearts of
young people, appealing to their capacity for generosity, commitment,
love and even heroism, and in this way inviting them to take up the
challenge of marriage with enthusiasm and courage.

—Francis, *Amoris laetitia*, 40 (citing his own Address to the United
Nations, September 24, 2015; and the Final Report of the 2015
Synod on the Family 2015, 29)

Christian marriage, as a reflection of the union between Christ and
his Church, is fully realized in the union between a man and a woman
who give themselves to each other in a free, faithful and exclusive love,
who belong to each other until death and are open to the transmission
of life, and are consecrated by the sacrament, which grants them the

grace to become a domestic church and a leaven of new life for society. Some forms of union radically contradict this ideal, while others realize it in at least a partial and analogous way. The Synod Fathers stated that the Church does not disregard the constructive elements in those situations which do not yet or no longer correspond to her teaching on marriage.

—Francis, *Amoris laetitia*, 292

The covenant of love between man and woman—a covenant for life—*cannot be improvised*. It isn't made up one day to the next. There is no marriage express: one needs to work on love, one needs to walk. The covenant of love between man and woman is something learned and refined. I venture to say it is a covenant carefully crafted. To make two lives one is almost a miracle of freedom and the heart entrusted to faith. Perhaps we should emphasize this point more, because our "emotional coordinates" have gone a bit askew. Those who claim to want everything right away, then back out of everything—right away—at the first difficulty (or at the first opportunity). There is no hope for the trust and fidelity entailed in the gift of self, if prevailing tendency is to consume love like some kind of "supplement" for mental and physical well-being. This is not love! Engagement focuses on the will to care for something together that must never be bought or sold, betrayed or abandoned, however tempting the offer may be.

—Francis, General Audience, May 27, 2015

First, there is the purely factual character of the relationship. It should be pointed out that these unions imply cohabitation that includes a sexual relationship (which distinguishes them from other forms of cohabitation), and a relative tendency toward stability (which distinguishes them from sporadic or occasional forms of cohabitation). *De facto* unions do not imply marital rights and duties, and they do not presume to have the stability that is based on the marriage bond. They are characterized by their strong assertion to not take on any ties. The constant instability that comes from the possibility of terminating the cohabitation is consequently a characteristic of *de facto* unions. . . .

Some other persons who live together justify this choice because of economic reasons or to avoid legal difficulties. The real motives are often much deeper. In using this type of pretext, there is often an underlying mentality that gives little value to sexuality. This is influenced more or less by pragmatism and hedonism, as well as by a conception of love detached from any responsibility. The commitment is avoided to the stability, the responsibilities, and the rights and duties that real conjugal love includes.

—Pontifical Council for the Family, *Family, Marriage, and "De Facto" Unions,* 4–5

A serenely impartial perspective free from any arbitrary or demagogical positions invites us to reflect very seriously in the different political communities on the essential differences between the vital and necessary contribution to the common good of the family based on marriage, and the other reality that exists in merely emotional forms of cohabitation. It does not seem reasonable to hold that the vital functions of family communities, whose nucleus is the stable and monogamous institution of marriage, can be carried out in a large-scale, stable and permanent way by merely emotional forms of cohabitation.

—Pontifical Council for the Family, *Family, Marriage, and "De Facto" Unions,* 9

Ethical discernment, pastoral action and Christian engagement in political realities will thus have to take into consideration the many real situations included under the common term "*de facto* unions" as we said earlier. Whatever the causes that give rise to these unions, they entail "serious pastoral problems, because of the grave religious and moral consequences that are derived from them (loss of the religious meaning of marriage seen in the light of God's Covenant with his People, deprivation of the sacramental grace, serious scandal), as well as social consequences (destruction of the concept of family, lessening of the significance of fidelity, also toward society, possible psychological traumas in the children, and the reaffirmation of selfishness)."

—Pontifical Council for the Family, *Family, Marriage, and "De Facto" Unions*, 39 (quoting John Paul II, *Familiaris consortio*, 81)

Consequently, sexuality, by means of which man and woman give themselves to one another through the acts which are proper and exclusive to spouses, is by no means something purely biological, but concerns the innermost being of the human person as such. It is realized in a truly human way only if it is an integral part of the love by which a man and a woman commit themselves totally to one another until death. The total physical self-giving would be a lie if it were not the sign and fruit of a total personal self-giving, in which the whole person, including the temporal dimension, is present: if the person were to withhold something or reserve the possibility of deciding otherwise in the future, by this very fact he or she would not be giving totally.

—John Paul II, *Familiaris consortio*, 11

A first example of an irregular situation is provided by what are called "trial marriages," which many people today would like to justify by attributing a certain value to them. But human reason leads one to see that they are unacceptable, by showing the unconvincing nature of carrying out an "experiment" with human beings, whose dignity demands that they should be always and solely the term of a self-giving love without limitations of time or of any other circumstance.

The Church, for her part, cannot admit such a kind of union, for further and original reasons which derive from faith. For, in the first place, the gift of the body in the sexual relationship is a real symbol of the giving of the whole person: such a giving, moreover, in the present state of things cannot take place with full truth without the concourse of the love of charity, given by Christ. In the second place, marriage between two baptized persons is a real symbol of the union of Christ and the Church, which is not a temporary or "trial" union but one which is eternally faithful. Therefore, between two baptized persons there can exist only an indissoluble marriage.

Such a situation cannot usually be overcome unless the human person, from childhood, with the help of Christ's grace and without fear, has been trained to dominate concupiscence from the beginning and to establish relationships of genuine love with other people. This cannot be secured without a true education in genuine love and in the right use of sexuality, such as to introduce the human person in every aspect, and therefore the bodily aspect too, into the fullness of the mystery of Christ.

—John Paul II, *Familiaris consortio*, 80

EDITORS' NOTE: "Concupiscence" refers to intense desires that are contrary to reason or the good of the person. This disordering of our desires is the result of original sin. Baptism removes the guilt of sin (original and actual) but not this disorder that inclines us toward sin. ✛

——— 29 ———

All our friends are living together and are pressuring us to do it also. Are there downsides to cohabitation?

This is hardly to suggest that we cease warning against a cultural decline that fails to promote love or self-giving. The consultation that took place prior to the last two Synods pointed to the various symptoms of a "culture of the ephemeral." Here I think, for example, of the speed with which people move from one affective relationship to another. They believe, along the lines of social networks, that love can be connected or disconnected at the whim of the consumer, and the relationship quickly "blocked." I think too of the fears associated with permanent commitment, the obsession with free time, and those relationships that weigh costs and benefits for the sake of remedying loneliness, providing protection, or offering some service. We treat affective relationships the way we treat material objects and the environment: everything is disposable; everyone uses and throws away, takes and breaks, exploits and squeezes to the last drop. Then, goodbye. Narcissism makes people incapable of looking beyond themselves, beyond their own desires and needs. Yet sooner or later, those who use others end up being used themselves, manipulated and discarded by that same mind-set. It is also worth noting that breakups often occur among older adults who seek a kind of "independence" and reject the ideal of growing old together, looking after and supporting one another.

—Francis, *Amoris laetitia*, 39

The Church, in her wisdom, guards the *distinction between being engaged and being spouses*—it's not the same—especially in view of the delicateness and depth of this test. Let us be careful not to disregard lightheartedly the wisdom of this teaching, which also comes from the experience of happy married life. The powerful symbols of the body hold the keys to the soul: We cannot treat the bonds of the flesh lightly, without opening some lasting wound in the spirit (cf. 1 Cor 6:15–20).

—Francis, General Audience, May 27, 2015

What about cohabiting and marriage? Overall, less than half of cohabiting couples ever marry. Those who do choose to marry are in some part counter-culture to the growing view that it is certainly not necessary and perhaps not good to marry. Those who choose to marry instead of continuing to cohabit are the "good news" in a culture that is increasingly anti-marriage. Those cohabiting couples who move to marriage seem to be the "best risk" of a high-risk group: they have fewer risk factors than those cohabitors who choose not to marry. Even so, they still divorce at a rate 50 percent higher than couples who have never cohabited. They are a high-risk group for divorce and their special risk factors need to be identified and addressed, especially at the time of marriage preparation, if the couples are to build solid marriages.

What are the factors that put cohabitors who marry at risk? Individuals who choose to cohabit have certain attitudes, issues and patterns that lead them to make the decision to cohabit. These same attitudes, issues and patterns often become the predisposing factors to put them at high risk for divorce when they do choose to move from cohabitation to marriage. The cohabitation experience itself creates risk factors, bad habits, that can sabotage the subsequent marriage. These attitudes and patterns can be identified and brought to the couple preparing for marriage for examination, decision-making, skill-building, change. Without creating "self-fulfilling prophecies," those preparing cohabiting couples for marriage can help them identify and work with issues around commitment, fidelity, individualism, pressure, appropriate expectations.

—U.S. Conference of Catholic Bishops, *Marriage Preparation and Cohabiting Couples*, I, 4–5

EDITORS' NOTE: While statements by the USCCB do not have magisterial authority, they provide helpful pastoral guidance and are included for their relevance. Though this document was released in 1999, the ideas cited here have largely been confirmed in more recent social scientific research (see the sources listed in the additional resources at the end of this volume). ⚘

At times it appears that concerted efforts are being made to present as "normal" and attractive, and even to glamorize, situations which are in fact "irregular." Indeed, they contradict "the truth and love" which should inspire and guide relationships between men and women, thus causing tensions and divisions in families, with grave consequences particularly for children. The moral conscience becomes darkened; what is true, good and beautiful is deformed; and freedom is replaced by what is actually enslavement. In view of all this, how relevant and thought-provoking are the words of the Apostle Paul about the freedom for which Christ has set us free, and the slavery which is caused by sin (cf. Gal 5:1)!

—John Paul II, Letter to Families *Gratissimam sane*, 5

———— 30 ————

We have been living together, but now we want to get married. Should we expect a lot of flak from the church during marriage preparation?

We know that there is "a continual increase in the number of those who, after having lived together for a long period, request the celebration of marriage in Church. Simply to live together is often a choice based on a general attitude opposed to anything institutional or definitive; it can also be done while awaiting more security in life (a steady job and steady income). In some countries, *de facto* unions are very numerous, not only because of a rejection of values concerning the family and matrimony, but primarily because celebrating a marriage is considered too expensive in the social circumstances. As a result, material poverty drives people into *de facto* unions." Whatever the case, "all these situations require a constructive response seeking to transform them into opportunities that can lead to the full reality of marriage and family in conformity with the Gospel. These couples need to be welcomed and guided patiently and discreetly." That is how Jesus treated the Samaritan woman (cf. Jn 4:1–26): he addressed her desire for true love, in order to free her from the darkness in her life and to bring her to the full joy of the Gospel.

—Francis, *Amoris laetitia*, 294

Two extremes are to be avoided: (1) Immediately confronting the couple and condemning their behavior and (2) Ignoring the cohabitation aspect of their relationship.... The majority of policies and practices follow a middle way between the two extremes, one that integrates general correction with understanding and compassion.... Marriage preparation is an opportunity for evangelization and catechesis.... While couples need to be welcomed with the gospel values of love, understanding, and acceptance, they also need to be challenged by the gospel message of commitment and faithfulness.... Because of the awkwardness of dealing with the situation, some chose to ignore the entire issue. Increasingly, however, pastoral ministers have abandoned this approach in favor of addressing the cohabitation gently but directly. The Church has consistently taught that human love "demands a total and definitive gift of persons to one another" that can only be made in marriage (*Catechism of the Catholic Church*, 2391). Since cohabitation violates the Church's teaching about sexual love and marriage, church ministers must speak and teach about it. Doing so, as one diocese points out, "is an act of love for the couple in the process of spiritual growth" (*Pastoral Care of Sexually Active/Co-Habiting Couples Before Marriage*, Diocese of Peoria, 1997). How can pastoral ministers know if a couple is cohabiting? This can be a delicate situation. Very few diocesan policies offer suggestions for surfacing this issue during marriage preparation. Given the potentially harmful effects of cohabitation on marital stability, however, pastoral ministers are beginning to recognize a responsibility to raise the issue. Certain tip-offs (e.g., giving the same address and/or telephone number) can alert the pastoral minister that the couple may be cohabiting. Some couples are quite open about their living arrangements. A pastoral minister who is sensitive but straightforward can encourage a similarly candid attitude on the part of the couple. Some pastoral ministers discuss cohabitation in general terms, noting the issues it raises and the potentially harmful effects on the marriage. However it surfaces, cohabitation should be discussed early in the marriage preparation process. If it is not possible or advisable to discuss it immediately, it should be flagged as an issue to be addressed at a subsequent face-to-face meeting.

—U.S. Conference of Catholic Bishops, *Marriage Preparation and Cohabiting Couples*, II, 1

—— 31 ——

What kind of ongoing support and formation do married couples need to live out their vocation?

Among the causes of broken marriages are unduly high expectations about conjugal life. Once it becomes apparent that the reality is more limited and challenging than one imagined, the solution is not to think quickly and irresponsibly about separation, but to come to the sober realization that married life is a process of growth, in which each spouse is God's means of helping the other to mature. Change, improvement, the flowering of the good qualities present in each person—all these are possible. Each marriage is a kind of "salvation history," which from fragile beginnings—thanks to God's gift and a creative and generous response on our part—grows over time into something precious and enduring. Might we say that the greatest mission of two people in love is to help one another become, respectively, more a man and more a woman? Fostering growth means helping a person to shape his or her own identity. Love is thus a kind of craftsmanship. When we read in the Bible about the creation of man and woman, we see God first forming Adam (cf. Gn 2:7); he realizes that something essential is lacking and so he forms Eve and then hears the man exclaim in amazement, "Yes, this one is just right for me!" We can almost hear the amazing dialogue that must have taken place when the man and the woman first encountered one another. In the life of married couples, even at difficult moments, one person can always surprise the other, and new doors can open for their relationship, as if they were meeting for the first time. At every new stage, they can keep "forming" one another. Love makes each wait for the other with the patience of a craftsman, a patience which comes from God.

—Francis, *Amoris laetitia*, 221

The pastoral care of the regularly established family signifies, in practice, the commitment of all the members of the local ecclesial community to helping the couple to discover and live their new vocation and mission. In order that the family may be ever more a true community of love, it is necessary that all its members should be helped and trained in their responsibilities as they face the new problems that arise, in mutual service, and in active sharing in family life.

This holds true especially for young families, which, finding themselves in a context of new values and responsibilities, are more vulnerable, especially in the first years of marriage, to possible difficulties, such as those created by adaptation to life together or by the birth of children. Young married couples should learn to accept willingly, and make good use of, the discreet, tactful and generous help offered by other couples that already have more experience of married and family life. Thus, within the ecclesial community—the great family made up of Christian families—there will take place a mutual exchange of presence and help among all the families, each one putting at the service of others its own experience of life, as well as the gifts of faith and grace. Animated by a true apostolic spirit, this assistance from family to family will constitute one of the simplest, most effective and most accessible means for transmitting from one to another those Christian values which are both the starting point and goal of all pastoral care. Thus young families will not limit themselves merely to receiving, but in their turn, having been helped in this way, will become a source of enrichment for other longer established families, through their witness of life and practical contribution.

—John Paul II, *Familiaris consortio*, 69

————— 32 —————

Why do we need to better form those
pastoral agents who minister to couples? How can
we give better preparation to parish pastoral associates
and mentor couples who work with the engaged
and with married couples?

"The main contribution to the pastoral care of families is offered by the parish, which is the family of families, where small communities, ecclesial movements and associations live in harmony." Along with a pastoral outreach aimed specifically at families, this shows the need for "a more adequate formation ... of priests, deacons, men and women religious, catechists and other pastoral workers." In the replies given to the worldwide consultation, it became clear that ordained ministers often lack the training needed to deal with the complex problems currently facing families. The experience of the broad oriental tradition of a married clergy could also be drawn upon.

Seminarians should receive a more extensive interdisciplinary, and not merely doctrinal, formation in the areas of engagement and marriage. Their training does not always allow them to explore their own psychological and affective background and experiences. Some come from troubled families, with absent parents and a lack of emotional stability. There is a need to ensure that the formation process can enable them to attain the maturity and psychological balance needed for their future ministry. Family bonds are essential for reinforcing healthy self-esteem. It is important for families to be part of the seminary process and priestly life, since they help to reaffirm these and to keep them well grounded in reality. It is helpful for seminarians to combine time in the seminary with time spent in parishes. There they can have greater contact with the concrete realities of family life, since in their future ministry they will largely be dealing with families. "The presence of lay people, families and especially the presence of women in priestly formation, promotes an appreciation of the diversity and complementarity of the different vocations in the Church."

—Francis, *Amoris laetitia*, 202–3 (citing the Final Report of the 2015 Synod on the Family 2015, 77 and 61)

PREPARING FOR THE WEDDING DAY

——— 33 ———

If the church teaches that my spouse and I "marry each other," why do we need a church wedding with a deacon or priest?

According to the Latin tradition, the spouses as ministers of Christ's grace mutually confer upon each other the sacrament of Matrimony by expressing their consent before the Church. In the traditions of the Eastern Churches, the priests (bishops or presbyters) are witnesses to the mutual consent given by the spouses, but for the validity of the sacrament their blessing is also necessary.

—*Catechism of the Catholic Church*, 1623

The priest (or deacon) who assists at the celebration of a marriage receives the consent of the spouses in the name of the Church and gives the blessing of the Church. The presence of the Church's minister (and also of the witnesses) visibly expresses the fact that marriage is an ecclesial reality.

—*Catechism of the Catholic Church*, 1630

Inasmuch as it is a sacramental action of sanctification, the celebration of marriage—inserted into the liturgy, which is the summit of the Church's action and the source of her sanctifying power—must be per se valid, worthy and fruitful. This opens a wide field for pastoral solicitude, in order that the needs deriving from the nature of the conjugal covenant, elevated into a sacrament, may be fully met, and also in order that the Church's discipline regarding free consent, impediments, the canonical form and the actual rite of the celebration may be faithfully observed. The celebration should be simple and dignified, according to the norms of the competent authorities of the Church. It is also for them—in accordance with concrete circumstances of time and place and in conformity with the norms issued by the Apostolic See—to include in the liturgical celebration such elements proper to each culture which serve to express more clearly the profound human and religious significance of the marriage contract, provided that such elements contain nothing that is not in harmony with Christian faith and morality.

Inasmuch as it is a sign, the liturgical celebration should be conducted in such a way as to constitute, also in its external reality, a proclamation of the word of God and a profession of faith on the part of the community of believers. Pastoral commitment will be expressed here through the intelligent and careful preparation of the Liturgy of the Word and through the education to faith of those participating in the celebration and in the first place the couple being married.

Inasmuch as it is a sacramental action of the Church, the liturgical celebration of marriage should involve the Christian community, with the full, active and responsible participation of all those present, according to the place and task of each individual: the bride and bridegroom, the priest, the witnesses, the relatives, the friends, the other members of the faithful, all of them members of an assembly that manifests and lives the mystery of Christ and His Church. For the celebration of Christian marriage in the sphere of ancestral cultures or traditions, the principles laid down above should be followed.

—John Paul II, *Familiaris consortio*, 67

Those who shall attempt to contract marriage otherwise than in the presence of the parish priest, or of some other priest by permission of the said parish priest, or of the Ordinary, and in the presence of two or three witnesses; the holy Synod renders such wholly incapable of thus contracting and declares such contracts invalid and null, as by the present decree It invalidates and annuls them.

—Council of Trent, *Tametsi*, chap. 1. The translation is from "The
Council of Trent, The Twenty-Fourth Session," in *The Canons
and Decrees of the Sacred and Oecumenical Council of Trent,*
ed. and trans. J. Waterworth (London: Dolman, 1848), 197.

—— 34 ——
Can we get married on the beach?

In the Latin Rite the celebration of marriage between two Catholic faithful normally takes place during Holy Mass, because of the connection of all the sacraments with the Paschal mystery of Christ. In the Eucharist the memorial of the New Covenant is realized, the New Covenant in which Christ has united himself forever to the Church, his beloved bride for whom he gave himself up. It is therefore fitting that the spouses should seal their consent to give themselves to each other through the offering of their own lives by uniting it to the offering of Christ for his Church made present in the Eucharistic sacrifice, and by receiving the Eucharist so that, communicating in the same Body and the same Blood of Christ, they may form but "one body" in Christ.

—*Catechism of the Catholic Church*, 1621 (citing 1 Cor 10:17)

EDITORS' NOTE: "Latin rite" refers to the Western or "Roman" Catholic Church, originating in the lands where Latin was once spoken. There are other liturgical rites in union with the pope and thus fully "Catholic," but they may have different guidelines. ↲

Sacramental marriage is a liturgical act. It is therefore appropriate that it should be celebrated in the public liturgy of the Church.

—*Catechism of the Catholic Church,* 1630

Christian marriage normally requires a liturgical celebration expressing in social and community form the essentially ecclesial and sacramental nature of the conjugal covenant between baptized persons.

Inasmuch as it is a sacramental action of sanctification, the celebration of marriage—inserted into the liturgy, which is the summit of the Church's action and the source of her sanctifying power—must be per se valid, worthy and fruitful. This opens a wide field for pastoral solicitude, in order that the needs deriving from the nature of the conjugal covenant, elevated into a sacrament, may be fully met, and also in order that the Church's discipline regarding free consent, impediments, the canonical form and the actual rite of the celebration may be faithfully observed. The celebration should be simple and dignified, according to the norms of the competent authorities of the Church. It is also for them—in accordance with concrete circumstances of time and place and in conformity with the norms issued by the Apostolic See—to include in the liturgical celebration such elements proper to each culture which serve to express more clearly the profound human and religious significance of the marriage contract, provided that such elements contain nothing that is not in harmony with Christian faith and morality.

Inasmuch as it is a sign, the liturgical celebration should be conducted in such a way as to constitute, also in its external reality, a proclamation of the word of God and a profession of faith on the part of the community of believers. Pastoral commitment will be expressed here through the intelligent and careful preparation of the Liturgy of the Word and through the education to faith of those participating in the celebration and in the first place the couple being married.

—John Paul II, *Familiaris consortio*, 67

—— 35 ——

Can we write our own vows?

EDITORS' NOTE: The rite provides different options for the vows—memorizing the form given or responding to questions from the presiding deacon or priest. It does not provide for the option of couples simply writing their own vows. However, they may add to or modify the usual vows provided that they still reflect the Church's understanding of the goods of marriage—permanence, fidelity, and openness to children. ⚓

"I, N., take you, N., to be my wife/husband. I promise to be faithful to you in good times and in bad, in sickness and in health, to love you and honor you all the days of my life."

The following alternative may also be used:

"I, N., take you, N., for my lawful wife/husband, to have and to hold, from this day forward, for better, for worse, for richer, for poorer, in sickness and in health, to love and to cherish, until death do us part."

—1990 *Order of Celebrating Matrimony*, Formula for Exchange of Consent, 2nd ed. New English Translation from 2016.

"I take you as my wife"; "I take you as my husband"—these words are at the center of the liturgy of marriage as a sacrament of the Church. These words spoken by the engaged couple are inserted in the following formula of consent: "I promise to be faithful to you always, in joy and in sorrow, in sickness and in health, and to love and honor you all the days of my life." With these words the engaged couple enter the marriage contract and at the same time receive the sacrament of which both are the ministers. Both of them, the man and the woman, administer the sacrament. They do it before witnesses. The priest is a qualified witness, and at the same time he blesses the marriage and presides over the whole sacramental liturgy. Moreover, all those participating in the marriage rite are in a certain sense witnesses, and some of them (usually two) are called specifically to act as witnesses in an official way. They must testify that the marriage was contracted before God and confirmed by the Church. In the ordinary course of events sacramental marriage is a public act by means of which two persons, a man and a woman, become husband and wife before the ecclesial society, that is, they become the actual subject of the marriage vocation and life.

—John Paul II, General Audience on the Theology of the Body, January 5, 1983

——— 36 ———
What do the wedding vows mean?

Husbands, love your wives, even as Christ loved the church and handed himself over for her to sanctify her, cleansing her by the bath of water with the word, that he might present to himself the church in splendor, without spot or wrinkle or any such thing, that she might be holy and without blemish. So [also] husbands should love their wives as their own bodies. He who loves his wife loves himself. For no one hates his own flesh but rather nourishes and cherishes it, even as Christ does the church, because we are members of his body.

For this reason a man shall leave [his] father and [his] mother and be joined to his wife,

and the two shall become one flesh.

This is a great mystery, but I speak in reference to Christ and the church.

—Ephesians 5:25–32, New American Bible Revised Edition

In their preparation for marriage, the couple should be encouraged to make the liturgical celebration a profound personal experience and to appreciate the meaning of each of its signs. In the case of two baptized persons, the commitment expressed by the words of consent and the bodily union that consummates the marriage can only be seen as signs of the covenantal love and union between the incarnate Son of God and his Church. In the baptized, words and signs become an eloquent language of faith. The body, created with a God-given meaning, "becomes the language of the ministers of the sacrament, aware that in the conjugal pact there is expressed and realized the mystery that has its origin in God himself."

At times, the couple does not grasp the theological and spiritual import of the words of consent, which illuminate the meaning of all the signs that follow. It needs to be stressed that these words cannot be reduced to the present; they include a totality that includes the future: "until death do us part."

—Francis, *Amoris laetitia*, 213–14 (citing John Paul II, General Audience on the Theology of the Body, June 27, 1984)

——— 37 ———

Why should Christians aim to celebrate their weddings simply and prayerfully?

Short-term preparations for marriage tend to be concentrated on invitations, clothes, the party and any number of other details that tend to drain not only the budget but energy and joy as well. The spouses come to the wedding ceremony exhausted and harried, rather than focused and ready for the great step that they are about to take. The same kind of preoccupation with a big celebration also affects certain *de facto* unions; because of the expenses involved, the couple, instead of being concerned above all with their love and solemnizing it in the presence of others, never get married. Here let me say a word to fiancés. Have the courage to be different. Don't let yourselves get swallowed up by a society of consumption and empty appearances. What is important is the love you share, strengthened and sanctified by grace. You are capable of opting for a more modest and simple celebration in which love takes precedence over everything else. Pastoral workers and the entire community can help make this priority the norm rather than the exception.

—Francis, *Amoris laetitia,* 212

Make it a real celebration—because marriage is a celebration—a Christian celebration, not a worldly feast! … What happened in Cana 2,000 years ago, happens today at every wedding celebration: that which makes your wedding full and profoundly true will be the presence of the Lord who reveals himself and gives his grace. It is his presence that offers the "good wine," he is the secret to full joy, that which truly warms the heart. It is the presence of Jesus at the celebration. May it be a beautiful celebration, but with Jesus! Not with a worldly spirit, no! You can feel it when the Lord is there.

At the same time, however, it is good that your wedding be simple and make what is truly important stand out. Some are more concerned with the exterior details, with the banquet, the photographs, the clothes, the flowers…. These are important for a celebration, but only if they point to the real reason for your joy: the Lord's blessing on your love. Make it so that, like the wine in Cana, the exterior signs of your celebration reveal the Lord's presence and remind you and everyone present of the origin and the reason for your joy.

—Francis, Address to Engaged Couples Preparing for Marriage, February 14, 2014

—— 38 ——

How is a Christian wedding an opportunity to evangelize?

The marriage liturgy is a unique event, which is both a family and a community celebration. The first signs of Jesus were performed at the wedding feast of Cana. The good wine, resulting from the Lord's miracle that brought joy to the beginning of a new family, is the new wine of Christ's covenant with the men and women of every age.... Frequently, the celebrant speaks to a congregation that includes people who seldom participate in the life of the Church, or who are members of other Christian denominations or religious communities. The occasion thus provides a valuable opportunity to proclaim the Gospel of Christ.

—Francis, *Amoris laetitia*, 216 (quoting the Final Report of the 2015 Synod on the Family, 59)

Inasmuch as it is a sign, the liturgical celebration should be conducted in such a way as to constitute, also in its external reality, a proclamation of the word of God and a profession of faith on the part of the community of believers.

—John Paul II, *Familiaris consortio*, 67

—— 39 ——

Is it best to have the wedding ceremony as part of a Mass?

In the Latin Rite the celebration of marriage between two Catholic faithful normally takes place during Holy Mass, because of the connection of all the sacraments with the Paschal mystery of Christ. In the Eucharist the memorial of the New Covenant is realized, the New Covenant in which Christ has united himself forever to the Church, his beloved bride for whom he gave himself up. It is therefore fitting that spouses should seal their consent to give themselves to each other through the offering of their own lives by uniting it to the offering of Christ for his Church made present in the Eucharistic sacrifice, and by receiving the Eucharist so that, communicating in the same Body and the same Blood of Christ, they may form but "one body" in Christ.

— *Catechism of the Catholic Church*, 1621

Inasmuch as it is a sacramental action of sanctification, the celebration of marriage—inserted into the liturgy, which is the summit of the church's action and the source of her sanctifying power—must be *per se* valid, worthy, and fruitful.

—John Paul II, *Familiaris consortio*, 67

―――― 40 ――――

Do we only receive the Sacrament of Matrimony on the day of our wedding, and not after?

The Kenyan Bishops have observed that "many [young people] concentrate on their wedding day and forget the life-long commitment they are about to enter into." They need to be encouraged to see the sacrament not as a single moment that then becomes a part of the past and its memories, but rather as a reality that permanently influences the whole of married life. The procreative meaning of sexuality, the language of the body, and the signs of love shown throughout married life, all become an "uninterrupted continuity of liturgical language" and "conjugal life becomes in a certain sense liturgical."

—Francis, *Amoris laetitia*, 215

Another great challenge of marriage preparation is to help couples realize that marriage is not something that happens once for all. Their union is real and irrevocable, confirmed and consecrated by the sacrament of matrimony. Yet in joining their lives, the spouses assume an active and creative role in a lifelong project. Their gaze now has to be directed to the future that, with the help of God's grace, they are daily called to build.

—Francis, *Amoris laetitia*, 218

"By reason of their state in life and of their order [Christian spouses], have their own special gifts in the People of God." This grace proper to the sacrament of Matrimony is intended to perfect the couple's love and to strengthen their indissoluble unity. By this grace they "help one another to attain holiness in their married life and in welcoming and educating their children."

Christ is the source of this grace. "Just as of old God encountered his people with a covenant of love and fidelity, so our Savior, the spouse of the Church, now encounters Christian spouses through the sacrament of Matrimony." Christ dwells with them, gives them the strength to take up their crosses and so follow him, to rise again after they have fallen, to forgive one another, to bear one another's burdens, to "be subject to one another out of reverence for Christ," and to love one another with supernatural, tender, and fruitful love. In the joys of their love and family life he gives them here on earth a foretaste of the wedding feast of the Lamb.

—*Catechism of the Catholic Church*, 1641–42 (citing the Second
      Vatican Council, *Lumen gentium*, 11)

By virtue of the sacramentality of their marriage, spouses are bound to one another in the most profoundly indissoluble manner. Their belonging to each other is the real representation, by means of the sacramental sign, of the very relationship of Christ with the Church.

Spouses are therefore the permanent reminder to the Church of what happened on the Cross; they are for one another and for the children witnesses to the salvation in which the sacrament makes them sharers. Of this salvation event marriage, like every sacrament, is a memorial, actuation and prophecy: "As a memorial, the sacrament gives them the grace and duty of commemorating the great works of God and of bearing witness to them before their children. As actuation, it gives them the grace and duty of putting into practice in the present, towards each other and their children, the demands of a love which forgives and redeems. As prophecy, it gives them the grace and duty of living and bearing witness to the hope of the future encounter with Christ."

—John Paul II, *Familiaris consortio*, 13 (citing his own Address to the Delegates of the Centre de Liason des Équipes de Recherche [November 3, 1979], 3)

Christ the Lord abundantly blessed this many-faceted love, welling up as it does from the fountain of divine love and structured as it is on the model of His union with His Church. For as God of old made Himself present to His people through a covenant of love and fidelity, so now the Savior of men and the Spouse of the Church comes into the lives of married Christians through the sacrament of matrimony. He abides with them thereafter so that just as He loved the Church and handed Himself over on her behalf, the spouses may love each other with perpetual fidelity through mutual self-bestowal.

Authentic married love is caught up into divine love and is governed and enriched by Christ's redeeming power and the saving activity of the Church, so that this love may lead the spouses to God with powerful effect and may aid and strengthen them in sublime office of being a father or a mother. For this reason Christian spouses have a special sacrament by which they are fortified and receive a kind of consecration in the duties and dignity of their state. By virtue of this sacrament, as spouses fulfill their conjugal and family obligation, they are penetrated with the spirit of Christ, which suffuses their whole lives with faith, hope and charity. Thus they increasingly advance the perfection of their own personalities, as well as their mutual sanctification, and hence contribute jointly to the glory of God.

—Second Vatican Council, *Gaudium et spes*, 48

CHAPTER 4

Then Come Kids

Having and Raising Children

The chapter on children covers questions about procreation, education, and childrearing. Topics include the moral and spiritual difference between natural family planning (NFP) and contraception; what constitutes serious reason for avoiding conception; questions about adoption; choosing between public school, Catholic school, and homeschooling; appropriate sex education; reflections on breastfeeding; and child discipline (e.g., to spank or not).

—— 41 ——

Do married couples have to have children? Can we get married if we don't want to have any?

God blessed them and God said to them: Be fertile and multiply; fill the earth and subdue it. Have dominion over the fish of the sea, the birds of the air, and all the living things that crawl on the earth.

—Genesis 1:28, New American Bible Revised Edition

Love always gives life. Conjugal love "does not end with the couple.... The couple, in giving themselves to one another, give not just themselves but also the reality of children, who are a living reflection of their love, a permanent sign of their conjugal unity and a living and inseparable synthesis of their being a father and a mother."

—Francis, *Amoris laetitia*, 165 (citing John Paul II, *Familiaris consortio*, 14)

Unity, indissolubility, and openness to fertility are essential to marriage.

—*Catechism of the Catholic Church*, 1664

Thus the fundamental task of the family is to serve life, to actualize in history the original blessing of the Creator—that of transmitting by procreation the divine image from person to person. Fecundity is the fruit and the sign of conjugal love, the living testimony of the full reciprocal self-giving of the spouses....

—John Paul II, *Familiaris consortio*, 28

By its very nature the institution of marriage and married love is ordered to the procreation and education of the offspring and it is in them that it finds its crowning glory.

—Second Vatican Council, *Gaudium et spes,* 48

Children are really the supreme gift of marriage and contribute very substantially to the welfare of their parents. The God Himself Who said, "it is not good for man to be alone" (Gn 2:18) and "Who made man from the beginning male and female" (Mt 19:4), wishing to share with man a certain special participation in His own creative work, blessed male and female, saying: "Increase and multiply" (Gn 1:28). Hence, while not making the other purposes of matrimony of less account, the true practice of conjugal love, and the whole meaning of the family life which results from it, have this aim: that the couple be ready with stout hearts to cooperate with the love of the Creator and the Savior. Who through them will enlarge and enrich His own family day by day.

Parents should regard as their proper mission the task of transmitting human life and educating those to whom it has been transmitted. They should realize that they are thereby cooperators with the love of God the Creator, and are, so to speak, the interpreters of that love.

—Second Vatican Council, *Gaudium et spes,* 50

If, one of the parties contracted marriage with the intention of limiting the matrimonial right itself to the periods of sterility, and not only its use, in such a manner that during the other days the other party would not even have the right to ask for the debt, than this would imply an essential defect in the marriage consent, which would result in the marriage being invalid, because the right deriving from the marriage contract is a permanent, uninterrupted and continuous right of husband and wife with respect to each other.

—Pius XII, Address to the Conference of the Italian Catholic
Union of Obstetricians, October 29, 1951

—— 42 ——

Can we get married if one or both of us is infertile? What about impotence?

Some couples are unable to have children. We know that this can be a cause of real suffering for them....

Adoption is a very generous way to become parents. I encourage those who cannot have children to expand their marital love to embrace those who lack a proper family situation. They will never regret having been generous. Adopting a child is an act of love, offering the gift of a family to someone who has none. It is important to insist that legislation help facilitate the adoption process, above all in the case of unwanted children, in order to prevent their abortion or abandonment. Those who accept the challenge of adopting and accepting someone unconditionally and gratuitously become channels of God's love. For he says, "Even if your mother forgets you, I will not forget you" (Is 49:15).

—Francis, *Amoris laetitia*, 178–79

We also do well to remember that procreation and adoption are not the only ways of experiencing the fruitfulness of love. Even large families are called to make their mark on society, finding other expressions of fruitfulness that in some way prolong the love that sustains them.

—Francis, *Amoris laetitia*, 181

Spouses to whom God has not granted children can nevertheless have a conjugal life full of meaning, in both human and Christian terms. Their marriage can radiate a fruitfulness of charity, of hospitality, and of sacrifice.

—*Catechism of the Catholic Church*, 1654

Antecedent and perpetual impotence to have intercourse, whether on the part of the man or the woman, whether absolute or relative, nullifies marriage by its very nature.

If the impediment of impotence is doubtful, whether by a doubt about the law or a doubt about a fact, a marriage must not be impeded nor, while the doubt remains, declared null. Sterility neither prohibits nor nullifies marriage....

—*Code of Canon Law,* c. 1084

EDITORS' NOTE: Impotence refers to the physical inability to engage in sexual intercourse. It is an impediment to entering marriage (although subsequent development of impotence does not invalidate the marriage—Catholic marriages are either "null" at the beginning or they are indissoluble). Neither infertility nor sterility is an impediment to marriage. ✦

Marriage to be sure is not instituted solely for procreation; rather, its very nature as an unbreakable compact between persons, and the welfare of the children, both demand that the mutual love of the spouses be embodied in a rightly ordered manner, that it grow and ripen. Therefore, marriage persists as a whole manner and communion of life, and maintains its value and indissolubility, even when despite the often intense desire of the couple, offspring are lacking.

—Second Vatican Council, *Gaudium et spes,* 50

——— 43 ———

Aren't children just a financial burden? Why are they considered a blessing?

Certainly sons are a gift from the LORD, the fruit of the womb, a reward.

—Psalm 127:3, New American Bible Revised Edition

The process from conception and growth in the mother's womb to birth makes it possible to create a space within which the new creature can be revealed as a "gift": indeed this is what it is from the very beginning. Could this frail and helpless being, totally dependent upon its parents and completely entrusted to them, be seen in any other way? The newborn child gives itself to its parents by the very fact of its coming into existence. Its existence is already a gift, the first gift of the Creator to the creature.

In the newborn child is realized the common good of the family. Just as the common good of spouses is fulfilled in conjugal love, ever ready to give and receive new life, so too the common good of the family is fulfilled through that same spousal love, as embodied in the newborn child. Part of the genealogy of the person is the genealogy of the family, preserved for posterity by the annotations in the Church's baptismal registers, even though these are merely the social consequence of the fact that "a man has been born into the world" (cf. Jn 16:21).

But is it really true that the new human being is a gift for his parents? A gift for society? Apparently nothing seems to indicate this. On occasion the birth of a child appears to be a simple statistical fact, registered like so many other data in demographic records. It is true that for the parents the birth of a child means more work, new financial burdens and further inconveniences, all of which can lead to the temptation not to want another birth. In some social and cultural contexts this temptation can become very strong. Does this mean that a child is not a gift? That it comes into the world only to take and not to give? These are some of the disturbing questions which men and women today find hard to escape. A child comes to take up room, when it seems that there is less and less room in the world. But is it really true that a child brings nothing to the family and society? Is not every child a "particle" of that common good without which human communities break down and risk extinction? Could this ever really be denied? The child becomes a gift to its brothers, sisters, parents and entire family. Its life becomes a gift for the very people who were givers of life and who cannot help but feel its presence, its sharing in their life and its contribution to their common good and to that of the community of the family. This truth is obvious in its simplicity and profundity, whatever the complexity and even the possible pathology of the psychological make-up of certain persons. The common good of the whole of society dwells in man; he is, as we recalled, "the way of the Church." Man is first of all the "glory of God": "*Gloria Dei vivens homo*," in the celebrated words of Saint Irenaeus, which might also be translated: "the glory of God is for man to be alive." It could be said that here we encounter the loftiest definition of man: the glory of God is the common good of all that exists; the common good of the human race.

—John Paul II, Letter to Families *Gratissimam sane*, 11

Acceptance, love, esteem, many-sided and united material, emotional, educational and spiritual concern for every child that comes into this world should always constitute a distinctive, essential characteristic of all Christians, in particular of the Christian family: thus children, while they are able to grow "in wisdom and in stature, and in favor with God and man," offer their own precious contribution to building up the family community and even to the sanctification of their parents.

—John Paul II, *Familiaris consortio*, 26

Thus amongst the blessings of marriage, the child holds the first place. And indeed the Creator of the human race Himself, Who in His goodness wishes to use men as His helpers in the propagation of life, taught this when, instituting marriage in Paradise, He said to our first parents, and through them to all future spouses: "Increase and multiply, and fill the earth. . . ."

How great a boon of God this is, and how great a blessing of matrimony is clear from a consideration of man's dignity and of his sublime end. For man surpasses all other visible creatures by the superiority of his rational nature alone. Besides, God wishes men to be born not only that they should live and fill the earth, but much more that they may be worshippers of God, that they may know Him and love Him and finally enjoy Him forever in heaven; and this end, since man is raised by God in a marvelous way to the supernatural order, surpasses all that eye hath seen, and ear heard, and all that hath entered into the heart of man. From which it is easily seen how great a gift of divine goodness and how remarkable a fruit of marriage are children born by the omnipotent power of God through the cooperation of those bound in wedlock.

But Christian parents must also understand that they are destined not only to propagate and preserve the human race on earth, indeed not only to educate any kind of worshippers of the true God, but children who are to become members of the Church of Christ, to raise up fellow-citizens of the Saints, and members of God's household, that the worshippers of God and Our Savior may daily increase.... Both husband and wife, however, receiving these children with joy and gratitude from the hand of God, will regard them as a talent committed to their charge by God, not only to be employed for their own advantage or for that of an earthly commonwealth, but to be restored to God with interest on the day of reckoning.

—Pius XI, *Casti connubii*, 11–13, 15 (citing Gn 1:28)

—— 44 ——

Does the church want you to have as many children as you can? How many children are "enough"? What are legitimate serious reasons for avoiding or delaying children?

Large families are a joy for the Church. They are an expression of the fruitfulness of love. At the same time, Saint John Paul II rightly explained that responsible parenthood does not mean "unlimited procreation or lack of awareness of what is involved in rearing children, but rather the empowerment of couples to use their inviolable liberty wisely and responsibly, taking into account social and demographic realities, as well as their own situation and legitimate desires."

—Francis, *Amoris laetitia*, 167 (citing John Paul II, General Audience, March 12, 1982)

For just reasons, spouses may wish to space the births of their children. It is their duty to make certain that their desire is not motivated by selfishness but is in conformity with the generosity appropriate to responsible parenthood. Moreover, they should conform their behavior to the objective criteria of morality.

—*Catechism of the Catholic Church*, 2368

However, profoundly different from any contraceptive practice is the behavior of married couples, who, always remaining fundamentally open to the gift of life, live their intimacy only in the unfruitful periods, when they are led to this course by serious motives of responsible parenthood. This is true both from the anthropological and moral points of view, because it is rooted in a different conception of the person and of sexuality. The witness of couples who for years have lived in harmony with the plan of the Creator, and who, for proportionately serious reasons, licitly use the methods rightly called "natural," confirms that it

is possible for spouses to live the demands of chastity and of married
life with common accord and full self-giving.

—Pontifical Council for the Family, *Vademecum for Confessors
Concerning Some Aspects of the Morality of Conjugal Life*, 2.6

If, then, there are serious motives to space out births, which derive
from the physical or psychological conditions of husband and wife,
or from external conditions, the Church teaches that it is then licit
to take into account the natural rhythms immanent in the generative
functions, for the use of marriage in the infecund periods only, and in
this way to regulate birth without offending the moral principles which
have been recalled earlier.

—Paul VI, *Humanae vitae*, 16

Let them thoughtfully take into account both their own welfare and
that of their children, those already born and those which the future
may bring. For this accounting they need to reckon with both the material and the spiritual conditions of the times as well as of their state
in life. Finally, they should consult the interests of the family group, of
temporal society, and of the Church herself. The parents themselves
and no one else should ultimately make this judgment in the sight of
God. But in their manner of acting, spouses should be aware that they
cannot proceed arbitrarily, but must always be governed according to
a conscience dutifully conformed to the divine law itself, and should
be submissive toward the Church's teaching office, which authentically
interprets that law in the light of the Gospel. That divine law reveals
and protects the integral meaning of conjugal love, and impels it toward
a truly human fulfillment. Thus, trusting in divine Providence and re-
fining the spirit of sacrifice, married Christians glorify the Creator and
strive toward fulfillment in Christ when with a generous human and
Christian sense of responsibility they acquit themselves of the duty to
procreate. Among the couples who fulfill their God-given task in this

way, those merit special mention who with a gallant heart and with wise and common deliberation, undertake to bring up suitably even a relatively large family.

—Second Vatican Council, *Gaudium et spes*, 50

——— 45 ———

I understand that the church's teaching allows couples to have intercourse if they "use the methods rightly called 'natural,'" but if my spouse and I are not actively trying to conceive a child, wouldn't the church prefer that we abstain from sex altogether? Isn't that the holier choice?

Now in regard to the matters about which you wrote: "It is a good thing for a man not to touch a woman," but because of cases of immorality every man should have his own wife, and every woman her own husband. The husband should fulfill his duty toward his wife, and likewise the wife toward her husband. A wife does not have authority over her own body, but rather her husband, and similarly a husband does not have authority over his own body, but rather his wife. Do not deprive each other, except perhaps by mutual consent for a time, to be free for prayer, but then return to one another, so that Satan may not tempt you through your lack of self-control. This I say by way of concession, however, not as a command. Indeed, I wish everyone to be as I am, but each has a particular gift from God, one of one kind and one of another.

—1 Corinthians 7:1–7, New American Bible Revised Edition

Consequently, "it is not a matter of diminishing the value of matrimony in favor of continence." "There is no basis for playing one off against the other.... If, following a certain theological tradition, one speaks of a 'state of perfection' (*status perfectionis*), this has to do not with continence in itself, but with the entirety of a life based on the evangelical counsels." A married person can experience the highest degree of charity and thus "reach the perfection which flows from charity, through fidelity to the spirit of those counsels. Such perfection is possible and accessible to every man and woman."

> —Francis, *Amoris laetitia*, 160 (citing John Paul II, General Audience on the Theology of the Body, April 7, 1982)

This outward expression of love in the home demands not only mutual help but must go further; must have as its primary purpose that man and wife help each other day by day in forming and perfecting themselves in the interior life, so that through their partnership in life they may advance ever more and more in virtue, and above all that they may grow in true love toward God and their neighbor, on which indeed "dependeth the whole Law and the Prophets." For all men of every condition, in whatever honorable walk of life they may be, can and ought to imitate that most perfect example of holiness placed before man by God, namely Christ Our Lord, and by God's grace to arrive at the summit of perfection, as is proved by the example set us of many saints.

This mutual molding of husband and wife, this determined effort to perfect each other, can in a very real sense, as the Roman Catechism teaches, be said to be the chief reason and purpose of matrimony, provided matrimony be looked at not in the restricted sense as instituted for the proper conception and education of the child, but more widely as the blending of life as a whole and the mutual interchange and sharing thereof.

> —Pius XI, *Casti connubii*, 23–24 (citing Matthew 22:40)

—— 46 ——

Because natural family planning and contraception both have the same goal— limiting the number of children—aren't they morally the same?

EDITORS' NOTE: Natural family planning refers to a variety of methods of fertility awareness which help couples to achieve or avoid pregnancy based on the timing of sexual intercourse. These methods can even help couples with limited fertility to become pregnant. Unlike the unreliable calendar rhythm method, they are based on the specific fertility signs of individual women and so are at least as effective as most forms of artificial contraception and carry none of the health risks. ✤

Moreover, "the use of methods based on the 'laws of nature and the incidence of fertility' (*Humanae vitae*, 11) are to be promoted, since 'these methods respect the bodies of the spouses, encourage tenderness between them and favor the education of an authentic freedom' (*Catechism of the Catholic Church*, 2370). Greater emphasis needs to be placed on the fact that children are a wonderful gift from God and a joy for parents and the Church. Through them, the Lord renews the world."

> —Francis, *Amoris laetitia*, 222 (citing the Final Report of the 2015 Synod on the Family, 63)

When couples, by means of recourse to contraception, separate these two meanings that God the Creator has inscribed in the being of man and woman and in the dynamism of their sexual communion [i. e., the unitive and procreative], they act as "arbiters" of the divine plan and they "manipulate" and degrade human sexuality—and with it themselves and their married partner—by altering its value of "total" self-giving. Thus the innate language that expresses the total reciprocal self-giving of husband and wife is overlaid, through contraception, by an objectively contradictory language, namely, that of not giving oneself totally to the other. This leads not only to a positive refusal to be open to life but also to a falsification of the inner truth of conjugal love, which is called upon to give itself in personal totality.

When, instead, by means of recourse to periods of infertility, the couple respect the inseparable connection between the unitive and procreative meanings of human sexuality, they are acting as "ministers" of God's plan and they "benefit from" their sexuality according to the original dynamism of "total" self-giving, without manipulation or alteration.

In the light of the experience of many couples and of the data provided by the different human sciences, theological reflection is able to perceive and is called to study further the difference, both anthropological and moral, between contraception and recourse to the rhythm of the cycle: it is a difference which is much wider and deeper than is usually thought, one which involves in the final analysis two irreconcilable concepts of the human person and of human sexuality. The choice of the natural rhythms involves accepting the cycle of the person, that is the woman, and thereby accepting dialogue, reciprocal respect, shared responsibility and self-control. To accept the cycle and to enter into dialogue means to recognize both the spiritual and corporal character of conjugal communion and to live personal love with its requirement of fidelity. In this context the couple comes to experience how conjugal communion is enriched with those values of tenderness and affection which constitute the inner soul of human sexuality, in its physical dimension also. In this way sexuality is respected and promoted in its truly and fully human dimension, and is never "used" as an "object" that, by breaking the personal unity of soul and body, strikes at God's creation itself at the level of the deepest interaction of nature and person.

—John Paul II, *Familiaris consortio*, 32

To use this divine gift destroying, even if only partially, its meaning and purpose is to contradict the nature both of man and of woman and of their most intimate relationship, and therefore it is to contradict also the plan of God and His will. On the other hand, to make use of the gift of conjugal love while respecting the laws of the generative process means to acknowledge oneself not to be the arbiter of the sources of human life, but rather the minister of the design established by the Creator. In fact, just as man does not have unlimited dominion over his body in general, so also, with particular reason, he has no such dominion over his generative faculties as such, because of their intrinsic ordination towards raising up life, of which God is the principle.

—Paul VI, *Humanae vitae*, 13

Any use whatsoever of matrimony exercised in such a way that the act is deliberately frustrated in its natural power to generate life is an offense against the law of God and of nature, and those who indulge in such are branded with the guilt of a grave sin.

—Pius XI, *Casti connubii*, 56

—— 47 ——

Isn't having a vasectomy or tubal ligation okay if I've already had enough children?

Except when performed for strictly therapeutic medical reasons, directly intended amputations, mutilations, and sterilizations performed on innocent persons are against the moral law.

—*Catechism of the Catholic Church*, 2297

Equally to be excluded, as the teaching authority of the Church has frequently declared, is direct sterilization, whether perpetual or temporary, whether of the man or of the woman.

—Paul VI, *Humanae vitae*, 14

EDITORS' NOTE: Direct sterilization refers to medical procedures whose primary aim is render a person infertile (e.g., a vasectomy or tubal ligation). This is distinct from treatment for a serious medical condition that has the foreseen but unintended result of leaving a person sterile. The former is only chosen for the sake of sterilization; the latter is chosen to treat a different condition, and the sterilization is simply a side effect. ⚓

It would be more than a mere lack of readiness in the service of life if an attack made by man were to concern not only a single act but should affect the organism itself to deprive it, by means of sterilization, of the faculty of procreating a new life. Here, too, you have a clear rule in the Church's teaching to guide your behavior both interiorly and exteriorly. Direct sterilization— that is, whose aim tends as a means or as an end at making procreation impossible—is a grave violation of the moral law and therefore unlawful. Not even public authority has any right, under the pretext of any "indication" whatsoever, to permit it, and less still to prescribe it or to have it used to the detriment of innocent human beings.

This principle is already proclaimed in the above-mentioned Encyclical of Pius XI on marriage. Thus when ten years or so ago sterilization came to be more widely applied, the Holy See saw the necessity of expressly and publicly declaring that direct sterilization, either perpetual or temporary, in either the male or the female, is unlawful according to natural law, from which, as you well know, not even the Church has the power to dispense.

—Pius XII, Address to the Conference of the Italian Catholic
Union of Obstetricians, October 29, 1951

Furthermore, Christian doctrine establishes, and the light of human reason makes it most clear, that private individuals have no other power over the members of their bodies than that which pertains to their natural ends; and they are not free to destroy or mutilate their members, or in any other way render themselves unfit for their natural functions, except when no other provision can be made for the good of the whole body.

—Pius XI, *Casti connubii*, 71

—— 48 ——

How does the church view government-mandated contraception, sterilization, and abortion?

It is irresponsible to view sexuality merely as a source of pleasure, and likewise to regulate it through strategies of mandatory birth control. In either case materialistic ideas and policies are at work, and individuals are ultimately subjected to various forms of violence. Against such policies, there is a need to defend the primary competence of the family in the area of sexuality, as opposed to the State and its restrictive policies, and to ensure that parents are suitably prepared to undertake their responsibilities.

—Benedict XVI, *Caritas in veritate*, 44

To claim the right to abortion, infanticide and euthanasia, and to recognize that right in law, means to attribute to human freedom a perverse and evil significance: that of an absolute power over others and against others. This is the death of true freedom: "Truly, truly, I say to you, everyone who commits sin is a slave to sin" (Jn 8:34). "Abortion and euthanasia are thus crimes which no human law can claim to legitimize. There is no obligation in conscience to obey such laws; instead there is a grave and clear obligation to oppose them by conscientious objection. From the very beginnings of the Church, the apostolic preaching reminded Christians of their duty to obey legitimately constituted public authorities (cf. Rom 13:1–7; 1 Pt 2:13–14), but at the same time it firmly warned that "we must obey God rather than men" (Acts 5:29).

—John Paul II, *Evangelium vitae*, 73

Finally, careful consideration should be given to the danger of this power passing into the hands of those public authorities who care little for the precepts of the moral law. Who will blame a government which in its attempt to resolve the problems affecting an entire country resorts to the same measures as are regarded as lawful by married people in the solution of a particular family difficulty? Who will prevent public authorities from favoring those contraceptive methods which they consider more effective? Should they regard this as necessary, they may even impose their use on everyone. It could well happen, therefore, that when people, either individually or in family or social life, experience the inherent difficulties of the divine law and are determined to avoid them, they may give into the hands of public authorities the power to intervene in the most personal and intimate responsibility of husband and wife.

—Paul VI, *Humanae vitae*, 17

EDITORS' NOTE: Government coercion can lessen the culpability of individuals for participating in such programs. However, it cannot make them morally good. Individuals sterilized or forced to undergo abortions against their will are not morally culpable for this violence against them. ⚘

——— 49 ———

What should I do if my spouse refuses to practice natural family planning and insists on contracepting?

Special difficulties are presented by cases of cooperation in the sin of a spouse who voluntarily renders the unitive act infecund. In the first place, it is necessary to distinguish cooperation in the proper sense, from violence or unjust imposition on the part of one of the spouses, which the other spouse in fact cannot resist. This cooperation can be licit when the three following conditions are jointly met:

1. when the action of the cooperating spouse is not already illicit in itself;
2. when proportionally grave reasons exist for cooperating in the sin of the other spouse;
3. when one is seeking to help the other spouse to desist from such conduct (patiently, with prayer, charity and dialogue; although not necessarily in that moment, nor on every single occasion).

Furthermore, it is necessary to carefully evaluate the question of cooperation in evil when recourse is made to means which can have an abortifacient effect.

—Pontifical Council for the Family, *Vademecum for Confessors Concerning Some Aspects of the Morality of Conjugal Life*, 13–14

Holy Church knows well that not infrequently one of the parties is sinned against rather than sinning, when for a grave cause he or she reluctantly allows the perversion of the right order. In such a case, there is no sin, provided that, mindful of the law of charity, he or she does not neglect to seek to dissuade and to deter the partner from sin.

—Pius XI, *Casti connubii*, 59

50

What if I have been using the Pill since my teen years to regulate a heavy period? Can I still use it now that I am married? Can I use the Pill for other medical conditions? Acne? PCOS (Polycystic Ovarian Syndrome)? Endometriosis?

The morality of human acts depends on: the object chosen; the end in view or the intention; the circumstances of the action. The object, the intention, and the circumstances make up the "sources," or constitutive elements, of the morality of human acts.

—*Catechism of the Catholic Church*, 1750

EDITORS' NOTE: The object refers to the intelligible good recognized by the mind and pursued by the will in a human act. An act bad in itself (i.e., objectively evil) cannot be made good by the agent's end or the circumstances surrounding it. A defect in any of these three fonts (object, end, or circumstances) renders an act morally bad. ✤

The Church, on the contrary, does not at all consider illicit the use of those therapeutic means truly necessary to cure diseases of the organism, even if an impediment to procreation, which may be foreseen, should result therefrom, provided such impediment is not, for whatever motive, directly willed.

— Paul VI, *Humanae vitae*, 15

They [the above-mentioned principles] also enable Us to resolve a question much discussed these days by doctors and moralists:

- Is it licit to prevent ovulation by means of pills used as remedies against excessive reactions of the uterus and of the organism, even though this medication by preventing ovulation also makes conception impossible? "An organism" is "a complete living unit." Hence, "the human system" would probably be its nearest equivalent in this context.
- Is this [treatment] allowed to the married woman who, despite this temporary sterility, wishes to have relations with her husband?
- The intention of the person determines the answer.

If the woman takes the medicament, not with the idea of preventing conception, but solely on the advice of her doctor as a necessary remedy for a disorder of the uterus or organism, she is causing an indirect sterilization, which is allowed according to the principle governing acts with a double effect.

— Pius XII, Address to Seventh International Congress of
Hematology, September 12, 1958

——— 51 ———

We are faithful Catholics and want to follow
church teaching. What constitutes "grave reason" for
using natural family planning to avoid conceiving?
What if a pregnancy poses a significant
health risk to the wife?

However, profoundly different from any contraceptive practice is the
behavior of married couples, who, always remaining fundamentally
open to the gift of life, live their intimacy only in the unfruitful periods, when they are led to this course by serious motives of responsible parenthood. This is true both from the anthropological and moral
points of view, because it is rooted in a different conception of the person and of sexuality. The witness of couples who for years have lived in
harmony with the plan of the Creator, and who, for proportionately serious reasons, licitly use the methods rightly called "natural," confirms
that it is possible for spouses to live the demands of chastity and of
married life with common accord and full self-giving.

—Pontifical Council for the Family, *Vademecum for Concerning
Some Aspects of the Morality of Conjugal Life*, 2.6

For just reasons, spouses may wish to space the births of their children.
It is their duty to make certain that their desire is not motivated by selfishness but is in conformity with the generosity appropriate to responsible parenthood. Moreover, they should conform their behavior to the
objective criteria of morality.

—*Catechism of the Catholic Church*, 2368

With regard to physical, economic, psychological and social conditions, responsible parenthood is exercised by those who prudently
and generously decide to have more children, and by those who, for
serious reasons and with due respect to moral precepts, decide not to

have additional children for either a certain or an indefinite period of time.

—Paul VI, *Humanae vitae*, 10

If therefore there are well-grounded reasons for spacing births, arising from the physical or psychological condition of husband or wife, or from external circumstances, the Church teaches that married people may then take advantage of the natural cycles immanent in the reproductive system and engage in marital intercourse only during those times that are infertile, thus controlling birth in a way which does not in the least offend the moral principles which We have just explained.

Neither the Church nor her doctrine is inconsistent when she considers it lawful for married people to take advantage of the infertile period but condemns as always unlawful the use of means which directly prevent conception, even when the reasons given for the later practice may appear to be upright and serious. In reality, these two cases are completely different. In the former the married couple rightly use a faculty provided them by nature. In the latter they obstruct the natural development of the generative process. It cannot be denied that in each case the married couple, for acceptable reasons, are both perfectly clear in their intention to avoid children and wish to make sure that none will result. But it is equally true that it is exclusively in the former case that husband and wife are ready to abstain from intercourse during the fertile period as often as for reasonable motives the birth of another child is not desirable. And when the infertile period recurs, they use their married intimacy to express their mutual love and safeguard their fidelity toward one another. In doing this they certainly give proof of a true and authentic love.

—Paul VI, *Humanae vitae*, 16

Serious motives, such as those which not rarely arise from medical, eugenic, economic and social so-called "indications," may exempt husband and wife from the obligatory, positive debt for a long period or even for the entire period of matrimonial life. From this it follows that the observance of the natural sterile periods may be lawful, from the moral viewpoint: and it is lawful in the conditions mentioned. If, however, according to a reasonable and equitable judgment, there are no such grave reasons either personal or deriving from exterior circumstances, the will to avoid the fecundity of their union, while continuing to satisfy to the full their sensuality, can only be the result of a false appreciation of life and of motives foreign to sound ethical principles.

—Pius XII, Address to the Conference of the Italian Catholic Union of Obstetricians, October 29, 1951

——— 52 ———
Do couples have a "right" to have children even if it means using reproductive technologies?

The predominant school of thought sometimes leads to "false compassion" which holds that it is a benefit to women to promote abortion; an act of dignity to perform euthanasia; a scientific breakthrough to "produce" a child, considered as a right rather than a gift to be welcomed; or to using human lives as laboratory animals, allegedly in order to save others. Instead, the compassion of the Gospel is what accompanies us in times of need, that compassion of the Good Samaritan, who "sees," "has compassion," draws near and provides concrete help (cf. Lk 10:33). Your mission as doctors places you in daily contact with so many forms of suffering. I encourage you to take them on as "Good Samaritans," caring in a special way for the elderly, the infirm and the disabled. Faithfulness to the Gospel of life and respect for life as a gift from God sometimes require brave choices that go against the current, which in particular circumstances may become points of conscientious objection. This faithfulness brings with it many social consequences.

We are living in a time of experimentation with life. But it is harmful experimentation. Making children, rather than accepting them as a gift, as I said. Playing with life. Be careful, because this is a sin against the Creator: against God the Creator, who created things this way.

—Francis, Address to the Italian Catholic Physicians Association,
November 15, 2014

On the part of the spouses, the desire for a child is natural: it express-es the vocation to fatherhood and motherhood inscribed in conjugal love. This desire can be even stronger if the couple is affected by ste-rility which appears incurable. Nevertheless, marriage does not con-fer upon the spouses the right to have a child, but only the right to perform those natural acts which are *per se* ordered to procreation. *A true and proper right to a child would be contrary to the child's dignity and nature. The child is not an object to which one has a right, nor can he be considered as an object of ownership: rather, a child is a gift, "the supreme gift" and the most gratuitous gift of marriage, and is a living testimony of the mutual giving of his parents. For this reason, the child has the right, as already mentioned, to be the fruit of the specific act of the conjugal love of his parents; and he also has the right to be respected as a person from the moment of his conception.*

—Congregation for the Doctrine of the Faith, *Donum vitae*, II.8
(citing the Second Vatican Council, *Gaudium et spes*, 58)

—— 53 ——

Does the church say anything about medical care during pregnancy and birth? Should we try to have a natural birth?

EDITORS' NOTE: The Church generally does not recommend specific forms of medical treatment, leaving such decisions to the counsel of physicians and the conscience of their patients in the light of general principles of Christian anthropology (the study of the human person). Instead the magisterium will describe as illicit certain procedures which violate human dignity or human life. ⚘

When a woman is in labor, she is in anguish because her hour has arrived; but when she has given birth to a child, she no longer remembers the pain because of her joy that a child has been born into the world.

—John 16:21, New American Bible Revised Edition

Scientific advances today allow us to know beforehand what color a child's hair will be or what illnesses they may one day suffer, because all the somatic traits of the person are written in his or her genetic code already in the embryonic stage. Yet only the Father, the Creator, fully knows the child; he alone knows his or her deepest identity and worth. Expectant mothers need to ask God for the wisdom fully to know their children and to accept them as they are. Some parents feel that their child is not coming at the best time. They should ask the Lord to heal and strengthen them to accept their child fully and wholeheartedly. It is important for that child to feel wanted. He or she is not an accessory or a solution to some personal need. A child is a human being of immense worth and may never be used for one's own benefit. So it matters little whether this new life is convenient for you, whether it has features that please you, or whether it fits into your plans and aspirations. For "children are a gift. Each one is unique and irreplaceable.... We love our children because they are children, not because they are beautiful, or look or think as we do, or embody our dreams. We love them because they are children. A child is a child." The love of parents is the means by which God our Father shows his own love. He awaits the birth of each child, accepts that child unconditionally, and welcomes him or her freely.

With great affection I urge all future mothers: keep happy and let nothing rob you of the interior joy of motherhood. Your child deserves your happiness. Don't let fears, worries, other people's comments or problems lessen your joy at being God's means of bringing a new life to the world. Prepare yourself for the birth of your child, but without obsessing, and join in Mary's song of joy: "My soul proclaims the greatness of the Lord and my spirit exults in God my Savior, for he has looked with favor on the lowliness of his servant" (Lk 1:46–48). Try to experience this serene excitement amid all your many concerns, and ask the Lord to preserve your joy, so that you can pass it on to your child.

—Francis, *Amoris laetitia*, 170–71

The dignity of a person must be recognized in every human being from conception to natural death. This fundamental principle expresses a great "yes" to human life and must be at the center of ethical reflection on biomedical research, which has an ever greater importance in today's world.

—Congregation for the Doctrine of the Faith,
Dignitatis personae, 1

Prenatal diagnosis, which presents no moral objections if carried out in order to identify the medical treatment which may be needed by the child in the womb, all too often becomes an opportunity for proposing and procuring an abortion. This is eugenic abortion, justified in public opinion on the basis of a mentality—mistakenly held to be consistent with the demands of "therapeutic interventions"—which accepts life only under certain conditions and rejects it when it is affected by any limitation, handicap or illness.

Following this same logic, the point has been reached where the most basic care, even nourishment, is denied to babies born with serious handicaps or illnesses. The contemporary scene, moreover, is becoming even more alarming by reason of the proposals, advanced here and there, to justify even infanticide, following the same arguments used to justify the right to abortion. In this way, we revert to a state of barbarism which one hoped had been left behind forever.

—John Paul II, *Evangelium vitae*, 14

Thus, in relation to life at birth or at death, man is no longer capable of posing the question of the truest meaning of his own existence, nor can he assimilate with genuine freedom these crucial moments of his own history. He is concerned only with "doing," and, using all kinds of technology, he busies himself with programming, controlling and dominating birth and death. Birth and death, instead of being primary experiences demanding to be "lived," become things to be merely "possessed" or "rejected."

—John Paul II, *Evangelium vitae*, 22

Since it must be treated from conception as a person, the embryo must be defended in its integrity, cared for, and healed, as far as possible, like any other human being.

Prenatal diagnosis is morally licit, "if it respects the life and integrity of the embryo and the human fetus and is directed toward its safeguarding or healing as an individual. . . . It is gravely opposed to the moral law when this is done with the thought of possibly inducing an abortion, depending upon the results: a diagnosis must not be the equivalent of a death sentence."

"One must hold as licit procedures carried out on the human embryo which respect the life and integrity of the embryo and do not involve disproportionate risks for it, but are directed toward its healing the improvement of its condition of health, or its individual survival." "It is immoral to produce human embryos intended for exploitation as disposable biological material." "Certain attempts to influence chromosomic or genetic inheritance are not therapeutic but are aimed at producing human beings selected according to sex or other predetermined qualities. Such manipulations are contrary to the personal dignity of the human being and his integrity and identity" which are unique and unrepeatable.

—*Catechism of the Catholic Church*, 2274–75 (citing the
Congregation for the Doctrine of the Faith, *Donum vitae*, I)

Infuse into the spirit and heart of the mother and father the esteem, desire, joy, and the loving welcome of the newly born right from its first cry. The child, formed in the mother's womb, is a gift of God, Who entrusts its care to the parents.... Immediately after birth, be quick to place the child in the father's arms—as the ancient Romans were wont to do—but with a spirit incomparably more elevated. For the Romans, it was the affirmation of the paternity and the authority which derived from it; here it is grateful homage to the Creator, the invocation of divine blessings, the promise to fulfill with devout affection the office which God has committed him. If the Lord praises and rewards the faithful servant for having yielded him five talents, what praise, what reward will He reserve for the father, who has guarded and raised for Him a human life entrusted to him, greater than all the gold and silver of the world?

Your apostolate, however, is directed above all to the mother. Undoubtedly nature's voice speaks in her and places in her heart the desire, joy, courage, love and will to care for the child; but to overcome the suggestions of fearfulness in all its forms, that voice must be strengthened and take on, so to say, a supernatural accent. It is your duty to cause the young mother to enjoy, less by your words than by your whole manner of acting, the greatness, beauty and nobility of that life which begins, is formed and lives in her womb, that child which she bears in her arms and suckles at her breast; to make shine in her eyes and heart the great gift of God's love for her and her child.

—Pius XII, Address to the Conference of the Italian Catholic
Union of Obstetricians, October 29, 1951

CATHOLIC PARENTHOOD

——— 54 ———

We had a baby before we got married. Can we still be a good Catholic family?

Jesus Christ is the face of the Father's mercy. These words might well sum up the mystery of the Christian faith. Mercy has become living and visible in Jesus of Nazareth, reaching its culmination in him. The Father, "rich in mercy" (Eph 2:4), after having revealed his name to Moses as "a God merciful and gracious, slow to anger, and abounding in steadfast love and faithfulness" (Ex 34:6), has never ceased to show, in various ways throughout history, his divine nature. In the "fullness of time" (Gal 4:4), when everything had been arranged according to his plan of salvation, he sent his only Son into the world, born of the Virgin Mary, to reveal his love for us in a definitive way. Whoever sees Jesus sees the Father (cf. Jn 14:9). Jesus of Nazareth, by his words, his actions, and his entire person reveals the mercy of God.

—Francis, *Misercordiae vultus*, 1

If a child comes into this world in unwanted circumstances, the parents and other members of the family must do everything possible to accept that child as a gift from God and assume the responsibility of accepting him or her with openness and affection. For "when speaking of children who come into the world, no sacrifice made by adults will be considered too costly or too great, if it means the child never has to feel that he or she is a mistake, or worthless or abandoned to the four winds and the arrogance of man." The gift of a new child, entrusted by the Lord to a father and a mother, begins with acceptance, continues with lifelong protection, and has as its final goal the joy of eternal life. By serenely contemplating the ultimate fulfillment of each human person, parents will be even more aware of the precious gift entrusted to them. For God allows parents to choose the name by which he himself will call their child for all eternity.

> —Francis, *Amoris laetitia*, 166 (citing his own catechesis of
> April 8, 2015)

All children, whether born in or out of wedlock, enjoy the same right to social protection, with a view to their integral personal development.

> —Pontifical Council for the Family, *Charter of the Rights of the
> Family*, article 4e

Every family has the right to live freely its own domestic religious life under the guidance of the parents, as well as the right to profess publicly and to propagate the faith, to take part in public worship and in freely chosen programs of religious instruction, without suffering discrimination.

> —Pontifical Council for the Family, *Charter of the Rights of the
> Family*, article 7

——— 55 ———

If a couple adopts a child is that child really "theirs"?

Adopting children, regarding and treating them as one's own children, means recognizing that the relationship between parents and children is not measured only by genetic standards. Procreative love is first and foremost a gift of self. There is a form of "procreation" which occurs through acceptance, concern and devotion. The resulting relationship is so intimate and enduring that it is in no way inferior to one based on a biological connection. When this is also juridically protected, as it is in adoption, in a family united by the stable bond of marriage, it assures the child that peaceful atmosphere and that paternal and maternal love which he needs for his full human development.

> —John Paul II, *Address to the Meeting of Adoptive Families* (September 5, 2000), 4

Adoption is a very generous way to become parents. I encourage those who cannot have children to expand their marital love to embrace those who lack a proper family situation. They will never regret having been generous. Adopting a child is an act of love, offering the gift of a family to someone who has none. It is important to insist that legislation help facilitate the adoption process, above all in the case of unwanted children, in order to prevent their abortion or abandonment. Those who accept the challenge of adopting and accepting someone unconditionally and gratuitously become channels of God's love. For he says, "Even if your mother forgets you, I will not forget you" (Is 49:15).

"The choice of adoption and foster care expresses a particular kind of fruitfulness in the marriage experience, and not only in cases of infertility. In the light of those situations where a child is desired at any cost, as a right for one's self-fulfillment, adoption and foster care, correctly understood, manifest an important aspect of parenting and the raising of children. They make people aware that children, whether natural, adoptive or taken in foster care, are persons in their own right who need to be accepted, loved and cared for, and not just brought into this world. The best interests of the child should always underlie any decision in adoption and foster care." On the other hand, "the trafficking of children between countries and continents needs to be prevented by appropriate legislative action and state control."

> —Francis, *Amoris laetitia*, 179–80 (citing the Final Report of the 2015 Synod on the Family, 65)

——— 56 ———

What does the church say
about breastfeeding?

Today the choir sings, but the most beautiful choir is the children making noise.... Some of them will cry, because they are uncomfortable or
because they are hungry: if they are hungry, mothers, feed them with
ease, because they are the most important ones here.

—Francis, Homily at Feast of Baptism of the Lord and
Administration of the Sacrament of Baptism, January 12, 2014

Worldwide surveys indicate that "two thirds of mothers still breast-
feed," at least to some extent. But statistics also show that there has
been a fall in the number of women who nourish their infants in this
way, not only in developed countries where the practice almost has to
be reinstituted, but also increasingly in developing countries.

This decline is traced to a combination of social factors such as ur-
banization and the increasing demands placed on women, to health-
care policies and practices, and to marketing strategies for alternate
forms of nourishment.

Yet the overwhelming body of research is in favor of natural feeding
rather than its substitutes. Responsible international agencies are calling on governments to ensure that women are enabled to breast-feed
their children for four to six months from birth and to continue this
practice, supplemented by other appropriate foods, up to the second
year of life or beyond (cf. UNICEF "Children and Development in the
1990s" on the occasion of the World Summit for Children, New York,
29–30 September 1990). Your meeting therefore intends to illustrate
the scientific bases for encouraging social policies and employment
conditions which allow mothers to do this.

In practical terms, what we are saying is that "mothers need time,
information and support." So much is expected of women in many so-

cieties that time to devote to breast-feeding and early care is not always available. Unlike other modes of feeding, no one can substitute for the mother in this natural activity. Likewise, women have a right to be informed truthfully about the advantages of this practice, as also about the difficulties involved in some cases. Health-care professionals too should be encouraged and properly trained to help women in these matters....

Even this brief reflection on the very individual and private act of a mother feeding her infant can lead us to a deep and far-ranging critical rethinking of certain social and economic presuppositions, the negative human and moral consequences of which are becoming more and more difficult to ignore. Certainly, "a radical re-examination of many aspects of prevailing socio-economic patterns of work, economic competitiveness and lack of attention to the needs of the family is urgently necessary."

—John Paul II, Address to Breastfeeding Study Group of the
Pontifical Academy of Sciences, May 12, 1995

We see in mothers those who exert the earliest and the most intimate influence upon the souls of the little ones and upon their growth in piety and virtue. Surely there is no art more difficult and strenuous than that of fashioning the souls of children; for those souls are so very tender, so easily disfigured through some thoughtless influence or wrong advice, so difficult to guide aright and so lightly led astray. This is the reason why, except where it is quite impossible, it is more desirable that the mother should feed her child at her own breast. Who shall say what mysterious influences are exerted upon the growth of that little creature by the mother upon whom it depends entirely for its development?

—Pius XII, Address, October 26, 1941. From *The Major Addresses of Pope Pius XII*, vol. 1, *Selected Addresses*, ed. Vincent A. Yzermans (St. Paul: North Central Publishing, 1961), 44.

—— 57 ——

Is spanking okay for Catholics? What sort of discipline is recommended?

Correction is also an incentive whenever children's efforts are appreciated and acknowledged, and they sense their parents' constant, patient trust. Children who are lovingly corrected feel cared for; they perceive that they are individuals whose potential is recognized. This does not require parents to be perfect, but to be able humbly to acknowledge their own limitations and make efforts to improve. Still, one of the things children need to learn from their parents is not to get carried away by anger. A child who does something wrong must be corrected, but never treated as an enemy or an object on which to take out one's own frustrations. Adults also need to realize that some kinds of misbehavior have to do with the frailty and limitations typical of youth. An attitude constantly prone to punishment would be harmful and not help children to realize that some actions are more serious than others. It would lead to discouragement and resentment: "Parents, do not provoke your children" (Eph 6:4; cf. Col 3:21).

It is important that discipline not lead to discouragement, but be instead a stimulus to further progress. How can discipline be best interiorized? How do we ensure that discipline is a constructive limit placed on a child's actions and not a barrier standing in the way of his or her growth? A balance has to be found between two equally harmful extremes. One would be to try to make everything revolve around the child's desires; such children will grow up with a sense of their rights but not their responsibilities. The other would be to deprive the child of an awareness of his or her dignity, personal identity and rights; such children end up overwhelmed by their duties and a need to carry out other people's wishes.

—Francis, *Amoris laetitia*, 269–70

A good father knows how to wait and knows how to forgive from the depths of his heart. Certainly, he also knows how to correct with firmness: he is not a weak father, submissive and sentimental. The father who knows how to correct without humiliating is the one who knows how to protect without sparing himself. Once I heard a father at a meeting on marriage say: "Sometimes I have to strike the children lightly ... but never in the face so as not to humiliate them." How beautiful! He has a sense of dignity. He must punish, but he does it in a just way, and moves on.

—Francis, General Audience, February 4, 2015

Parents have the first responsibility for the education of their children. They bear witness to this responsibility first by creating a home where tenderness, forgiveness, respect, fidelity, and disinterested service are the rule. The home is well suited for education in the virtues.... Parents have a grave responsibility to give good example to their children. By knowing how to acknowledge their own failings to their children, parents will be better able to guide and correct them: "He who loves his son will not spare the rod.... He who disciplines his son will profit by him." "Fathers, do not provoke your children to anger, but bring them up in the discipline and instruction of the Lord."

—*Catechism of the Catholic Church*, 2223 (citing Sirach 30:1–2 and Eph 6:4)

In addition to those characteristics, it cannot be forgotten that the most basic element, so basic that it qualifies the most educational role of parents, is parental love, which finds fulfillment in the task of education as it completes and perfects its service to life. As well as being a source, the parents' love is also the animating principle and therefore the norm inspiring and guiding all concrete educational activity, enriching it with the values of kindness, constancy, goodness, service, disinterestedness and self-sacrifice that are the most precious fruit of love.

—John Paul II, *Familiaris consortio*, 36

——— 58 ———
Shouldn't I let my kids
decide for themselves what
they believe?

Raising children calls for an orderly process of handing on the faith. This is made difficult by current lifestyles, work schedules and the complexity of today's world, where many people keep up a frenetic pace just to survive. Even so, the home must continue to be the place where we learn to appreciate the meaning and beauty of the faith, to pray and to serve our neighbor. This begins with baptism, in which, as Saint Augustine said, mothers who bring their children "cooperate in the sacred birthing." Thus begins the journey of growth in that new life. Faith is God's gift, received in baptism, and not our own work, yet parents are the means that God uses for it to grow and develop. Hence "it is beautiful when mothers teach their little children to blow a kiss to Jesus or to Our Lady. How much love there is in that! At that moment the child's heart becomes a place of prayer." Handing on the faith presumes that parents themselves genuinely trust God, seek him and sense their need for him, for only in this way does "one generation laud your works to another, and declare your mighty acts" (Ps 144:4) and "fathers make known to children your faithfulness" (Is 38:19). This means that we need to ask God to act in their hearts, in places where we ourselves cannot reach. A mustard seed, small as it is, becomes a great tree (cf. Mt 13:31–32); this teaches us to see the disproportion between our actions and their effects. We know that we do not own the gift, but that its care is entrusted to us. Yet our creative commitment is itself an offering which enables us to cooperate with God's plan. For this reason, "couples and parents should be properly appreciated as active agents in catechesis.... Family catechesis is of great assistance as an effective method in training young parents to be aware of their mission as the evangelizers of their own family."

> —Francis, *Amoris laetitia*, 287 (citing his own catechesis of August 26, 2015; and the Final Report of the 2015 Synod on the Family, 89)

Parents are the first heralds of the gospel to their children.

> —John Paul II, *Familiaris consortio*, 30

The ministry of evangelization carried out by Christian parents is original and irreplaceable. It assumes the characteristics typical of family life itself, which should be interwoven with love, simplicity, practicality and daily witness.

The family must educate the children for life in such a way that each one may fully perform his or her role according to the vocation received from God. Indeed, the family that is open to transcendent values, that serves its brothers and sisters with joy, that fulfills its duties with generous fidelity, and is aware of its daily sharing in the mystery of the glorious Cross of Christ, becomes the primary and most excellent seed-bed of vocations to a life of consecration to the Kingdom of God.

The parents' ministry of evangelization and catechesis ought to play a part in their children's lives also during adolescence and youth, when the children, as often happens, challenge or even reject the Christian faith received in earlier years. Just as in the Church the work of evangelization can never be separated from the sufferings of the apostle, so in the Christian family parents must face with courage and great interior serenity the difficulties that their ministry of evangelization sometimes encounters in their own children.

> —John Paul II, *Familiaris consortio*, 53

For no one can fail to see that children are incapable of providing wholly for themselves, even in matters pertaining to their natural life, and much less in those pertaining to the supernatural, but require for many years to be helped, instructed, and educated by others. Now it is certain that both by the law of nature and of God this right and duty of educating their offspring belongs in the first place to those who began the work of nature by giving them birth, and they are indeed forbidden to leave unfinished this work and so expose it to certain ruin....

Since, however, We have spoken fully elsewhere on the Christian education of youth, let Us sum it all up by quoting once more the words of St. Augustine: "As regards the offspring it is provided that they should be begotten lovingly and educated religiously,"—and this is also expressed succinctly in the Code of Canon Law—"The primary end of marriage is the procreation and the education of children."

—Pius XI, *Casti connubii*, 16–17 (citing *Divini illius Magistri*, 1929; St. Augustine, *De Genesis ad litt.*, Bk 9, ch. 7, n. 12; and the 1917 Code of Canon Law, c. 1013 and 7)

———— 59 ————

Can I send my children to public schools, or should I always prefer Catholic schools? What about homeschooling?

The right and duty of parents to give education is essential, since it is connected with the transmission of human life; it is original and primary with regard to the educational role of others on account of the uniqueness of the loving relationship between parents and children; and it is irreplaceable and inalienable and therefore incapable of being entirely delegated to others or usurped by others.

—John Paul II, *Familiaris consortio*, 36

The family is the primary but not the only and exclusive educating community. Man's community aspect itself—both civil and ecclesial— demands and leads to a broader and more articulated activity resulting from well-ordered collaboration between the various agents of education. All these agents are necessary, even though each can and should play its part in accordance with the special competence and contribution proper to itself.

The educational role of the Christian family therefore has a very important place in organic pastoral work. This involves a new form of cooperation between parents and Christian communities, and between the various educational groups and pastors. In this sense, the renewal of the Catholic school must give special attention both to the parents of the pupils and to the formation of a perfect educating community.

The right of parents to choose an education in conformity with their religious faith must be absolutely guaranteed.

The State and the Church have the obligation to give families all possible aid to enable them to perform their educational role properly. Therefore both the Church and the State must create and foster the institutions and activities that families justly demand, and the aid must be in proportion to the families' needs. However, those in society who are in charge of schools must never forget that the parents have been appointed by God Himself as the first and principal educators of their children and that their right is completely inalienable.

But corresponding to their right, parents have a serious duty to commit themselves totally to a cordial and active relationship with the teachers and the school authorities.

If ideologies opposed to the Christian faith are taught in the schools, the family must join with other families, if possible through family associations, and with all its strength and with wisdom help the young not to depart from the faith. In this case the family needs special assistance from pastors of souls, who must never forget that parents have the inviolable right to entrust their children to the ecclesial community.

—John Paul II, *Familiaris consortio*, 40

The absolute need for family catechesis emerges with particular force in certain situations that the Church unfortunately experiences in some places: "In places where anti-religious legislation endeavors even to prevent education in the faith, and in places where widespread unbelief or invasive secularism makes real religious growth practically impossible, 'the Church of the home' remains the one place where children and young people can receive an authentic catechesis."

—John Paul II, *Familiaris consortio*, 52

Since parents have conferred life on their children, they have a most solemn obligation to educate their offspring. Hence, parents must be acknowledged as the first and foremost educators of their children. Their role as educators is so decisive that scarcely anything can compensate for their failure in it.

—Second Vatican Council, *Gravissimum educationis*, 3

EDITORS' NOTE: The Church's understanding is that whether or not parents choose a Catholic school, another private school, homeschool, or public school, they still have the primary responsibility to oversee their children's education, whatever setting they choose. The collaboration of schools—whether Catholic or public—should not undermine this parental role. ⤶

——— 60 ———

Can my kids attend "sex ed" in public school?

Frequently, sex education deals primarily with "protection" through the practice of "safe sex." Such expressions convey a negative attitude towards the natural procreative finality of sexuality, as if an eventual child were an enemy to be protected against. This way of thinking promotes narcissism and aggressivity in place of acceptance. It is always irresponsible to invite adolescents to toy with their bodies and their desires, as if they possessed the maturity, values, mutual commitment and goals proper to marriage. They end up being blithely encouraged to use other persons as a means of fulfilling their needs or limitations. The important thing is to teach them sensitivity to different expressions of love, mutual concern and care, loving respect and deeply meaningful communication. All of these prepare them for an integral and generous gift of self that will be expressed, following a public commitment, in the gift of their bodies. Sexual union in marriage will thus appear as a sign of an all-inclusive commitment, enriched by everything that has preceded it.

—Francis, *Amoris laetitia*, 283

In particular, there is a need for education about the value of life from its very origins. It is an illusion to think that we can build a true culture of human life if we do not help the young to accept and experience sexuality and love and the whole of life according to their true meaning and in their close interconnection. Sexuality, which enriches the whole person, "manifests its inmost meaning in leading the person to the gift of self in love." The trivialization of sexuality is among the principal factors which have led to contempt for new life. Only a true love is able to protect life. There can be no avoiding the duty to offer, especially to adolescents and young adults, an authentic education in sexuality and in love, an education which involves training in chastity as a virtue which fosters personal maturity and makes one capable of respecting the "spousal" meaning of the body.

—John Paul II, *Evangelium vitae*, 97 (citing *Familiaris consortio*, 37)

Education, in the first place, is the duty of the family, which "is the school of richest humanity." It is, in fact, the best environment to accomplish the obligation of securing a gradual education in sexual life. The family has an affective dignity which is suited to making acceptable

without trauma the most delicate realities and to integrating them harmoniously in a balanced and rich personality.

> —Sacred Congregation for Catholic Education, *Educational*
> *Guidance in Human Love*, 48

It being understood from what has been said on the primary duty of
the family, the role of the school should be that of assisting and com-
pleting the work of the parents, furnishing children and adolescents
with an evaluation of "sexuality as value and task of the whole person,
created male and female in the image of God."

> —Sacred Congregation for Catholic Education, *Educational*
> *Guidance in Human Love*, 69

Sex education is not reducible to simple teaching material, nor to theoretical knowledge alone, nor does it consist of a program to be carried
out progressively, but it has a specific objective in view: that affective
maturation of the pupil, of self-control, and of correct behavior in social relationships.

> —Sacred Congregation for Catholic Education, *Educational*
> *Guidance in Human Love*, 70

Only a strict collaboration between the school and the family will be
able to guarantee an advantageous exchange of experience between
parents and teachers for the good of the pupils. It is the responsibility
of Bishops, taking account of school legislation and local circumstances, to establish guidelines for sex education in groups, above all if they
are mixed.

> —Sacred Congregation for Catholic Education, *Educational*
> *Guidance in Human Love*, 72

Sex education, which is a basic right and duty of parents, must always
be carried out under their attentive guidance whether at home or in
educational centers chosen and controlled by them. In this regard, the

church reaffirms the law of subsidiarity, which the school is bound to observe when it cooperates in sex education, by entering into the same spirit that animates the parents.... In view of the close links between the sexual dimension of the person and his or her ethical values, education must bring the children to a knowledge of and respect for the moral norms as the necessary and highly valuable guarantee for responsible personal growth in human sexuality.

For this reason, the church is firmly opposed to an often widespread form of imparting sex information dissociated from moral principles. That would merely be an introduction to the experience of pleasure and a stimulus leading to the loss of serenity—while still in the years of innocence—by opening the way to vice.

—John Paul II, *Familiaris consortio*, 37

───── 61 ─────

How can I prepare my children for the challenges of dating and courtship?

By keeping open a confident dialogue that encourages a sense of responsibility and respects their children's legitimate and necessary autonomy, parents will always be their reference point, through both advice and example, so that the process of broader socialization will make it possible for them to achieve a mature and integrated personality, internally and socially. In a special way, care should be taken that children do not discontinue their faith relationship with the Church and her activities which, on the contrary, should be intensified. They should learn how to choose models of thought and life for their future and how to become committed in the cultural and social area as Christians, without fear of professing that they are Christians and without losing a sense of vocation and the search for their own vocation....

Parents should avoid adopting the widespread mentality whereby girls are given every recommendation regarding virtue and the value of virginity, while the same is not required for boys, as if everything were licit for them.

For a Christian conscience and a vision of marriage and the family, St. Paul's recommendation to the Philippians holds for every type of vocation: "… whatever is true, whatever is honorable, whatever is just, whatever is pure, whatever is lovely, whatever is gracious, if there is any excellency, if there is anything worthy of praise, think about these things" (Phil 4:8).

> —Pontifical Council for the Family, *The Truth and Meaning of Human Sexuality*, 110–11

Especially in the heart of their own families, young people should be aptly and seasonably instructed in the dignity, duty and work of married love. Trained thus in the cultivation of chastity, they will be able at a suitable age to enter a marriage of their own after an honorable courtship.

> —Second Vatican Council, *Gaudium et spes*, 49

——— 62 ———

Why is it important for children to have a mother and a father to help to raise them?

"Children, once born, begin to receive, along with nourishment and care, the spiritual gift of knowing with certainty that they are loved. This love is shown to them through the gift of their personal name, the sharing of language, looks of love and the brightness of a smile. In this way, they learn that the beauty of human relationships touches our soul, seeks our freedom, accepts the difference of others, recognizes and respects them as a partner in dialogue…. Such is love, and it contains a spark of God's love!" Every child has a right to receive love from mother and a father; both are necessary for a child's integral and harmonious development. As the Australian Bishops have observed, each of the spouses "contributes in a distinct way to the upbringing of a child. Respecting a child's dignity means affirming his or her need and natural right to have a mother and a father." We are speaking not simply of the love of father and mother as individuals, but also of their mutual love, perceived as the source of one's life and the solid foundation of the family. Without this, a child could become a mere plaything. Husband and wife, father and mother, both "cooperate with the love of God the Creator, and are, in a certain sense, his interpreters." They show their children the maternal and paternal face of the Lord. Together they teach the value of reciprocity, of respect for differences and of being able to give and take. If for some inevitable reason one parent should be lacking, it is important to compensate for this loss, for the sake of the child's healthy growth to maturity.

> —Francis, *Amoris laetitia*, 172 (citing his own catechesis of
> October 15, 2015; the Australian Bishops, Pastoral Letter
> *Don't Mess with Marriage*; and the Second Vatican Council,
> *Gaudium et spes*, 50)

It is necessary first to promote the fundamental pillars that govern a nation: its non-material goods. The family is the foundation of co-existence and a remedy against social fragmentation. Children have a right to grow up in a family with a father and a mother capable of creating a suitable environment for the child's development and emotional maturity....

> —Francis, Address to the Humanum Conference,
> November 17, 2014

The eternal mystery of generation, which is in God himself, the one and Triune God (cf. Eph 3:14–15), is reflected in the woman's motherhood and in the man's fatherhood. Human parenthood is something shared by both the man and the woman. Even if the woman, out of love for her husband, says: "I have given you a child," her words also mean: "This is our child." Although both of them together are parents of their child, the woman's motherhood constitutes a special "part" in this shared parenthood, and the most demanding part. Parenthood—even though it belongs to both—is realized much more fully in the woman, especially in the prenatal period. It is the woman who "pays" directly for this shared generation, which literally absorbs the energies of her body and soul. It is therefore necessary that the man be fully aware that in their shared parenthood he owes a special debt to the woman. No program of "equal rights" between women and men is valid unless it takes this fact fully into account.

Motherhood involves a special communion with the mystery of life, as it develops in the woman's womb. The mother is filled with wonder at this mystery of life, and "understands" with unique intuition what is happening inside her. In the light of the "beginning," the mother accepts and loves as a person the child she is carrying in her womb. This unique contact with the new human being developing within her gives rise to an attitude towards human beings—not only towards her own child, but every human being—which profoundly marks the woman's personality. It is commonly thought that women are more capable than men of paying attention to another person, and that motherhood develops this predisposition even more. The man—even with all his sharing in parenthood—always remains "outside" the process of pregnancy and the baby's birth; in many ways he has to learn his own "fatherhood" from the mother. One can say that this is part of the normal human dimension of parenthood, including the stages that follow the birth of the baby, especially the initial period. The child's upbringing, taken as a whole, should include the contribution of both parents: the maternal and paternal contribution. In any event, the mother's contribution is decisive in laying the foundation for a new human personality.

—John Paul II, *Mulieris dignitatem*, 18

A mother who watches over her child with tenderness and compassion helps him or her to grow in confidence and to experience that the world is a good and welcoming place. This helps the child to grow in self-esteem and, in turn, to develop a capacity for intimacy and empathy. A father, for his part, helps the child to perceive the limits of life, to be open to the challenges of the wider world, and to see the need for hard work and strenuous effort. A father possessed of a clear and serene masculine identity who demonstrates affection and concern for his wife is just as necessary as a caring mother.

—Francis, *Amoris laetitia*, 175

——— 63 ———

Why are grandparents and other extended family members important for a married couple and their children?

Saint John Paul II asked us to be attentive to the role of the elderly in our families, because there are cultures which, "especially in the wake of disordered industrial and urban development, have both in the past and in the present set the elderly aside in unacceptable ways." The elderly help us to appreciate "the continuity of the generations," by their "charism of bridging the gap." Very often it is grandparents who ensure that the most important values are passed down to their grandchildren, and "many people can testify that they owe their initiation into the Christian life to their grandparents." Their words, their affection or simply their presence help children to realize that history did not begin with them, that they are now part of an age-old pilgrimage and that they need to respect all that came before them. Those who would break all ties with the past will surely find it difficult to build stable relationships and to realize that reality is bigger than they are. Attention to the elderly makes the difference in a society. Does a society show concern for the elderly? Does it make room for the elderly? Such a society will move forward if it respects the wisdom of the elderly.

> —Francis, *Amoris laetitia,* 192 (citing John Paul II, *Familiaris consortio,* 27; the Final Report of the 2015 Synod on the Family, 18; and his own catechesis of March 4, 2016)

The prayer of grandparents and of the elderly is a great gift for the Church! The prayer of grandparents and of the elderly is a great gift for the Church, it is a treasure! A great injection of wisdom for the whole of human society: above all for one which is too busy, too taken, too distracted....

How beautiful, however, is the encouragement an elderly person manages to pass on to a young person who is seeking the meaning of faith and of life! It is truly the mission of grandparents, the vocation of the elderly. The words of grandparents have special value for the young. And the young know it. I still carry with me, always, in my breviary, the words my grandmother consigned to me in writing on the day of my priestly ordination. I read them often and they do me good.

How I would like a Church that challenges the throw-away culture with the overflowing joy of a new embrace between young and old! This is what I ask of the Lord today, this embrace!

> —Pope Francis, General Audience, March 11, 2015

The Church has always paid special attention to grandparents, recognizing them as a great treasure from both the human and social, as well as religious and spiritual viewpoints. My venerable Predecessors Paul VI and John Paul II—we have just celebrated the third anniversary of the latter's death—emphasized on various occasions the Ecclesial Community's respect for the elderly, for their dedication and their spirituality....

Your Plenary Assembly has discussed the theme of grandparents' presence in the family, the Church and society with a look that can include the past, present and future. Let us briefly analyze these three moments. In the past, grandparents had an important role in the life and growth of the family. Even with their advancing age they continued to be present with their children, their grandchildren and even their great-grandchildren, giving a living witness of caring, sacrifice and a daily gift of themselves without reserve. They were witnesses of a personal and community history that continued to live on in their memories and in their wisdom....

In the face of the crisis of the family, might it not be possible to set out anew precisely from the presence and witness of these people—grandparents—whose values and projects are more resilient? Indeed, it is impossible to plan the future without referring to a past full of significant experiences and spiritual and moral reference points. Thinking of grandparents, of their testimony of love and fidelity to life, reminds us of the Biblical figures of Abraham and Sarah, of Elizabeth and Zechariah, of Joachim and Anne, as well as of the elderly Simeon and Anna and even Nicodemus: they all remind us that at every age the Lord asks each one for the contribution of his or her own talents.

—Benedict XVI, Address to Plenary Assembly of the Pontifical
Council for the Family, April 5, 2008

CHAPTER 5

Making "Ends" Meet

Balancing Work, Family, and Finances

Supporting a family takes a lot of work, both inside and outside the home. This chapter treats questions about parents working outside the home, working on Sundays, staying connected with relatives, caring for elderly parents, and teaching children about stewardship.

—— 64 ——

Should mothers stay home if possible, at least in the
early years of childhood? Does the church look down on
mothers of young children who work?

There can be a certain flexibility of roles and responsibilities, depending on the concrete circumstances of each particular family. But the
clear and well-defined presence of both figures, female and male, creates the environment best suited to the growth of the child.

—Francis, *Amoris laetitia*, 175

The Christian seed at the root of equality between spouses must bear
new fruit today. The witness of the social dignity of marriage shall become persuasive precisely in this way, the way of a testimony which
attracts, the way of reciprocity between them, of complementarity between them.

For this reason, as Christians, we must become more demanding
in this regard. For example: firmly support the right to equal pay for
equal work; why is it taken for granted that women should earn less
than men? No! They have the same rights. This disparity is an absolute
disgrace! At the same time, recognize women's motherhood and men's
fatherhood as an always precious treasure, for the good of their children above all.

—Francis, General Audience, April 29, 2015

Above all, it is necessary to respect the right and duty of woman as
mother to carry out her specific tasks in the family, without being
forced by need to take on an additional job. What would society truly
gain—even at the economic level—if a short-sighted labor policy were
to prejudice the family's endurance and functions?

The safeguarding of this basic good, however, cannot be an alibi with regard to the principle of equal opportunity for men and women also in work outside the family. Flexible and balanced solutions should be found which can harmonize the different needs.

—John Paul II, Angelus Message, August 20, 1995

Of course, the employment of women outside the family, especially during the period when they are fulfilling the most delicate tasks of motherhood, must be done with respect for this fundamental duty. However, apart from this requirement, it is necessary to strive convincingly to ensure that the widest possible space is open to women in all areas of culture, economics, politics, and ecclesial life itself, so that all human society is increasingly enriched by the gifts proper to masculinity and femininity.

—John Paul II, Angelus Message, July 23, 1995

Thank you, women who are mothers! You have sheltered human beings within yourselves in a unique experience of joy and travail. This experience makes you become God's own smile upon the newborn child, the one who guides your child's first steps, who helps it to grow and who is the anchor as the child makes its way along the journey of life....

Thank you, women who work! You are present and active in every area of life—social, economic, cultural, artistic and political. In this way you make an indispensable contribution to the growth of a culture which unites reason and feeling, to a model of life ever open to the sense of "mystery," to the establishment of economic and political structures ever more worthy of humanity.

—John Paul II, *Letter to Women*, 2

It is a disservice not only to children, but also to women and society itself, when a woman is made to feel guilty for wanting to remain in the home and nurture and care for her children. A mother's presence in the family, so critical to the stability and growth of that basic unit

of society, should instead be recognized, applauded, and supported in
every possible way. By the same token society needs to call husbands
and fathers to their family responsibilities, and ought to strive for a situation in which they will not be forced by economic circumstances to
move away from the home in search of work.

> —John Paul II, Letter to Gertrude Mongella, Secretary General of
> the Fourth World Conference on Women, May 26, 1995

Much remains to be done to prevent discrimination against those who
have chosen to be wives and mothers. As far as personal rights are concerned, there is an urgent need to achieve real equality in every area:
equal pay for equal work, protection for working mothers, fairness in
career advancements, equality of spouses with regard to family rights
and the recognition of everything that is part of the rights and duties of
citizens in a democratic state.

> —John Paul II, *Mulieris dignitatem*, 4

Therefore, the Church gives thanks for each and every woman ... for
women who watch over the human persons in the family, which is the
fundamental sign of the human community; for women who work pro-
fessionally, and who at times are burdened by a great social responsibility....

> —John Paul II, *Mulieris dignitatem*, 31

This means of checking concerns above all the family. Just remuneration for the work of an adult who is responsible for a family means
remuneration which will suffice for establishing and properly maintain-
ing a family and for providing security for its future. Such remuneration
can be given either through what is called a family wage—that is, a single salary given to the head of the family for his work, sufficient for the
needs of the family without the other spouse having to take up gainful
employment outside the home—or through other social measures
such as family allowances or grants to mothers devoting themselves ex-

clusively to their families. These grants should correspond to the actual needs, that is, to the number of dependents for as long as they are not in a position to assume proper responsibility for their own lives.

Experience confirms that there must be a social re-evaluation of the mother's role, of the toil connected with it, and of the need that children have for care, love and affection in order that they may develop into responsible, morally and religiously mature and psychologically stable persons. It will redound to the credit of society to make it possible for a mother—without inhibiting her freedom, without psychological or practical discrimination, and without penalizing her as compared with other women—to devote herself to taking care of her children and educating them in accordance with their needs, which vary with age. Having to abandon these tasks in order to take up paid work outside the home is wrong from the point of view of the good of society and of the family when it contradicts or hinders these primary goals of the mission of a mother.

In this context, it should be emphasized that, on a more general level, the whole labor process must be organized and adapted in such a way as to respect the requirements of the person and his or her forms of life, above all life in the home, taking into account the individual's age and sex. It is a fact that in many societies women work in nearly every sector of life. But it is fitting that they should be able to fulfill their tasks in accordance with their own nature, without being discriminated against and without being excluded from jobs for which they are capable, but also without lack of respect for their family aspirations and for their specific role in contributing, together with men, to the good of society. The true advancement of women requires that labor should be structured in such a way that women do not have to pay for their advancement by abandoning what is specific to them and at the expense of the family, in which women as mothers have an irreplaceable role.

—John Paul II, *Laborem exercens*, 19

—— 65 ——

Why are the gifts of women needed in economic and public life as well as in the home?

The sense of being orphaned that affects many children and young people today is much deeper than we think. Nowadays we acknowledge as legitimate and indeed desirable that women wish to study, work, develop their skills and have personal goals. At the same time, we cannot ignore the need that children have for a mother's presence, especially in the first months of life. Indeed, "the woman stands before the man as a mother, the subject of the new human life that is conceived and develops in her, and from her is born into the world." The weakening of this maternal presence with its feminine qualities poses a grave risk to our world. I certainly value feminism, but one that does not demand uniformity or negate motherhood. For the grandeur of women includes all the rights derived from their inalienable human dignity but also from their feminine genius, which is essential to society. Their specifically feminine abilities—motherhood in particular—also grant duties, because womanhood also entails a specific mission in this world, a mission that society needs to protect and preserve for the good of all.

—Francis, *Amoris laetitia*, 173 (citing John Paul II, General Audience on the Theology of the Body, March 12, 1980)

It is thus my hope, dear sisters, that you will reflect carefully on what it means to speak of the "genius of women," not only in order to be able to see in this phrase a specific part of God's plan which needs to be accepted and appreciated, but also in order to let this genius be more fully expressed in the life of society as a whole, as well as in the life of the Church.

—John Paul II, *Letter to Women*, 10

Necessary emphasis should be placed on the "genius of women," not only by considering great and famous women of the past or present, but also those ordinary women who reveal the gift of their womanhood by placing themselves at the service of others in their everyday lives. For in giving themselves to others each day women fulfill their deepest vocation. Perhaps more than men, women acknowledge the person, because they see persons with their hearts. They see them independently of various ideological or political systems. They see others in their greatness and limitations; they try to go out to them and help them. In this way, the basic plan of the Creator takes flesh in the history of humanity and there is constantly revealed, in the variety of vocations, that beauty—not merely physical, but above all spiritual—which God bestowed from the very beginning on all, and in a particular way on women.

—John Paul II, *Letter to Women*, 12

When women are able fully to share their gifts with the whole community, the very way in which society understands and organizes itself is improved and comes to reflect in a better way the substantial unity of the human family.

—John Paul II, World Day of Peace Message (January 1, 1995), 9

In our own time, the successes of science and technology make it possible to attain material well-being to a degree hitherto unknown. While this favors some, it pushes others to the edges of society. In this way, unilateral progress can also lead to a gradual loss of sensitivity for man, that is, for what is essentially human. In this sense, our time in particular awaits the manifestation of that "genius" which belongs to women, and which can ensure sensitivity for human beings in every circumstance: because they are human!—and because "the greatest of these is love" (cf. 1 Cor 13:13).

—John Paul II, *Mulieris dignitatem*, 30

—— 66 ——

Does the church have anything to say about being a "stay-at-home dad"?

A father, for his part, helps the child to perceive the limits of life, to be open to the challenges of the wider world, and to see the need for hard work and strenuous effort. A father possessed of a clear and serene masculine identity who demonstrates affection and concern for his wife is just as necessary as a caring mother. There can be a certain flexibility of roles and responsibilities, depending on the concrete circumstances of each particular family. But the clear and well-defined presence of both figures, female and male, creates the environment best suited to the growth of the child.

—Francis, *Amoris laetitia*, 175

And indeed work, in its many forms, beginning with that in the home, is also concerned with the common good. Where does one learn this hard-working lifestyle? First of all, one learns it in the family. The family teaches work through the example of the parents: the father and the mother who work for the good of the family and of society.

—Francis, General Audience, August 19, 2015

At her side in the Holy Family of Nazareth, stands the figure of Saint Joseph. Through his work and generous presence, he cared for and defended Mary and Jesus, delivering them from the violence of the unjust by bringing them to Egypt. The Gospel presents Joseph as a just man, hard-working and strong. But he also shows great tenderness, which is not a mark of the weak but of those who are genuinely strong, fully aware of reality and ready to love and serve in humility.

—Francis, *Laudato Si'*, 242

Now, on this common journey of reflection on the family, I would like to say to all Christian communities that we must be more attentive: the absent father figure in the life of little ones and young people causes gaps and wounds that may even be very serious. And, in effect, delinquency among children and adolescents can be largely attributed to this lack, to the shortage of examples and authoritative guidance in their everyday life, a shortage of closeness, a shortage of love from the father. And the feeling of orphanhood that so many young people live with is more profound than we think.

They are orphaned in the family, because their fathers are often absent, also physically, from the home, but above all because, when they are present, they do not behave like fathers. They do not converse with their children. They do not fulfill their role as educators. They do not set their children a good example with their words, principles, values, those rules of life which they need like bread.

—Francis, General Audience, January 28, 2015

Work was the daily expression of love in the life of the Family of Nazareth. The Gospel specifies the kind of work Joseph did in order to support his family: he was a carpenter. This simple word sums up Joseph's entire life. For Jesus, these were hidden years, the years to which Luke refers after recounting the episode that occurred in the Temple: "And he went down with them and came to Nazareth, and was obedient to them" (Lk 2:51). This "submission" or obedience of Jesus in the house of Nazareth should be understood as a sharing in the work of Joseph. Having learned the work of his presumed father, he was known as "the carpenter's son." If the Family of Nazareth is an example and model for human families, in the order of salvation and holiness, so too, by analogy, is Jesus' work at the side of Joseph the carpenter. In our own day, the Church has emphasized this by instituting the liturgical memorial of St. Joseph the Worker on May 1. Human work, and especially manual labor, receive special prominence in the Gospel. Along with the humanity of the Son of God, work too has been taken up in the mystery of the Incarnation, and has also been redeemed in a special way. At the workbench where he plied his trade together with Jesus, Joseph brought human work closer to the mystery of the Redemption.

In the human growth of Jesus "in wisdom, age and grace," the virtue of industriousness played a notable role, since "work is a human good" which "transforms nature" and makes man "in a sense, more human."

The importance of work in human life demands that its meaning be known and assimilated in order to "help all people to come closer to God, the Creator and Redeemer, to participate in his salvific plan for man and the world, and to deepen ... friendship with Christ in their lives, by accepting, through faith, a living participation in his threefold mission as Priest, Prophet and King."

—John Paul II, *Redemptoris custos*, 22–23 (citing *Laborem exercens*, 9 and 24)

—— 67 ——
How involved should dads be in raising their children?

We often hear that ours is a society without fathers. In Western culture, the father figure is said to be symbolically absent, missing or vanished. Manhood itself seems to be called into question. The result has been an understandable confusion. "At first, this was perceived as a liberation: liberation from the father as master, from the father as the representative of a law imposed from without, from the father as the arbiter of his children's happiness and an obstacle to the emancipation and autonomy of young people. In some homes authoritarianism once reigned and, at times, even oppression." Yet, "as often happens, one goes from one extreme to the other. In our day, the problem no longer seems to be the overbearing presence of the father so much as his absence, his not being there. Fathers are often so caught up in themselves and their work, and at times in their own self-fulfillment, that they neglect their families. They leave the little ones and the young to themselves." The presence of the father, and hence his authority, is also impacted by the amount of time given over to the communications and entertainment media. Nowadays authority is often considered suspect and adults treated with impertinence. They themselves become uncertain and so fail to offer sure and solid guidance to their children. A reversal of the roles of parents and children is unhealthy, since it hinders the proper process of development that children need to experience, and it denies them the love and guidance needed to mature.

God sets the father in the family so that by the gifts of his masculinity he can be "close to his wife and share everything, joy and sorrow, hope and hardship. And to be close to his children as they grow—when they play and when they work, when they are carefree and when they are distressed, when they are talkative and when they are silent, when they are daring and when they are afraid, when they stray and when they get back on the right path. To be a father who is always present. When I say 'present,' I do not mean 'controlling.' Fathers who are too controlling overshadow their children, they don't let them develop. Some fathers feel they are useless or unnecessary, but the fact is that 'children need to find a father waiting for them when they return home with their problems. They may try hard not to admit it, not to show it, but they need it.'" It is not good for children to lack a father and to grow up before they are ready.

—Francis, *Amoris laetitia*, 175–76 (citing his General Audience of January 28, 2015)

Love for his wife as mother of their children and love for the children themselves are for the man the natural way of understanding and fulfilling his own fatherhood. Above all where social and cultural conditions so easily encourage a father to be less concerned with his family or at any rate less involved in the work of education, efforts must be made to restore socially the conviction that the place and task of the father in and for the family is of unique and irreplaceable importance. As experience teaches, the absence of a father causes psychological and moral imbalance and notable difficulties in family relationships, as does, in contrary circumstances, the oppressive presence of a father, especially where there still prevails the phenomenon of "machismo," or a wrong superiority of male prerogatives which humiliates women and inhibits the development of healthy family relationships.

In revealing and in reliving on earth the very fatherhood of God, a man is called upon to ensure the harmonious and united development of all the members of the family: he will perform this task by exercising generous responsibility for the life conceived under the heart of the mother, by a more solicitous commitment to education, a task he shares with his wife, by work which is never a cause of division in the family but promotes its unity and stability, and by means of the witness he gives of an adult Christian life which effectively introduces the children into the living experience of Christ and the Church.

—John Paul II, *Familiaris consortio*, 25

—— 68 ——

What does scripture mean when it says that men are the "heads" of their families? What about wives "being submissive" to their husbands?

The author of the Letter to the Ephesians sees no contradiction between an exhortation formulated in this way and the words: "Wives, be subject to your husbands, as to the Lord. For the husband is the head of the wife" (5:22–23). The author knows that this way of speaking, so profoundly rooted in the customs and religious tradition of the time, is to be understood and carried out in a new way: as a "mutual subjection out of reverence for Christ" (cf. Eph 5:21). This is especially true because the husband is called the "head" of the wife as Christ is the head of the Church; he is so in order to give "himself up for her" (Eph 5:25), and giving himself up for her means giving up even his own life. However, whereas in the relationship between Christ and the Church the subjection is only on the part of the Church, in the relationship between husband and wife the "subjection" is not one-sided but mutual.

In relation to the "old" this is evidently something "new": it is an innovation of the Gospel. We find various passages in which the apostolic writings express this innovation, even though they also communicate what is "old": what is rooted in the religious tradition of Israel, in its way of understanding and explaining the sacred texts, as for example the second chapter of the Book of Genesis.

The apostolic letters are addressed to people living in an environment marked by that same traditional way of thinking and acting. The "innovation" of Christ is a fact: it constitutes the unambiguous content of the evangelical message and is the result of the Redemption. However, the awareness that in marriage there is mutual "subjection of the spouses out of reverence for Christ," and not just that of the wife to the husband, must gradually establish itself in hearts, consciences, behavior and customs. This is a call which from that time onwards, does not cease to challenge succeeding generations; it is a call which people have to accept ever anew....

But the challenge presented by the "ethos" of the Redemption is clear and definitive. All the reasons in favor of the "subjection" of woman to man in marriage must be understood in the sense of a "mutual subjection" of both "out of reverence for Christ." The measure of true spousal love finds its deepest source in Christ, who is the Bridegroom of the Church, his Bride.

—John Paul II, *Mulieris dignitatem*, 24

Every form of sexual submission must be clearly rejected. This includes all improper interpretations of the passage in the Letter to the Ephesians where Paul tells women to "be subject to your husbands" (Eph 5:22). This passage mirrors the cultural categories of the time, but our concern is not with its cultural matrix but with the revealed message that it conveys. As Saint John Paul II wisely observed: "Love excludes every kind of subjection whereby the wife might become a servant or a slave of the husband.... The community or unity which they should establish through marriage is constituted by a reciprocal donation of self, which is also a mutual subjection." Hence Paul goes on to say that "husbands should love their wives as their own bodies" (Eph 5:28). The biblical text is actually concerned with encouraging everyone to overcome a complacent individualism and to be constantly mindful of others: "Be subject to one another" (Eph 5:21). In marriage, this reciprocal "submission" takes on a special meaning, and is seen as a freely chosen mutual belonging marked by fidelity, respect and care. Sexuality is inseparably at the service of this conjugal friendship, for it is meant to aid the fulfillment of the other.

—Francis, *Amoris laetita*, 156 (citing John Paul II, General Audience
on the Theology of the Body, August 11, 1982)

This subjection, however, does not deny or take away the liberty which fully belongs to the woman both in view of her dignity as a human person, and in view of her most noble office as wife and mother and companion; nor does it bid her obey her husband's every request if not in harmony with right reason or with the dignity due to wife; nor, in fine, does it imply that the wife should be put on a level with those persons who in law are called minors, to whom it is not customary to allow free exercise of their rights on account of their lack of mature judgment, or of their ignorance of human affairs. But it forbids that exaggerated liberty which cares not for the good of the family; it forbids that in this body which is the family, the heart be separated from the head to the great detriment of the whole body and the proximate danger of ruin. For if the man is the head, the woman is the heart, and as he occupies the chief place in ruling, so she may and ought to claim for herself the chief place in love.

—Pius XI, *Casti connubii*, 27

——— 69 ———

How much effort should we put into staying connected with our relatives, in-laws, grandparents, and our own parents when we're so busy with work and our own kids?

The nuclear family needs to interact with the wider family made up of parents, aunts and uncles, cousins and even neighbors. This greater family may have members who require assistance, or at least companionship and affection, or consolation amid suffering. The individualism so prevalent today can lead to creating small nests of security, where others are perceived as bothersome or a threat. Such isolation, however, cannot offer greater peace or happiness; rather, it straitens the heart of a family and makes its life all the more narrow.

—Francis, *Amoris laetitia*, 187

The family, which is founded and given life by love, is a community of persons: of husband and wife, of parents and children, of relatives. Its first task is to live with fidelity the reality of communion in a constant effort to develop an authentic community of persons.

The inner principle of that task, its permanent power and its final goal is love: without love the family is not a community of persons and, in the same way, without love the family cannot live, grow and perfect itself as a community of persons. What I wrote in the Encyclical *Redemptor hominis* applies primarily and especially within the family as such: "Man cannot live without love. He remains a being that is incomprehensible for himself, his life is senseless, if love is not revealed to him, if he does not encounter love, if he does not experience it and make it his own, if he does not participate intimately in it."

The love between husband and wife and, in a derivatory and broader way, the love between members of the same family—between parents and children, brothers and sisters and relatives and members of the household—is given life and sustenance by an unceasing inner dynamism leading the family to ever deeper and more intense communion, which is the foundation and soul of the community of marriage and the family.

—John Paul II, *Familiaris consortio*, 18

―――― 70 ――――

How can I best provide care for my aging parents? What does our Catholic faith say about our attitude toward the elderly?

Benedict XVI, visiting a home for the elderly, used clear and prophetic words, saying in this way: "The quality of a society, I mean of a civilization, is also judged by how it treats elderly people and by the place it gives them in community life" (12 November 2012). It's true, attention to the elderly makes the difference in a civilization. Is there attention to the elderly in a civilization? Is there room for the elderly? This civilization will move forward if it knows how to respect wisdom, the wisdom of the elderly. In a civilization in which there is no room for the elderly or where they are thrown away because they create problems, this society carries with it the virus of death....

I remember, when I was visiting a retirement home, I spoke with each person and I frequently heard this: "How are you? And your children? Well, well. How many do you have? Many. And do they come to visit you? Oh sure, yes, always, yes, they come. When was the last time they came?" I remember an elderly woman who said to me: "Mmm, for Christmas." It was August! Eight months without being visited by her children, abandoned for eight months! This is called mortal sin, understand? ...

In the tradition of the Church there is a *wealth of wisdom* that has always supported a culture of *closeness to the elderly*, a disposition of warm and supportive companionship in this final phase of life. This tradition is rooted in Sacred Scripture, as these passages from the Book of Sirach attest: "Do not disregard the discourse of the aged, for they themselves learned from their fathers; because from them you will gain understanding and learn how to give an answer in time of need" (Sir 8:9).

The Church cannot and does not want to conform to a mentality of impatience, and much less of indifference and contempt, towards old age. We must reawaken the *collective sense of gratitude*, of appreciation, of hospitality, which makes the elder feel like a living part of his community.

Our elders are men and women, fathers and mothers, who came before us on our own road, in our own house, in our daily battle for a worthy life. They are men and women from whom we have received so much. The elder is not an alien. We are that elder: in the near or far future, but inevitably, even if we don't think it. And if we don't learn how to treat the elder better, that is how we will be treated.

We old people are all a little fragile. Some, however, are *particularly weak*, many are alone, and stricken by illness. Some depend on the indispensable care and attention of others. Are we going to take a step back? Abandon them to their fate? A society without *proximity*, where *gratuity* and affection *without compensation*—between strangers as well—is disappearing, is a perverse society. The Church, faithful to the Word of God, cannot tolerate such degeneration. A Christian community in which proximity and gratuity are no longer considered indispensable is a society which would lose her soul. Where there is no honor for the elderly, there is no future for the young.

—Pope Francis, General Audience, March 4, 2015

There are cultures which manifest a unique veneration and great love for the elderly: far from being outcasts from the family or merely tolerated as a useless burden, they continue to be present and to take an active and responsible part in family life, though having to respect the autonomy of the new family; above all they carry out the important mission of being a witness to the past and a source of wisdom for the young and for the future.

Other cultures, however, especially in the wake of disordered industrial and urban development, have both in the past and in the present set the elderly aside in unacceptable ways. This causes acute suffering to them and spiritually impoverishes many families.

The pastoral activity of the Church must help everyone to discover and to make good use of the role of the elderly within the civil and ecclesial community, in particular within the family. In fact, "the life of the aging helps to clarify a scale of human values; it shows the continuity of generations and marvelously demonstrates the interdependence of God's people. The elderly often have the charism to bridge generation gaps before they are made: how many children have found understanding and love in the eyes and words and caresses of the aging! And how many old people have willingly subscribed to the inspired word that the 'crown of the aged is their children's children' (Prv. 17:6)!"

—John Paul II, *Familiaris consortio*, 27 (citing his own Address to the Participants in the International Forum on Active Aging, September 5, 1980, 5)

WEALTH AND FAMILY HEALTH

—— 71 ——

Our family has so many financial pressures. Are we morally required to give sacrificially to our parish? What about saving for our retirement and our children's educations and futures—is that a moral issue?

First question: "Do I give?" Second: "How much do I give?" Third question: "How do I give?" Do I give as Jesus gives, with the caress of love, or as one who pays a tax? How do I give? "But father, what do you mean by that?" When you help someone, do you look that person in the eye? Do you touch that person's hand? Theirs is Christ's own flesh, that person is your brother, your sister. At that moment you are like the Father who does not leave the birds of the air to go without food. With what love the Father gives! Let us ask God for the grace to be free of this idolatry, the attachment to wealth: let us ask the grace to look at Him, so rich in His love and so rich in generosity, in His mercy; and let us ask the grace to help others with the exercise of almsgiving, but as He does it. "But, Father, He has not let Himself be deprived of anything!" Jesus Christ, being equal to God, deprived Himself of this: He lowered Himself, He made Himself nothing — [yes,] He too deprived Himself of something.

—Francis, Homily, October 19, 2015

The fifth precept ("You shall help to provide for the needs of the Church") means that the faithful are obliged to assist with the material needs of the Church, each according to his own ability.

The faithful also have the duty of providing for the material needs of the Church, each according to his own abilities.

—*Catechism of the Catholic Church*, 2043

"In his use of things man should regard the external goods he legitimately owns not merely as exclusive to himself but common to others also, in the sense that they can benefit others as well as himself." The ownership of any property makes its holder a steward of Providence, with the task of making it fruitful and communicating its benefits to others, first of all his family.

—*Catechism of the Catholic Church*, 2404

—— 72 ——

How do I balance work, family, and lifestyle?

This, certainly, is not a good approach; but, as often happens, one goes from one extreme to the other. In our day, the problem no longer seems to be the invasive presence of the father so much as his absence, his inaction. Fathers are sometimes so concentrated on themselves and on their work and at times on their career that they even forget about the family. And they leave the little ones and the young ones to themselves. As Bishop of Buenos Aires I sensed the feeling of orphanhood that children are experiencing today, and I often asked fathers if they played with their children, if they had the courage and love to spend time with their kids. And the answer was negative in most cases: "But I can't, because I have so much work...." And the father was absent from the little child growing up, he did not play with him, no, he did not waste time with him.

Now, on this common journey of reflection on the family, I would like to say to all Christian communities that we must be more attentive: the absent father figure in the life of little ones and young people causes gaps and wounds that may even be very serious. And, in effect, delinquency among children and adolescents can be largely attributed to this lack, to the shortage of examples and authoritative guidance in their everyday life, a shortage of closeness, a shortage of love from the father. And the feeling of orphanhood that so many young people live with is more profound than we think.

They are orphaned in the family, because their fathers are often absent, also physically, from the home, but above all because, when they are present, they do not behave like fathers. They do not converse with their children. They do not fulfill their role as educators. They do not set their children a good example with their words, principles, values, those rules of life which they need like bread. The educative quality of the time the father spends raising the child is all the more necessary when he is forced to stay away from home because of work.

—Francis, General Audience, January 28, 2015

—— 73 ——

Is it a sin to work on Sundays unnecessarily? What is involved in keeping the Sabbath day holy? Why?

On the seventh day God completed the work he had been doing; he rested on the seventh day from all the work he had undertaken. God blessed the seventh day and made it holy, because on it he rested from all the work he had done in creation.

—Genesis 2:2–3, New American Bible Revised Edition

Observe the sabbath day—keep it holy, as the LORD, your God, commanded you. Six days you may labor and do all your work, but the seventh day is a sabbath of the LORD your God. You shall not do any work, either you, your son or your daughter, your male or female slave, your ox or donkey or any work animal, or the resident alien within your gates, so that your male and female slave may rest as you do.

—Deuteronomy 5:12–14, New American Bible Revised Edition

Then he said to them, "Is it lawful to do good on the sabbath rather than to do evil, to save life rather than to destroy it?"

—Mark 3:4a–c, New American Bible Revised Edition

I would like here to recall what I said in defense of time for the family, threatened by a sort of "dictatorship" of work commitments: Sunday is the day of the Lord and of men and women, a day in which everyone must be able to be free, free for the family and free for God. In defending Sunday we defend human freedom!

—Benedict XVI, General Audience, June 6, 2012

Sunday is a day which is at the very heart of the Christian life. From the beginning of my Pontificate, I have not ceased to repeat: "Do not be afraid! Open, open wide the doors to Christ!" In the same way, today I would strongly urge everyone to rediscover Sunday: Do not be afraid to give your time to Christ! Yes, let us open our time to Christ, that he may cast light upon it and give it direction. He is the One who knows the secret of time and the secret of eternity, and he gives us "his day" as an ever new gift of his love. The rediscovery of this day is a grace which we must implore, not only so that we may live the demands of faith to the full, but also so that we may respond concretely to the deepest human yearnings. Time given to Christ is never time lost, but is rather time gained, so that our relationships and indeed our whole life may become more profoundly human.

Unfortunately, when Sunday loses its fundamental meaning and becomes merely part of a "weekend," it can happen that people stay locked within a horizon so limited that they can no longer see "the heavens." Hence, though ready to celebrate, they are really incapable of doing so.

The disciples of Christ, however, are asked to avoid any confusion between the celebration of Sunday, which should truly be a way of keeping the Lord's Day holy, and the "weekend," understood as a time of simple rest and relaxation. This will require a genuine spiritual maturity, which will enable Christians to "be what they are," in full accordance with the gift of faith, always ready to give an account of the hope which is in them (cf. 1 Pt 3:15). In this way, they will be led to a deeper understanding of Sunday, with the result that, even in difficult situations, they will be able to live it in complete docility to the Holy Spirit.

—John Paul II, *Dies domini*, 4

In our own historical context, there remains the obligation to ensure that everyone can enjoy the freedom, rest and relaxation which human dignity requires, together with the associated religious, family, cultural and interpersonal needs which are difficult to meet if there is no guarantee of at least one day of the week on which people can both rest and celebrate.

—John Paul II, *Dies domini*, 66

Through Sunday rest, daily concerns and tasks can find their proper perspective: the material things about which we worry give way to spiritual values; in a moment of encounter and less pressured exchange, we see the true face of the people with whom we live. Even the beauties of nature—too often marred by the desire to exploit, which turns against man himself—can be rediscovered and enjoyed to the full. As the day on which man is at peace with God, with himself and with others, Sunday becomes a moment when people can look anew upon the wonders of nature, allowing themselves to be caught up in that marvelous and mysterious harmony which, in the words of Saint Ambrose, weds the many elements of the cosmos in a "bond of communion and peace" by "an inviolable law of concord and love." Men and women then come to a deeper sense, as the Apostle says, that "everything created by God is good and nothing is to be rejected if it is received with thanksgiving, for then it is consecrated by the word of God and prayer" (1 Tm 4:4–5). If after six days of work—reduced in fact to five for many people—people look for time to relax and to pay more attention to other aspects of their lives, this corresponds to an authentic need which is in full harmony with the vision of the Gospel message. Believers are therefore called to satisfy this need in a way consistent with the manifestation of their personal and community faith, as expressed in the celebration and sanctification of the Lord's Day.

—John Paul II, *Dies domini*, 67

Just as God "rested on the seventh day from all his work which he had done," human life has a rhythm of work and rest. The institution of the Lord's Day helps everyone enjoy adequate rest and leisure to cultivate their familial, cultural, social, and religious lives.

On Sundays and other holy days of obligation, the faithful are to refrain from engaging in work or activities that hinder the worship owed to God, the joy proper to the Lord's Day, the performance of the works of mercy, and the appropriate relaxation of mind and body. Family needs or important social service can legitimately excuse from the obligation of Sunday rest. The faithful should see to it that legitimate excuses do not lead to habits prejudicial to religion, family life, and health.

The charity of truth seeks holy leisure—the necessity of charity accepts just work.

Those Christians who have leisure should be mindful of their brethren who have the same needs and the same rights, yet cannot rest from work because of poverty and misery. Sunday is traditionally consecrated by Christian piety to good works and humble service of the sick, the infirm, and the elderly. Christians will also sanctify Sunday by devoting time and care to their families and relatives, often difficult to do on other days of the week. Sunday is a time for reflection, silence, cultivation of the mind, and meditation which furthers the growth of the Christian interior life.

Sanctifying Sundays and holy days requires a common effort. Every Christian should avoid making unnecessary demands on others that would hinder them from observing the Lord's Day. Traditional activities (sport, restaurants, etc.), and social necessities (public services, etc.), require some people to work on Sundays, but everyone should still take care to set aside sufficient time for leisure.

—*Catechism of the Catholic Church*, 2184–88

—— 74 ——

Should we teach our children about money management and stewardship? What virtues can we teach them in these areas?

In the family too, we can rethink our habits of consumption and join in caring for the environment as our common home. "The family is the principal agent of an integral ecology, because it is the primary social subject which contains within it the two fundamental principles of human civilization on earth: the principle of communion and the principle of fruitfulness." In the same way, times of difficulty and trouble in the lives of family life can teach important lessons.

—Francis, *Amoris laetitia*, 277

The home is the natural environment for initiating a human being into solidarity and communal responsibilities. Parents should teach children to avoid the compromising and degrading influences which threaten human societies.

—*Catechism of the Catholic Church*, 2224

Having thus confirmed the personal dimension of human work, we must go on to the second sphere of values which is necessarily linked to work. Work constitutes a foundation for the formation of family life, which is a natural right and something that man is called to. These two spheres of values—one linked to work and the other consequent on the family nature of human life—must be properly united and must properly permeate each other. In a way, work is a condition for making it possible to found a family, since the family requires the means of subsistence which man normally gains through work. Work and industriousness also influence the whole process of education in the family, for the very reason that everyone "becomes a human being" through, among other things, work, and becoming a human being is precisely the main purpose of the whole process of education. Obviously, two aspects of work in a sense come into play here: the one making family life and its upkeep possible, and the other making possible the achievement of the purposes of the family, especially education. Nevertheless, these two aspects of work are linked to one another and are mutually complementary in various points.

It must be remembered and affirmed that the family constitutes one of the most important terms of reference for shaping the social and ethical order of human work. The teaching of the Church has always devoted special attention to this question, and in the present document we shall have to return to it. In fact, the family is simultaneously a community made possible by work and the first school of work, within the home, for every person.

—John Paul II, *Laborem exercens*, 10

—— 75 ——
Should I get my children a smartphone or other electronic device?

In our own day, dominated by stress and rapid technological advances, one of the most important tasks of families is to provide an education in hope. This does not mean preventing children from playing with electronic devices, but rather finding ways to help them develop their critical abilities and not to think that digital speed can apply to everything in life. Postponing desires does not mean denying them but simply deferring their fulfillment. When children or adolescents are not helped to realize that some things have to be waited for, they can become obsessed with satisfying their immediate needs and develop the vice of "wanting it all now." This is a grand illusion which does not favor freedom but weakens it. On the other hand, when we are taught to postpone some things until the right moment, we learn self-mastery and detachment from our impulses. When children realize that they have to be responsible for themselves, their self-esteem is enriched. This in turn teaches them to respect the freedom of others. Obviously, this does not mean expecting children to act like adults, but neither does it mean underestimating their ability to grow in responsible freedom. In a healthy family, this learning process usually takes place through the demands made by life in common.

—Francis, *Amoris laetitia*, 276

The educational process that occurs between parents and children can be helped or hindered by the increasing sophistication of the communications and entertainment media. When well used, these media can be helpful for connecting family members who live apart from one another. Frequent contacts help to overcome difficulties. Still, it is clear that these media cannot replace the need for more personal and direct dialogue, which requires physical presence or at least hearing the voice of the other person. We know that sometimes they can keep people apart rather than together, as when at dinnertime everyone is surfing on a mobile phone, or when one spouse falls asleep waiting for the other who spends hours playing with an electronic device. This is also something that families have to discuss and resolve in ways which encourage interaction without imposing unrealistic prohibitions. In any event, we cannot ignore the risks that these new forms of communication pose for children and adolescents; at times they can foster apathy and disconnect from the real world. This "technological disconnect" exposes them more easily to manipulation by those who would invade their private space with selfish interests.

—Francis, *Amoris laetitia*, 278

Conviviality is a sure barometer for measuring the health of relationships: if in a family something has gone awry, or there is some hidden wound, it is immediately understood at the table. A family that hardly ever eats together, or that does not talk at the table but watches television, or looks at a smartphone, is a "barely familial" family. When children are engrossed with a computer at the table, or a mobile phone, and do not talk to each other, this is not a family, it is like a boarding house.

—Francis, General Audience, November 11, 2015

Children must grow up with a correct attitude of freedom with regard to material goods, by adopting a simple and austere lifestyle and by being fully convinced that "man is more precious for what he is than for what he has."

—John Paul II, *Familiaris consortio*, 37

------ 76 ------

It feels so hard to manage all of the electronic media in our home. Should we just get rid of our television?

Now we, I understand that the times have changed; we live in an age of images. And this is very important. In an age of images we must do what was done in the age of books: choose what is good for me! Out of this come two consequences: the responsibility of television networks to offer programs which encourage the good, which promote values, which build up society, which help us advance, not ones that drag us down. And then to produce programs that help us so that values, true values, may be reinforced and may help to prepare us for life. This is the responsibility of television networks. Secondly: knowing how to choose what programs to watch, and this is our responsibility. If I watch a program that is not good for me, that disparages my values, that leads me to become vulgar, even filthy, I need to change the channel.

As was done in my Stone Age: ... when a book was [not] good for you, you would throw it away. And this leads to a third point: the point of evil fantasy, of those fantasies which kill the soul. If you who are young live attached to your computers and become slaves to the computer, you lose your freedom! And if you use your computer to look for dirty programs, you lose your dignity.

Watch television, use the computer, but for beautiful reasons, for great things, things which help us to grow. This is good. Thank you!

—Francis, Meeting with Young People in Sarajevo, June 6, 2015

In the prevailing culture, priority is given to the outward, the immediate, the visible, the quick, the superficial and the provisional. What is real gives way to appearances. In many countries globalization has meant a hastened deterioration of their own cultural roots and the invasion of ways of thinking and acting proper to other cultures which are economically advanced but ethically debilitated. This fact has been brought up by bishops from various continents in different Synods. The African bishops, for example, taking up the Encyclical *Sollicitudo Rei Socialis*, pointed out years ago that there have been frequent attempts to make the African countries "parts of a machine, cogs on a gigantic wheel. This is often true also in the field of social communications which, being run by centers mostly in the northern hemisphere, do not always give due consideration to the priorities and problems of such countries or respect their cultural make-up." By the same token, the bishops of Asia "underlined the external influences being brought to bear on Asian cultures. New patterns of behavior are emerging as a result of over-exposure to the mass media.... As a result, the negative aspects of the media and entertainment industries are threatening traditional values, and in particular the sacredness of marriage and the stability of the family."

—Francis, *Evangelii gaudium*, 62 (citing John Paul II, *Ecclesia in Africa*, 52, and *Ecclesia in Asia*, 7)

This very important category in modern life deserves a word of its own. It is well known that the means of social communication "affect, and often profoundly, the minds of those who use them, under the affective and intellectual aspect and also under the moral and religious aspect," especially in the case of young people. They can thus exercise a beneficial influence on the life and habits of the family and on the education of children, but at the same time they also conceal "snares and dangers that cannot be ignored." They could also become a vehicle— sometimes cleverly and systematically manipulated, as unfortunately happens in various countries of the world—for divisive ideologies and distorted ways of looking at life, the family, religion and morality, attitudes that lack respect for man's true dignity and destiny.

This danger is all the more real inasmuch as "the modern life style—especially in the more industrialized nations—all too often causes families to abandon their responsibility to educate their children. Evasion of this duty is made easy for them by the presence of television and certain publications in the home, and in this way they keep their children's time and energies occupied." Hence "the duty ... to protect the young from the forms of aggression they are subjected to by the mass media," and to ensure that the use of the media in the family is carefully regulated. Families should also take care to seek for their children other forms of entertainment that are more wholesome, useful and physically, morally and spiritually formative, "to develop and use to advantage the free time of the young and direct their energies."

Furthermore, because the means of social communication, like the school and the environment, often have a notable influence on the formation of children, parents as recipients must actively ensure the moderate, critical, watchful and prudent use of the media, by discovering what effect they have on their children and by controlling the use of the media in such a way as to "train the conscience of their children to express calm and objective judgments, which will then guide them in the choice or rejection of programs available."

> —John Paul II, *Familiaris consortio*, 76 (citing Pope Paul VI's Message for Third World Social Communications Day, April 7, 1969; and his own messages for this event for May 1, 1980, and May 10, 1981)

—— 77 ——

How do we teach our children that pornography is a poison for their minds, hearts, and relationships?

This does not mean preventing children from playing with electronic devices, but rather finding ways to help them develop their critical abilities and not to think that digital speed can apply to everything in life.

> —Francis, *Amoris laetitia*, 275

There are two different things here: the medium and the content. Concerning the medium, there is one thing that hurts the soul and that is, to be too attached to computers. Too attached to the computer! This damages the soul and takes away freedom: it makes you a slave of the computer. It's curious: many mothers and fathers tell me that, in their families, they are together at the dining table with their children but the children have their telephones and are in another world. It's true that the virtual language is a reality and we cannot ignore it; but we must direct it in the right way, because it does represent human progress. But when this leads us away from a common life, from family life, from social life, and also from sports, from the arts, and we are glued to our computer … this is a psychological illness. I am sure of it! Secondly, the question of content. Yes, there are dirty things, from various degrees of pornography, to empty and valueless shows, such as relativistic, hedonistic, consumerist ones, which foment these things. We know that consumerism is a cancer on society, that relativism is a cancer on society. I will speak about this in the forthcoming encyclical, to be published this month. I don't know if I have answered your question. I used the word "filth" in a general way, but we all know this. There are parents who are so concerned that they do not allow their children to have computers in their room; the computers must be in a common area of the house. These are small ways that help parents to avoid precisely this problem.

—Francis, In-Flight Press Conference from Sarajevo to Rome, June 6, 2015

The practice of decency and modesty in speech, action and dress is very important for creating an atmosphere suitable to the growth of chastity, but this must be well motivated by respect for one's own body and the dignity of others. Parents, as we have said, should be watchful so that certain immoral fashions and attitudes do not violate the integrity of the home, especially through misuse of the mass media....

Another circumstance that facilitates this is the fact that both parents are busy with their work, in and outside the home. "The result is that these young people are in most need of help in developing their responsible freedom. There is the duty—especially for believers, for men and women who love freedom, to protect the young from the aggressions they are subjected to by the media. May no one shirk from this duty by using the excuse that he or she is not involved. Parents as recipients must actively ensure the moderate, critical, watchful and prudent use of the media."

—Pontifical Council for the Family, *The Truth and Meaning of Human Sexuality*, 56

It is well known that through all these elements the fundamental intentionality of the work of art or of the product of the respective media becomes, in a way, accessible to the viewer, as to the listener or the reader.

If our personal sensitivity reacts with objection and disapproval, it is because in that fundamental intentionality, together with the concretizing of man and his body, we discover as indispensable for the work of art or its reproduction, his simultaneous reduction to the level of an object. He becomes an object of "enjoyment," intended for the satisfaction of concupiscence itself. This is contrary to the dignity of man also in the intentional order of art and reproduction. By analogy, the same thing must be applied to the various fields of artistic activity—according to the respective specific character—as also to the various audiovisual media.

> —John Paul II, General Audience on the Theology of the Body, May 6, 1981

Fascinated and devoid of defense before the world and adults, children are naturally ready to accept whatever is offered them, whether good or bad.... They are attracted by the "small screen"; they follow each gesture which is portrayed, and they perceive, before and better than every other person, the emotions and feelings which result.

> —John Paul II, Message for the 13th World Communications Day, May 23, 1979

CHAPTER 6

When the Going Gets Tough

Difficult Situations and Hard Questions

Real family life is not always happily ever after; boots on the ground of family life get muddy when things don't turn out as hoped. In this chapter, questions treat difficulties such as not being able to find a spouse, loving a child with same-sex attraction, and what to do when an adult child marries outside the church or leaves the church. Other questions deal with addictions and abuse, divorce and annulment, and widowhood.

Why hasn't God given me a spouse,
even though I pray for one daily?

That is why Jesus urges us to pray and "not to lose heart." We all go through times of tiredness and discouragement, especially when our prayers seem ineffective. But Jesus assures us: unlike the dishonest judge, God promptly answers his children, even though this doesn't mean he will necessarily do it when and how we would like. Prayer does not work like a magic wand! It helps us keep faith in God, and to entrust ourselves to him even when we do not understand his will. In this, Jesus himself—who prayed constantly!—is our model. The Letter to the Hebrews reminds us that "In the days of his flesh, Jesus offered up prayers and supplications, with loud cries and tears, to him [God] who was able to save him from death, and he was heard for his godly fear" (5:7). At first glance this statement seems far-fetched, because Jesus died on the Cross. Yet, the Letter to the Hebrews makes no mistake: God has indeed saved Jesus from death by giving him complete victory over it, but the path to that [victory] is through death itself! The supplication that God has answered referred to Jesus' prayer in Gethsemane. Assailed by looming anguish, Jesus prays to the Father to deliver him of this bitter cup of the Passion, but his prayer is pervaded by trust in the Father and he entrusts himself entirely to his will: "not as I will," Jesus says, "but as thou wilt" (Mt 26:39). The object of prayer is of secondary importance; what matters above all is his relationship with the Father. This is what prayer does: it transforms the desire and models it according to the will of God, whatever that may be, because the one who prays aspires first of all to union with God, who is merciful Love.

—Francis, General Audience, May 25, 2016

Dear brothers and sisters, in reading this account each one of us is called to understand that in our prayers of petition to the Lord we must not expect an immediate fulfillment of what we ask, of our own will. Rather, we must entrust ourselves to the Father's will, interpreting every event in the perspective of his glory, of his plan of love, which to our eyes is often mysterious. For this reason, we too must join in our prayers, petitions, praise and thanksgiving, even when it seems to us that God is not responding to our real expectations.

Abandoning ourselves to God's love which always precedes and accompanies us is one of the basic attitudes for our dialogue with him. On Jesus' prayer in the account of the raising of Lazarus the *Catechism of the Catholic Church* comments: "Jesus' prayer, characterized by thanksgiving, reveals to us how to ask: before the gift is given, Jesus commits himself to the One who in giving gives himself. The Giver is more precious than the gift; he is the 'treasure'; in him abides his Son's heart; the gift is given 'as well' (cf. Mt 6:21, 33)" (n. 2604). To me this seems very important: before the gift is given, committing ourselves to the One who gives. The Giver is more precious than the gift. For us too, therefore, over and above what God bestows on us when we call on him, the greatest gift that he can give us is his friendship, his presence and his love. He is the precious treasure to ask for and to preserve forever.

—Benedict XVI, General Audience, December 14, 2011

In the first place, we ought to be astonished by this fact: when we praise God or give him thanks for his benefits in general, we are not particularly concerned whether or not our prayer is acceptable to him. On the other hand, we demand to see the results of our petitions. What is the image of God that motivates our prayer: an instrument to be used? or the Father of our Lord Jesus Christ?

Are we convinced that "we do not know how to pray as we ought"? Are we asking God for "what is good for us"? Our Father knows what we need before we ask him, but he awaits our petition because the dignity of his children lies in their freedom. We must pray, then, with his Spirit of freedom, to be able truly to know what he wants.

"You ask and do not receive, because you ask wrongly, to spend it on your passions." If we ask with a divided heart, we are "adulterers"; God cannot answer us, for he desires our well-being, our life. "Or do you suppose that it is in vain that the scripture says, 'He yearns jealously over the spirit which he has made to dwell in us?'" That our God is "jealous" for us is the sign of how true his love is. If we enter into the desire of his Spirit, we shall be heard.

Do not be troubled if you do not immediately receive from God what you ask him; for he desires to do something even greater for you, while you cling to him in prayer. God wills that our desire should be exercised in prayer, that we may be able to receive what he is prepared to give.

—*Catechism of the Catholic Church,* 2735–37 (citing Rom 8:26;
Jas 4:3, 4:4, 4:5; Evagrius Ponticus, *De oratione* 34; and Augustine,
Ep. 130, 8, 17)

———— 79 ————

We are undocumented immigrants and cannot legally marry without risking deportation. What should we do? Can the church marry us "in secret"?

For a grave and urgent cause, the local ordinary can permit a marriage to be celebrated secretly.

Permission to celebrate a marriage secretly entails the following:

1. the investigations which must be conducted before the marriage are done secretly;

2. the local ordinary, the one assisting, the witnesses, and the spouses observe secrecy about the marriage celebrated.

—*Code of Canon Law,* cc. 1130–31

Just as in Jonah's time, so too today may we commit ourselves to conversion; may we be signs lighting the way and announcing salvation. I know of the work of countless civil organizations working to support the rights of migrants. I know too of the committed work of so many men and women religious, priests and lay people in accompanying migrants and in defending life. They are on the front lines, often risking their own lives. By their very lives they are prophets of mercy; they are the beating heart and the accompanying feet of the Church that opens its arms and sustains.

— Francis, Homily at Ciudad Juárez Fair Grounds, Mexico,
February 17, 2016

VIOLENCE AND ABUSE

—— 80 ——

How am I called to help families who are wounded or struggling in some way?

"Christian couples are, for each other, for their children and for their relatives, cooperators of grace and witnesses of the faith." God calls them to bestow life and to care for life. For this reason, the family "has always been the nearest 'hospital.'" So let us care for one another, guide and encourage one another, and experience this as a part of our family spirituality. Life as a couple is a daily sharing in God's creative work, and each person is for the other a constant challenge from the Holy Spirit. God's love is proclaimed "through the living and concrete word whereby a man and the woman express their conjugal love." The two are thus mutual reflections of that divine love which comforts with a word, a look, a helping hand, a caress, an embrace. For this reason, "to want to form a family is to resolve to be a part of God's dream, to choose to dream with him, to want to build with him, to join him in this saga of building a world where no one will feel alone."

All family life is a "shepherding" in mercy. Each of us, by our love and care, leaves a mark on the life of others; with Paul, we can say: "You are our letter of recommendation, written on your hearts ... not with ink, but with the Spirit of the living God" (2 Cor 3:2–3). Each of us is a "fisher of men" (Lk 5:10) who in Jesus' name "casts the nets" (cf. Lk 5:5) to others, or a farmer who tills the fresh soil of those whom he or she loves, seeking to bring out the best in them. Marital fruitfulness involves helping others, for "to love anybody is to expect from him something which can neither be defined nor foreseen; it is at the same time in some way to make it possible for him to fulfill this expectation." This is itself a way to worship God, who has sown so much good in others in the hope that we will help make it grow.

> —Francis, *Amoris laetitia*, 321–22 (citing Dietrich
> Bonhoeffer, *Life Together* [New York: HarperOne,
> 1954], 27; *Apostolicam actuositaem*, 11; his own catechesis
> of June 10, 2015; John Paul II, *Familiaris consortio*, 12; and
> his own Address at the Prayer Vigil of the Festival of
> Families, September 28, 2015)

The biblical icon of the Good Shepherd (Jn 10:11–18) summarizes the mission that Jesus received from the Father: that of giving his life for the sheep. This attitude is also a model for the Church, which embraces her children as a mother who gives her life for them. "The Church is called to be the house of the Father, with doors always wide open." ... No closed doors! No closed doors! "Everyone can share in some way in the life of the Church; everyone can be part of the community." ... The Church "is the house of the Father, where there is a place for everyone, with all their problems."

In the same way, all Christians are called to imitate the Good Shepherd. Especially Christian families can cooperate with Him by taking care of wounded families, accompanying them in the life of faith of the community. Each one must do his part in taking on the attitude of the

Good Shepherd, who knows each one of his sheep and excludes no one from his infinitive love!

—Francis, General Audience, August 5, 2015 (citing *Evangelii gaudium*, 47)

The *works of mercy* are charitable actions by which we come to the aid of our neighbor in his spiritual and bodily necessities. Instructing, advising, consoling, comforting are spiritual works of mercy, as are forgiving and bearing wrongs patiently. The corporal works of mercy consist especially in feeding the hungry, sheltering the homeless, clothing the naked, visiting the sick and imprisoned, and burying the dead. Among all these, giving alms to the poor is one of the chief witnesses to fraternal charity: it is also a work of justice pleasing to God: He who has two coats, let him share with him who has none and he who has food must do likewise. But give for alms those things which are within; and behold, everything is clean for you. If a brother or sister is ill-clad and in lack of daily food, and one of you says to them, "Go in peace, be warmed and filled," without giving them the things needed for the body, what does it profit?

"In its various forms—material deprivation, unjust oppression, physical and psychological illness and death—*human misery* is the obvious sign of the inherited condition of frailty and need for salvation in which man finds himself as a consequence of original sin. This misery elicited the compassion of Christ the Savior, who willingly took it upon himself and identified himself with the least of his brethren. Hence, those who are oppressed by poverty are the object of *a preferential love* on the part of the Church which, since her origin and in spite of the failings of many of her members, has not ceased to work for their relief, defense, and liberation through numerous works of charity which remain indispensable always and everywhere."

—*Catechism of the Catholic Church*, 2447–48 (citing Lk 3:11, 11:41; Jas 2:15–16; Congregation for the Doctrine of the Faith, *Libertatis conscientia*, 68)

—— 81 ——

My spouse is physically abusive. What should I do? We married "for better or for worse," and I'm supposed to forgive, so do I just need to accept this as my cross?

In some cases, respect for one's own dignity and the good of the children requires not giving in to excessive demands or preventing a grave injustice, violence or chronic ill-treatment. In such cases, "separation becomes inevitable. At times, it even becomes morally necessary, precisely when it is a matter of removing the more vulnerable spouse or young children from serious injury due to abuse and violence, from humiliation and exploitation, and from disregard and indifference." Even so, "separation must be considered as a last resort, after all other reasonable attempts at reconciliation have proved vain."

> —Francis, *Amoris laetitia*, 241 (citing his own catechesis of June 24, 2015; and John Paul II, *Familiaris consortio*, 83)

At this time, when so many families are separated or forced to emigrate, when so many are suffering due to poverty, corruption, domestic violence, drug trafficking, the crisis of values and increased crime, we come to Mary in search of consolation, strength and hope. She is the Mother of the true God, who invites us to stay with faith and charity beneath her mantle, so as "to overcome in this way all evil and to establish a more just and fraternal society."

> —Benedict XVI, Angelus Message in León, Mexico, March 25, 2012

Yet there are some situations in which living together becomes practically impossible for a variety of reasons. In such cases the Church permits the physical separation of the couple and their living apart. The spouses do not cease to be husband and wife before God and so are not free to contract a new union. In this difficult situation, the best solution would be, if possible, reconciliation. The Christian community is called to help these persons live out their situation in a Christian manner and in fidelity to their marriage bond which remains indissoluble.

—*Catechism of the Catholic Church*, 1649

At the root of every act of violence against one's neighbor there is a concession to the "thinking" of the evil one, the one who "was a murderer from the beginning" (Jn 8:44). As the Apostle John reminds us: "For this is the message which you have heard from the beginning, that we should love one another, and not be like Cain who was of the evil one and murdered his brother" (1 Jn 3:11–12). Cain's killing of his brother at the very dawn of history is thus a sad witness of how evil spreads with amazing speed: man's revolt against God in the earthly paradise is followed by the deadly combat of man against man.

—John Paul II, *Evangelium vitae*, 8

If either of the *spouses* causes grave mental or physical danger to the other spouse or to the offspring or otherwise renders common life too difficult, that spouse gives the other a legitimate cause for leaving, either by decree of the local ordinary or even on his or her own authority if there is danger in delay.

In all cases, when the cause for the separation ceases, conjugal living must be restored unless ecclesiastical authority has established otherwise.

After the separation of the spouses has taken place, the adequate support and education of the children must always be suitably provided.

The innocent spouse laudably can readmit the other spouse to conjugal life; in this case the innocent spouse renounces the right to separate.

—*Code of Canon Law*, cc. 1153–55

—— 82 ——

Is it possible for spouses to be sexually abusive toward one another? According to scripture, don't their bodies "belong to each other"?

We also know that, within marriage itself, sex can become a source of suffering and manipulation. Hence it must be clearly reaffirmed that "a conjugal act imposed on one's spouse without regard to his or her condition, or personal and reasonable wishes in the matter, is no true act of love, and therefore offends the moral order in its particular application to the intimate relationship of husband and wife." The acts proper to the sexual union of husband and wife correspond to the nature of sexuality as willed by God when they take place in "a manner which is truly human." Saint Paul insists: "Let no one transgress and wrong his brother or sister in this matter" (1 Thes 4:6). Even though Paul was writing in the context of a patriarchal culture in which women were considered completely subordinate to men, he nonetheless taught that sex must involve communication between the spouses: he brings up the possibility of postponing sexual relations for a period, but "by agreement" (1 Cor 7:5).

> —Francis, *Amoris laetitia*, 154 (citing Paul VI, *Humanae vitae*, 13; and the Second Vatican Council, *Gaudium et spes*, 49)

Every form of sexual submission must be clearly rejected. This includes all improper interpretations of the passage in the Letter to the Ephesians where Paul tells women to "be subject to your husbands" (Eph 5:22). This passage mirrors the cultural categories of the time, but our concern is not with its cultural matrix but with the revealed message that it conveys. As Saint John Paul II wisely observed: "Love excludes every kind of subjection whereby the wife might become a servant or a slave of the husband.... The community or unity which they should establish through marriage is constituted by a reciprocal donation of self, which is also a mutual subjection." Hence Paul goes on to say that "husbands should love their wives as their own bodies" (Eph 5:28). The biblical text is actually concerned with encouraging everyone to overcome a complacent individualism and to be constantly mindful of others: "Be subject to one another" (Eph 5:21). In marriage, this reciprocal "submission" takes on a special meaning, and is seen as a freely chosen mutual belonging marked by fidelity, respect and care. Sexuality is inseparably at the service of conjugal friendship, for it is meant to aid the fulfillment of the other.

— Francis, *Amoris laetitia*, 156 (citing John Paul II, General Audience on the Theology of the Body, August 11, 1982)

---- 83 ----

Does the church say anything about the problem of violence within families?

As the Bishops of Mexico have pointed out, violence within families breeds new forms of social aggression, since "family relationships can also explain the tendency to a violent personality. This is often the case with families where communication is lacking, defensive attitudes predominate, the members are not supportive of one another, family activities that encourage participation are absent, the parental relationship is frequently conflictual and violent, and relationships between parents and children are marked by hostility. Violence within the family is a breeding-ground of resentment and hatred in the most basic human relationships."

— Francis, *Amoris laetitia*, 51 (citing Mexican Bishops' Conference, *Que en Cristo Nuestra Paz Mexico tenga vida digna*, 67)

Surely it is legitimate and right to reject older forms of the traditional family marked by authoritarianism and even violence, yet this should not lead to a disparagement of marriage itself, but rather to the rediscovery of its authentic meaning and its renewal. The strength of the family "lies in its capacity to love and to teach how to love. For all a family's problems, it can always grow, beginning with love."

—Francis, *Amoris laetitia*, 53 (citing the Final Report of the 2015 Synod on the Family)

Unacceptable customs still need to be eliminated. I think particularly of the shameful ill-treatment to which women are sometimes subjected, domestic violence and various forms of enslavement which, rather than a show of masculine power, are craven acts of cowardice. The verbal, physical, and sexual violence that women endure in some marriages contradicts the very nature of the conjugal union.

—Francis, *Amoris laetitia*, 54

ANNULMENTS, DIVORCE, REMARRIAGE, AND THE DEATH OF A SPOUSE

—— 84 ——

My wife left me; she had an untreated addiction and was irresponsible. Can I get a second chance at marriage with someone else? Do I have to stay single to honor a legitimate wedding vow?

The Synod Fathers noted that "special discernment is indispensable for the pastoral care of those who are separated, divorced or abandoned. Respect needs to be shown especially for the sufferings of those who have unjustly endured separation, divorce or abandonment, or those who have been forced by maltreatment from a husband or a wife to interrupt their life together. To forgive such an injustice that has been suffered is not easy, but grace makes this journey possible. Pastoral care must necessarily include efforts at reconciliation and mediation,

through the establishment of specialized counselling centers in dioces-
es." At the same time, "divorced people who have not remarried, and
often bear witness to marital fidelity, ought to be encouraged to find
in the Eucharist the nourishment they need to sustain them in their
present state of life."

> —Francis, *Amoris laetitia*, 242 (citing the *Relatio synodi* of the 2014
> Synod on the Family, 47 and 50)

Yet there are some situations in which living together becomes practically impossible for a variety of reasons. In such cases the Church permits the physical *separation* of the couple and their living apart. The
spouses do not cease to be husband and wife before God and so are not
free to contract a new union. In this difficult situation, the best solution
would be, if possible, reconciliation. The Christian community is called
to help these persons live out their situation in a Christian manner and
in fidelity to their marriage bond which remains indissoluble.

> —*Catechism of the Catholic Church*, 1649–50

Various reasons can unfortunately lead to the often irreparable break-
down of valid marriages. These include mutual lack of understanding
and the inability to enter into interpersonal relationships. Obviously,
separation must be considered as a last resort, after all other reasonable
attempts at reconciliation have proved vain.

Loneliness and other difficulties are often the lot of separated
spouses, especially when they are the innocent parties. The ecclesial
community must support such people more than ever. It must give
them much respect, solidarity, understanding and practical help, so
that they can preserve their fidelity even in their difficult situation; and
it must help them to cultivate the need to forgive which is inherent in
Christian love, and to be ready perhaps to return to their former married life.

The situation is similar for people who have undergone divorce, but, being well aware that the valid marriage bond is indissoluble, re-frain from becoming involved in a new union and devote themselves solely to carrying out their family duties and the responsibilities of Christian life. In such cases their example of fidelity and Christian con-sistency takes on particular value as a witness before the world and the Church. Here it is even more necessary for the Church to offer contin-ual love and assistance, without there being any obstacle to admission to the sacraments.

Daily experience unfortunately shows that people who have ob-tained a divorce usually intend to enter into a new union, obviously not with a Catholic religious ceremony. Since this is an evil that, like the others, is affecting more and more Catholics as well, the problem must be faced with resolution and without delay. The Synod Fathers studied it expressly. The Church, which was set up to lead to salvation all people and especially the baptized, cannot abandon to their own de-vices those who have been previously bound by sacramental marriage and who have attempted a second marriage. The Church will therefore make untiring efforts to put at their disposal her means of salvation.

Pastors must know that, for the sake of truth, they are obliged to exercise careful discernment of situations. There is in fact a difference between those who have sincerely tried to save their first marriage and have been unjustly abandoned, and those who through their own grave fault have destroyed a canonically valid marriage. Finally, there are those who have entered into a second union for the sake of the children's upbringing, and who are sometimes subjectively certain in conscience that their previous and irreparably destroyed marriage had never been valid.

—John Paul II, *Familiaris consortio*, 83–84

—— 85 ——

Does an annulment dissolve a sacramental marriage? If someone is divorced, why does he or she need an annulment?

The consent must be an act of the will of each of the contracting parties, free of coercion or grave external fear. No human power can substitute for this consent. If this freedom is lacking the marriage is invalid.

For this reason (or for other reasons that render the marriage null and void) the Church, after an examination of the situation by the competent ecclesiastical tribunal, can declare the nullity of a marriage, i.e., that the marriage never existed. In this case the contracting parties are free to marry, provided the natural obligations of a previous union are discharged.

—*Catechism of the Catholic Church*, 1628–29

Today there are numerous Catholics in many countries who have recourse to civil *divorce* and contract new civil unions. In fidelity to the words of Jesus Christ—"Whoever divorces his wife and marries another, commits adultery against her; and if she divorces her husband and marries another, she commits adultery"—the Church maintains that a new union cannot be recognized as valid, if the first marriage was. If the divorced are remarried civilly, they find themselves in a situation that objectively contravenes God's law. Consequently, they cannot receive Eucharistic communion as long as this situation persists. For the same reason, they cannot exercise certain ecclesial responsibilities. Reconciliation through the sacrament of Penance can be granted only to those who have repented for having violated the sign of the covenant and of fidelity to Christ, and who are committed to living in complete continence.

—*Catechism of the Catholic Church*, 1650

—— 86 ——

How has the annulment process
been streamlined?

A few fundamental criteria stand out that have guided the work of reform.

I. A single executive sentence in favor of nullity is effective.—First of all, it seemed that a double conforming decision in favor of the nullity of a marriage was no longer necessary to enable the parties to enter into a new canonical marriage. Rather, moral certainty on the part of the first judge in accord with the norm of law is sufficient.

II. A sole judge under the responsibility of the bishop.—In the first instance, the responsibility of appointing a sole judge, who must be a cleric, is entrusted to the bishop, who in the pastoral exercise of his judicial power must guard against all laxism.

III. The bishop himself as judge.—In order that a teaching of the Second Vatican Council regarding a certain area of great importance finally be put into practice, it has been decided to declare openly that the bishop himself, in the church over which he has been appointed shepherd and head, is by that very fact the judge of those faithful entrusted to his care. It is thus hoped that the bishop himself, be it of a large or small diocese, stand as a sign of the conversion of ecclesiastical structures, and that he does not delegate completely the duty of deciding marriage cases to the offices of his curia. This is especially true in the streamlined process for handling cases of clear nullity being established in the present document.

IV. Briefer process.—For indeed, in simplifying the ordinary process for handling marriage cases, a sort of briefer process was devised—besides the current documentary procedure—to be applied in those cases where the alleged nullity of marriage is supported by particularly clear arguments.

—Francis, *Mitis iudex dominus Iesus*, Introduction

—— 87 ——

Why does my non-Catholic fiancé need an annulment for his first marriage?

The intimate partnership of married life and love has been established by the Creator and qualified by His laws, and is rooted in the conjugal covenant of irrevocable personal consent. Hence by that human act whereby spouses mutually bestow and accept each other a relationship arises which by divine will and in the eyes of society too is a lasting one. For the good of the spouses and their offspring as well as of society, the existence of the sacred bond no longer depends on human decisions alone. For, God Himself is the author of matrimony, endowed as it is with various benefits and purposes.... By their very nature, the institution of matrimony itself and conjugal love are ordained for the procreation and education of children, and find in them their ultimate crown. Thus a man and a woman, who by their compact of conjugal love "are no longer two, but one flesh" (Mt 19:ff), render mutual help and service to each other through an intimate union of their persons and of their actions. Through this union they experience the meaning of their oneness and attain to it with growing perfection day by day. As a mutual gift of two persons, this intimate union and the good of the children impose total fidelity on the spouses and argue for an unbreakable oneness between them.

Christ the Lord abundantly blessed this many-faceted love, welling up as it does from the fountain of divine love and structured as it is on the model of His union with His Church. For as God of old made Himself present to His people through a covenant of love and fidelity, so now the Savior of men and the Spouse of the Church comes into the lives of married Christians through the sacrament of matrimony. He abides with them thereafter so that just as He loved the Church and handed Himself over on her behalf, the spouses may love each other with perpetual fidelity through mutual self-bestowal.

—Second Vatican Council, *Gaudium et spes*, 48

The internal consent of the mind is presumed to conform to the words and signs used in celebrating the marriage. If, however, either or both of the parties by a positive act of the will exclude marriage itself, some essential element of marriage, or some essential property of marriage, the party contracts invalidly.

—*Code of Canon Law*, c. 1101

Marriage possesses the favor of law; therefore, in a case of doubt, the validity of a marriage must be upheld until the contrary is proven.

—*Code of Canon Law*, c. 1060

——— 88 ———
Can divorced and remarried Catholics receive Communion?

If we consider the immense variety of concrete situations such as those I have mentioned, it is understandable that neither the Synod nor this Exhortation could be expected to provide a new set of general rules, canonical in nature and applicable to all cases.

—Francis, *Amoris laetitia*, 300

In certain cases, this can include the help of the sacraments. Hence, "I want to remind priests that the confessional must not be a torture chamber, but rather an encounter with the Lord's mercy" (*Evangelii gaudium*, no. 44). I would also point out that the Eucharist "is not a prize for the perfect, but a powerful medicine and nourishment for the weak (*Evangelii gaudium*, no. 47).

—Francis, *Amoris Laetitia*, 305, footnote 351

In order to avoid all misunderstanding, I would point out that in no way must the Church desist from proposing the full ideal of marriage, God's plan in all its grandeur: "Young people who are baptized should be encouraged to understand that the sacrament of marriage can enrich their prospects of love and that they can be sustained by the grace of Christ in the sacrament and by the possibility of participating fully in the life of the Church." A lukewarm attitude, any kind of relativism, or an undue reticence in proposing that ideal, would be a lack of fidelity to the Gospel and also of love on the part of the Church for young people themselves.

—Francis, *Amoris laetitia*, 307

EDITORS' NOTE: Theologians and bishops continue to debate how to best understand Pope Francis's teaching in *Amoris laetitia*, chapter 8. Given the Holy Father's express declarations in the document and elsewhere that he is not altering the doctrine of the indissolubility of marriage and making no general changes to the church's practice, it is important to read this teaching in continuity with that of his predecessors. The considerations concerning gradualism, discernment, mitigating factors, rules and exceptions, and "the logic of pastoral mercy" introduced in this chapter are in the service of adopting a more pastoral tone toward those who have divorced and entered civil marriages. This more merciful and welcoming tone is a wider concern of the document (see *Amoris laetitia,*, nos. 38 and 49). The mention of reception of the sacraments in specific cases in footnote 351 may refer to "the conflict case" of a couple who sincerely believe their previous marriage to be invalid (referenced in *Amoris laetitia*, no. 298) but who for various reasons are unable to prove it before a tribunal. ⚓

If the Eucharist expresses the irrevocable nature of God's love in Christ for his Church, we can then understand why it implies, with regard to the sacrament of Matrimony, that indissolubility to which all true love necessarily aspires. There was good reason for the pastoral attention that the Synod gave to the painful situations experienced by some of the faithful who, having celebrated the sacrament of Matrimony, then divorced and remarried. This represents a complex and troubling pastoral problem, a real scourge for contemporary society, and one which increasingly affects the Catholic community as well. The Church's pastors, out of love for the truth, are obliged to discern different situations carefully, in order to be able to offer appropriate spiritual guidance to the faithful involved. The Synod of Bishops confirmed the Church's practice, based on Sacred Scripture (cf. Mk 10:2–12), of not admitting the divorced and remarried to the sacraments, since their state and their condition of life objectively contradict the loving union of Christ and the Church signified and made present in the Eucharist. Yet the divorced and remarried continue to belong to the Church, which accompanies them with special concern and encourages them to live as fully as possible the Christian life through regular participation at Mass, albeit without receiving communion, listening to the word of God, eucharistic adoration, prayer, participation in the life of the community, honest dialogue with a priest or spiritual director, dedication to the life of charity, works of penance, and commitment to the education of their children.

When legitimate doubts exist about the validity of the prior sacramental marriage, the necessary investigation must be carried out to establish if these are well founded. Consequently there is a need to ensure, in full respect for canon law, the presence of local ecclesiastical tribunals, their pastoral character, and their correct and prompt functioning. Each Diocese should have a sufficient number of persons with the necessary preparation, so that the ecclesiastical tribunals can operate in an expeditious manner. I repeat that "it is a grave obligation to bring the Church's institutional activity in her tribunals ever closer to the faithful." At the same time, pastoral care must not be understood as if it were somehow in conflict with the law. Rather, one should begin by assuming that the fundamental point of encounter between the law and pastoral care is love for the truth: truth is never something purely abstract, but "a real part of the human and Christian journey of every member of the faithful." Finally, where the nullity of the marriage bond is not declared and objective circumstances make it impossible to cease cohabitation, the Church encourages these members of the faithful to commit themselves to living their relationship in fidelity to the demands of God's law, as friends, as brother and sister; in this way they will be able to return to the table of the Eucharist, taking care to observe the Church's established and approved practice in this regard. This path, if it is to be possible and fruitful, must be supported by pastors and by adequate ecclesial initiatives, nor can it ever involve the blessing of these relations, lest confusion arise among the faithful concerning the value of marriage.

—Benedict XVI, *Sacramentum caritatis*, 29

The mistaken conviction of a divorced-and-remarried person that he may receive holy communion normally presupposes that personal conscience is considered in the final analysis to be able, on the basis of one's own convictions, to come to a decision about the existence or absence of a previous marriage and the value of the new union. However, such a position is inadmissible. Marriage, in fact, both because it is the image of the spousal relationship between Christ and his church as well as the fundamental core and an important factor in the life of civil society, is essentially a public reality.

—Congregation for the Doctrine of the Faith, *Concerning the Reception of Holy Communion by Divorced-and-Remarried Members of the Faithful*, 7

Together with the Synod, I earnestly call upon pastors and the whole community of the faithful to help the divorced, and with solicitous care to make sure that they do not consider themselves as separated from the Church, for as baptized persons they can, and indeed must, share in her life. They should be encouraged to listen to the word of God, to attend the Sacrifice of the Mass, to persevere in prayer, to contribute to works of charity and to community efforts in favor of justice, to bring up their children in the Christian faith, to cultivate the spirit and practice of penance and thus implore, day by day, God's grace. Let the Church pray for them, encourage them and show herself a merciful mother, and thus sustain them in faith and hope.

However, the Church reaffirms her practice, which is based upon Sacred Scripture, of not admitting to Eucharistic Communion divorced persons who have remarried. They are unable to be admitted thereto from the fact that their state and condition of life objectively contradict that union of love between Christ and the Church which is signified and effected by the Eucharist. Besides this, there is another special pastoral reason: if these people were admitted to the Eucharist, the faithful would be led into error and confusion regarding the Church's teaching about the indissolubility of marriage.

Reconciliation in the sacrament of Penance which would open the way to the Eucharist, can only be granted to those who, repenting of having broken the sign of the Covenant and of fidelity to Christ, are sincerely ready to undertake a way of life that is no longer in contradiction to the indissolubility of marriage. This means, in practice, that when, for serious reasons, such as for example the children's upbringing, a man and a woman cannot satisfy the obligation to separate, they "take on themselves the duty to live in complete continence, that is, by abstinence from the acts proper to married couples."

  —John Paul II, *Familiaris consortio,* 84

—— 89 ——

My husband died. Are we still married in heaven? I feel like I am his forever. How can I give myself totally to him and have that end when he dies?

Set me as a seal upon your heart, as a seal upon your arm; For Love is strong as Death, longing is fierce as Sheol. Its arrows are arrows of fire, flames of the divine.

—Song of Songs 8:6, New American Bible Revised Edition

Some Sadducees, those who deny that there is a resurrection, came forward and put this question to him, saying, "Teacher, Moses wrote for us, 'If someone's brother dies leaving a wife but no child, his brother must take the wife and raise up descendants for his brother.' Now there were seven brothers; the first married a woman but died childless. Then the second and the third married her, and likewise all the seven died childless. Finally the woman also died. Now at the resurrection whose wife will that woman be? For all seven had been married to her.' Jesus said to them, 'The children of this age marry and are given in marriage; but those who are deemed worthy to attain to the coming age and to the resurrection of the dead neither marry nor are given in marriage. They can no longer die, for they are like angels; and they are the children of God because they are the ones who will rise.' That the dead will rise even Moses made known in the passage about the bush, when he called 'Lord' the God of Abraham, the God of Isaac, and the God of Jacob; and he is not God of the dead, but of the living, for to him all are alive."

—Luke 20:27–38, New American Bible Revised Edition

I, N., take you, N., to be my wife/husband. I promise to be faithful to you in good times and in bad, in sickness and in health, to love you and honor you all the days of my life.

—1990 *Order of Celebrating Matrimony*, Formula for Exchange of Consent, 2nd ed. New English Translation from 2016.

The consent by which the spouses mutually give and receive one another is sealed by God himself. From their covenant arises "an institution, confirmed by the divine law, ... even in the eyes of society." The covenant between the spouses is integrated into God's covenant with man: "Authentic married love is caught up into divine love."

Thus *the marriage bond* has been established by God himself in such a way that a marriage concluded and consummated between baptized persons can never be dissolved. This bond, which results from the free human act of the spouses and their consummation of the marriage, is a reality, henceforth irrevocable, and gives rise to a covenant guaranteed by God's fidelity. The Church does not have the power to contravene this disposition of divine wisdom.

—*Catechism of the Catholic Church*, 1639–40 (citing the Second Vatican Council, *Gaudium et spes*, 48)

By matrimony, therefore, the souls of the contracting parties are joined and knit together more directly and more intimately than are their bodies, and that not by any passing affection of sense of spirit, but by a deliberate and firm act of the will; and from this union of souls by God's decree, a sacred and inviolable bond arises.

—Pius XI, *Casti connubii*, 7

EDITORS' NOTE: The traditional understanding of Western churches has been that the bond of marriage is dissolved by the death of a spouse ("till death do us part"). Some in the Eastern churches, however, hold that the bond of marriage continues in heaven in some form. ✠

——— 90 ———

What is my place in the church now that I am a widow? Does widowhood have a value?

Widowhood, accepted bravely as a continuation of the marriage vocation, should be esteemed by all.

—Second Vatican Council, *Gaudium et spes*, 48

I can understand the anguish felt by those who have lost a much-loved person, a spouse with whom they have shared so much. Jesus himself was deeply moved and began to weep at the death of a friend (cf. Jn 11:33, 35). And how can we even begin to understand the grief of parents who have lost a child? "It is as if time stops altogether: a chasm opens to engulf both past and future," and "at times we even go so far as to lay the blame on God. How many people—I can understand them—get angry with God." "Losing one's spouse is particularly difficult.... From the moment of enduring a loss, some display an ability to concentrate their energies in a greater dedication to their children and grandchildren, finding in this experience of love a renewed sense of mission in raising their children.... Those who do not have relatives to spend time with and to receive affection from, should be aided by the Christian community with particular attention and availability, especially if they are poor."

—Francis, *Amoris laetitia*, 254 (citing his own catechesis of June 17, 2015; and the Final Report of the 2015 Synod on the Family)

From apostolic times Christian virgins and widows, called by the Lord to cling only to him with greater freedom of heart, body, and spirit, have decided with the Church's approval to live in the respective status of virginity or perpetual chastity "for the sake of the Kingdom of heaven."

—*Catechism of the Catholic Church*, 922 (citing Mt 19:12)

LOVING (GROWN) CHILDREN

——— 91 ———

Should I go to my child's wedding if both parties are Catholic but they are not marrying in the church?

When they become adults, children have the right and duty to choose their profession and state of life. They should assume their new responsibilities within a trusting relationship with their parents, willingly asking and receiving their advice and counsel. Parents should be careful not to exert pressure on their children either in the choice of a profession or in that of a spouse. This necessary restraint does not prevent them—quite the contrary—from giving their children judicious advice, particularly when they are planning to start a family.

—*Catechism of the Catholic Church*, 2230

Only those marriages [involving a baptized Catholic] are valid which are contracted before the local [bishop], pastor or a priest or deacon delegated by either of them who assist, and before two witnesses.

—*Code of Canon Law*, c. 1108, §1

Sin is a personal act. Moreover, we have a responsibility for the sins committed by others when we cooperate in them:
- by participating directly and voluntarily in them;
- by ordering, advising, praising, or approving them;
- by not disclosing or not hindering them when we have an obligation to do so;
- by protecting evil-doers.

—*Catechism of the Catholic Church*, 1868

Scandal is an attitude or behavior which leads another to do evil. The person who gives scandal becomes his neighbor's tempter. He damages virtue and integrity; he may even draw his brother into spiritual death. Scandal is a grave offense if by deed or omission another is deliberately led into a grave offense.

Scandal can be provoked by laws or institutions, by fashion or opinion.

Therefore, they are guilty of scandal who establish laws or social structures leading to the decline of morals and the corruption of religious practice, or to "social conditions that, intentionally or not, make Christian conduct and obedience to the Commandments difficult and practically impossible." This is also true of business leaders who make rules encouraging fraud, teachers who provoke their children to anger, or manipulators of public opinion who turn it away from moral values.

Anyone who uses the power at his disposal in such a way that it leads others to do wrong becomes guilty of scandal and responsible for the evil that he has directly or indirectly encouraged. "Temptations to sin are sure to come; but woe to him by whom they come!"

—*Catechism of the Catholic Church*, 2284, 2286–87 (quoting
Pius XII, Discourse [June 1, 1941]; and Lk 17:1)

By their baptismal consecration, they were enabled to join in marriage as the Lord's ministers and thus to respond to God's call. Hence, when two non-Christian spouses receive baptism, they need not renew their marriage vows; they need simply not reject them, since by the reception of baptism their union automatically becomes sacramental. Canon Law also recognizes the validity of certain unions celebrated without the presence of an ordained minister. The natural order has been so imbued with the redemptive grace of Jesus that "a valid matrimonial contract cannot exist between the baptized without it being by that fact a sacrament." The Church can require that the wedding be celebrated publicly, with the presence of witnesses and other conditions that have varied over the course of time, but this does not detract from the fact that the couple who marry are the ministers of the sacrament.

—Pope Francis, *Amoris laetitia*, 75 (citing the *Code of Canon Law*, c. 1055)

EDITORS' NOTE: Such cases require the judgment of a well-formed conscience to balance showing love and support for children with concerns of scandal and cooperation with evil done by others. ⚜

——— 92 ———

If my child is attracted to members of his or her own sex or claims a nonbiological gender identity, what does this mean for me as a parent?

Children in turn contribute to the growth in holiness of their parents. Each and everyone should be generous and tireless in forgiving one another for offenses, quarrels, injustices, and neglect. Mutual affection suggests this. The charity of Christ demands it.

—*Catechism of the Catholic Church*, 2227

From this multi-faceted approach there are numerous advantages to be gained, not the least of which is the realization that a homosexual person, as every human being, deeply needs to be nourished at many different levels simultaneously.

The human person, made in the image and likeness of God, can hardly be adequately described by a reductionist reference to his or her sexual orientation. Every one living on the face of the earth has personal problems and difficulties, but challenges to growth, strengths, talents and gifts as well. Today, the Church provides a badly needed context for the care of the human person when she refuses to consider the person as a "heterosexual" or a "homosexual" and insists that every person has a fundamental Identity: the creature of God, and by grace, his child and heir to eternal life.

—Congregation for the Doctrine of the Faith, *Letter to the Bishops of the Catholic Church on the Pastoral Care of Homosexual Persons*, 16

In the pastoral field, these homosexuals must certainly be treated with understanding and sustained in the hope of overcoming their personal difficulties and their inability to fit into society. Their culpability will be judged with prudence. But no pastoral method can be employed which would give moral justification to these acts on the grounds that they would be consonant with the condition of such people. For according to the objective moral order, homosexual relations are acts which lack an essential and indispensable finality. In Sacred Scripture, they are condemned as a serious depravity and even presented as the sad consequence of rejecting God. This judgment of Scripture does not of course permit us to conclude that all those who suffer from this anomaly are personally responsible for it, but it does attest to the fact that homosexual acts are intrinsically disordered and can in no case be approved of.

—Congregation for the Doctrine of the Faith, *Persona humana*, 8

—— 93 ——

What should I do if my child or family member says he or she is same-sex attracted or claims a new gender?

The Church makes her own the attitude of the Lord Jesus, who offers his boundless love to each person without exception. During the Synod, we discussed the situation of families whose members include persons who experience same-sex attraction, a situation not easy either for parents or for children. We would like before all else to reaffirm that every person, regardless of sexual orientation, ought to be respected in his or her dignity and treated with consideration, while "every sign of unjust discrimination" is to be carefully avoided, particularly any form of aggression and violence. Such families should be given respectful pastoral guidance, so that those who manifest a homosexual orientation can receive the assistance they need to understand and fully carry out God's will in their lives.

—Francis, *Amoris laetitia*, 250

An authentic pastoral program will assist homosexual persons at all levels of the spiritual life: through the sacraments, and in particular through the frequent and sincere use of the sacrament of Reconciliation, through prayer, witness, counsel and individual care. In such a way, the entire Christian community can come to recognize its own call to assist its brothers and sisters, without deluding them or isolating them.

From this multi-faceted approach there are numerous advantages to be gained, not the least of which is the realization that a homosexual person, as every human being, deeply needs to be nourished at many different levels simultaneously.

The human person, made in the image and likeness of God, can hardly be adequately described by a reductionist reference to his or her sexual orientation. Every one living on the face of the earth has personal problems and difficulties, but challenges to growth, strengths, talents and gifts as well. Today, the Church provides a badly needed context for the care of the human person when she refuses to consider the person as a "heterosexual" or a "homosexual" and insists that every person has a fundamental Identity: the creature of God, and by grace, his child and heir to eternal life.

—Congregation for the Doctrine of the Faith, *Letter to the Bishops of the Catholic Church on the Pastoral Care of Homosexual Persons*, 15–16

—— 94 ——

How should I treat my child's homosexual partner?

The Church makes her own the attitude of the Lord Jesus, who offers his boundless love to each person without exception. During the Synod, we discussed the situation of families whose members include persons who experience same-sex attraction, a situation not easy either for parents or for children. We would like before all else to reaffirm that every person, regardless of sexual orientation, ought to be respected in his or her dignity and treated with consideration, while "every sign of unjust discrimination" is to be carefully avoided, particularly any form of aggression and violence. Such families should be given respectful pastoral guidance, so that those who manifest a homosexual orientation can receive the assistance they need to understand and fully carry out God's will in their lives.

—Francis, *Amoris laetitia*, 250

In discussing the dignity and mission of the family, the Synod Fathers observed that, as for proposals to place unions between homosexual persons on the same level as marriage, there are absolutely no grounds for considering homosexual unions to be in any way similar or even remotely analogous to God's plan for marriage and family."

—Francis, *Amoris laetitia*, 251

Where the government's policy is *de facto* tolerance and there is no explicit legal recognition of homosexual unions, it is necessary to distinguish carefully the various aspects of the problem. Moral conscience requires that, in every occasion, Christians give witness to the whole moral truth, which is contradicted both by approval of homosexual acts and unjust discrimination against homosexual persons. Therefore, discreet and prudent actions can be effective; these might involve: unmasking the way in which such tolerance might be exploited or used in the service of ideology; stating clearly the immoral nature of these unions; reminding the government of the need to contain the phenomenon within certain limits so as to safeguard public morality; and, above all, to avoid exposing young people to erroneous ideas about sexuality and marriage that would deprive them of their necessary defenses and contribute to the spread of the phenomenon. Those who would move from tolerance to the legitimization of specific rights for cohabiting homosexual persons need to be reminded that the approval or legalization of evil is something far different from the toleration of evil.

In those situations where homosexual unions have been legally recognized or have been given the legal status and rights belonging to marriage, clear and emphatic opposition is a duty. One must refrain from any kind of formal cooperation in the enactment or application of such gravely unjust laws and, as far as possible, from material cooperation on the level of their application. In this area, everyone can exercise the right to conscientious objection.

—Congregation for the Doctrine of the Faith, *Considerations Regarding Proposals to Give Legal Recognition to Unions between Homosexual Persons*, 5

The number of men and women who have deep-seated homosexual tendencies is not negligible. This inclination, which is objectively disordered, constitutes for most of them a trial. They must be accepted with respect, compassion, and sensitivity. Every sign of unjust discrimination in their regard should be avoided. These persons are called to fulfill God's will in their lives and, if they are Christians, to unite to the sacrifice of the Lord's Cross the difficulties they may encounter from their condition.

Homosexual persons are called to chastity. By the virtues of self-mastery that teach them inner freedom, at times by the support of disinterested friendship, by prayer and sacramental grace, they can and should gradually and resolutely approach Christian perfection.

—*Catechism of the Catholic Church*, 2358–59

EDITORS' NOTE: In the tradition of Catholic moral analysis, the technical term "objectively disordered" refers to that which cannot be directed toward an objectively good end or telos regardless of the subject's intentions. It should be noted that all persons have disordered desires and inclinations because of the effects of original sin. Furthermore, scripture says more about disordered inclinations of opposite-sex-attracted persons than same-sex-attracted persons. This language does not refer to the dignity of the person experiencing the inclination. Each human person is created in the image and likeness of God and possesses an inviolable dignity. ☙

—— 95 ——

How can I bring my children back to the church?

Mary of Magdala went and announced to the disciples, "I have seen the Lord," and what he told her.

—John 20:18, New American Bible Revised Edition

I recall your sincere faith that first lived in your grandmother Lois and in your mother Eunice and that I am confident lives also in you. For this reason, I remind you to stir into flame the gift of God that you have through the imposition of my hands. For God did not give us a spirit of cowardice but rather of power and love and self-control. So do not be ashamed of your testimony to our Lord, nor to me, a prisoner for his sake; but bear your share of hardship for the gospel with the strength that comes from God.

—2 Timothy 1:5–8, New American Bible Revised Edition

The church sometimes has locked itself up in small things, in small-minded rules. The most important thing is the first proclamation: Jesus Christ has saved you. And the ministers of the church must be ministers of mercy above all. The confessor, for example, is always in danger of being either too much of a rigorist or too lax. Neither is merciful, because neither of them really takes responsibility for the person. The rigorist washes his hands so that he leaves it to the commandment. The loose minister washes his hands by simply saying, "This is not a sin" or something like that. In pastoral ministry we must accompany people, and we must heal their wounds.

How are we treating the people of God? I dream of a church that is a mother and shepherdess. The church's ministers must be merciful, take responsibility for the people and accompany them like the good Samaritan, who washes, cleans and raises up his neighbor. This is pure Gospel. God is greater than sin. The structural and organizational reforms are secondary—that is, they come afterward. The first reform must be the attitude. The ministers of the Gospel must be people who can warm the hearts of the people, who walk through the dark night with them, who know how to dialogue and to descend themselves into their people's night, into the darkness, but without getting lost....

Instead of being just a church that welcomes and receives by keeping the doors open, let us try also to be a church that finds new roads, that is able to step outside itself and go to those who do not attend Mass, to those who have quit or are indifferent. The ones who quit sometimes do it for reasons that, if properly understood and assessed, can lead to a return. But that takes audacity and courage....

The church's pastoral ministry cannot be obsessed with the transmission of a disjointed multitude of doctrines to be imposed insistently. Proclamation in a missionary style focuses on the essentials, on the necessary things: this is also what fascinates and attracts more, what makes the heart burn, as it did for the disciples at Emmaus. We have to find a new balance; otherwise even the moral edifice of the church is likely to fall like a house of cards, losing the freshness and fragrance of the Gospel. The proposal of the Gospel must be more simple, profound, radiant. It is from this proposition that the moral consequences then flow.

> —Francis, Interview, September 21, 2013, in *God Is Always Near: Conversations with Pope Francis* (Huntington, Ind.: Our Sunday Visitor, 2015).

In the exercise of my ministry as the Successor of Peter, I have come to America to confirm you, my brothers and sisters, in the faith of the Apostles (cf. Lk 22:32). I have come to proclaim anew, as Peter proclaimed on the day of Pentecost, that Jesus Christ is Lord and Messiah, risen from the dead, seated in glory at the right hand of the Father, and established as judge of the living and the dead (cf. Acts 2:14ff.). I have come to repeat the Apostle's urgent call to conversion and the forgiveness of sins, and to implore from the Lord a new outpouring of the Holy Spirit upon the Church in this country. As we have heard throughout this Easter season, the Church was born of the Spirit's gift of repentance and faith in the risen Lord. In every age she is impelled by the same Spirit to bring to men and women of every race, language and people (cf. Rv 5:9) the good news of our reconciliation with God in Christ.

Here I wish to offer a special word of gratitude and encouragement to all those who have taken up the challenge of the Second Vatican Council, so often reiterated by Pope John Paul II, and committed their lives to the new evangelization. I thank my brother Bishops, priests and deacons, men and women religious, parents, teachers and catechists. The fidelity and courage with which the Church in this country will respond to the challenges raised by an increasingly secular and materialistic culture will depend in large part upon your own fidelity in handing on the treasure of our Catholic faith. Young people need to be helped to discern the path that leads to true freedom: the path of a sincere and generous imitation of Christ, the path of commitment to justice and peace. Much progress has been made in developing solid programs of catechesis, yet so much more remains to be done in forming the hearts and minds of the young in knowledge and love of the Lord. The challenges confronting us require a comprehensive and sound instruction in the truths of the faith. But they also call for cultivating a mindset, an intellectual "culture," which is genuinely Catholic, confident in the profound harmony of faith and reason, and prepared to bring the richness of faith's vision to bear on the urgent issues which affect the future of American society.

　　—Benedict XVI, Homily at Washington Nationals Stadium,
　　April 17, 2008

We have come to believe in God's love: in these words the Christian can express the fundamental decision of his life. Being Christian is not the result of an ethical choice or a lofty idea, but the encounter with an event, a person, which gives life a new horizon and a decisive direction.

　　—Benedict XVI, *Deus caritas est*, 1

All forms of missionary activity are marked by an awareness that one is furthering human freedom by proclaiming Jesus Christ. The Church must be faithful to Christ, whose body she is, and whose mission she continues. She must necessarily "go the same road that Christ went— namely a road of poverty, obedience, service and self-sacrifice even unto death, from which he emerged a victor through his resurrection." The Church is thus obliged to do everything possible to carry out her mission in the world and to reach all peoples. And she has the right to do this, a right given her by God for the accomplishment of his plan. Religious freedom, which is still at times limited or restricted, remains the premise and guarantee of all the freedoms that ensure the common good of individuals and peoples. It is to be hoped that authentic religious freedom will be granted to all people everywhere. The Church strives for this in all countries, especially in those with a Catholic majority, where she has greater influence. But it is not a question of the religion of the majority or the minority, but of an inalienable right of each and every human person.

On her part, the Church addresses people with full respect for their freedom. Her mission does not restrict freedom but rather promotes it. The Church proposes; she imposes nothing. She respects individuals and cultures, and she honors the sanctuary of conscience.

—John Paul II, *Redemptoris missio*, 39 (citing the Second Vatican Council, *Ad gentes*, 5)

CHAPTER 7

Facing Outward
The Domestic Church and the Common Good

The domestic church chapter gathers questions about praying as a family and discovering the family's identity as a domestic church.

—— 96 ——

How does living authentic Catholic family life contribute to the wider society?

Within the "people of life and the people for life," the family has a decisive responsibility. This responsibility flows from its very nature as a community of life and love, founded upon marriage, and from its mission to "guard, reveal and communicate love." Here it is a matter of God's own love, of which parents are co-workers and as it were interpreters when they transmit life and raise it according to his fatherly plan. This is the love that becomes selflessness, receptiveness and gift. Within the family each member is accepted, respected and honored precisely because he or she is a person; and if any family member is in greater need, the care which he or she receives is all the more intense and attentive.

The family has a special role to play throughout the life of its members, from birth to death. It is truly "the sanctuary of life: the place in which life—the gift of God—can be properly welcomed and protected against the many attacks to which it is exposed, and can develop in accordance with what constitutes authentic human growth." Consequently, the role of the family in building a culture of life is decisive and irreplaceable.

As the domestic church, the family is summoned to proclaim, celebrate and serve the Gospel of life. This is a responsibility which first concerns married couples, called to be givers of life, on the basis of an ever greater awareness of the meaning of procreation as a unique event which clearly reveals that human life is a gift received in order then to be given as a gift. In giving origin to a new life, parents recognize that the child, "as the fruit of their mutual gift of love, is, in turn, a gift for both of them, a gift which flows from them."

It is above all in raising children that the family fulfills its mission to proclaim the Gospel of life. By word and example, in the daily round of relations and choices, and through concrete actions and signs, parents lead their children to authentic freedom, actualized in the sincere gift of self, and they cultivate in them respect for others, a sense of justice, cordial openness, dialogue, generous service, solidarity and all the other values which help people to live life as a gift. In raising children Christian parents must be concerned about their children's faith and help them to fulfill the vocation God has given them. The parents' mission as educators also includes teaching and giving their children an example of the true meaning of suffering and death. They will be able to do this if they are sensitive to all kinds of suffering around them and, even more, if they succeed in fostering attitudes of closeness, assistance and sharing towards sick or elderly members of the family.

The family celebrates the Gospel of life through daily prayer, both individual prayer and family prayer. The family prays in order to glorify and give thanks to God for the gift of life, and implores his light and strength in order to face times of difficulty and suffering without losing hope. But the celebration which gives meaning to every other form of prayer and worship is found in the family's actual daily life together, if it is a life of love and self-giving.

This celebration thus becomes a service to the Gospel of life, expressed through solidarity as experienced within and around the family in the form of concerned, attentive and loving care shown in the humble, ordinary events of each day. A particularly significant expression of solidarity between families is a willingness to adopt or take in children abandoned by their parents or in situations of serious hardship. True parental love is ready to go beyond the bonds of flesh and blood in order to accept children from other families, offering them whatever is necessary for their well-being and full development. Among the various forms of adoption, consideration should be given to adoption-at-a-distance, preferable in cases where the only reason for giving up the child is the extreme poverty of the child's family. Through this type of adoption, parents are given the help needed to support and raise their children, without their being uprooted from their natural environment.

As "a firm and persevering determination to commit oneself to the common good," solidarity also needs to be practiced through participation in social and political life. Serving the Gospel of life thus means that the family, particularly through its membership of family associations, works to ensure that the laws and institutions of the State in no way violate the right to life, from conception to natural death, but rather protect and promote it.

—John Paul II, *Evangelium vitae*, 92–93 (citing *Familiaris consortio*, 17; *Centesimus annus*, 39; and *Solicitudo rei socialis*, 38)

——— 97 ———
How should my faith impact the way I participate in politics?

John Paul II, continuing the constant teaching of the Church, has re-iterated many times that those who are directly involved in lawmaking bodies have a "grave and clear obligation to oppose" any law that attacks human life. For them, as for every Catholic, it is impossible to promote such laws or to vote for them....

In this context, it must be noted also that a well-formed Christian conscience does not permit one to vote for a political program or an individual law which contradicts the fundamental contents of faith and morals. The Christian faith is an integral unity, and thus it is incoherent to isolate some particular element to the detriment of the whole of Catholic doctrine. A political commitment to a single isolated aspect of the Church's social doctrine does not exhaust one's responsibility towards the common good. Nor can a Catholic think of delegating his Christian responsibility to others; rather, the Gospel of Jesus Christ gives him this task, so that the truth about man and the world might be proclaimed and put into action.

When political activity comes up against moral principles that do not admit of exception, compromise or derogation, the Catholic commitment becomes more evident and laden with responsibility. In the face of fundamental and inalienable ethical demands, Christians must recognize that what is at stake is the essence of the moral law, which concerns the integral good of the human person. This is the case with laws concerning abortion and euthanasia (not to be confused with the decision to forgo extraordinary treatments, which is morally legitimate). Such laws must defend the basic right to life from conception to natural death. In the same way, it is necessary to recall the duty to respect and protect the rights of the human embryo. Analogously, the family needs to be safeguarded and promoted, based on monogamous marriage between a man and a woman, and protected in its unity and stability in the face of modern laws on divorce: in no way can other forms of cohabitation be placed on the same level as marriage, nor can they receive legal recognition as such. The same is true for the freedom of parents regarding the education of their children; it is an inalienable right recognized also by the Universal Declaration on Human Rights. In the same way, one must consider society's protection of minors and freedom from modern forms of slavery (drug abuse and prostitution, for example). In addition, there is the right to religious freedom and the development of an economy that is at the service of the human person and of the common good, with respect for social justice, the principles of human solidarity and subsidiarity, according to which "the rights of all individuals, families, and organizations and their practical implementation must be acknowledged."

> —Congregation for the Doctrine of the Faith, *Doctrinal Note on Some Questions Regarding the Participation of Catholics in Political Life*, 4

—— 98 ——

What is a "family politics" and how can I promote it? Am I supposed to be volunteering or leading political campaigns in addition to all my family responsibilities?

"Participation" is the voluntary and generous engagement of a person in social interchange. It is necessary that all participate, each according to his position and role, in promoting the common good. This obligation is inherent in the dignity of the human person.

—*Catechism of the Catholic Church*, 1913

As far as possible citizens should take an active part in public life. The manner of this participation may vary from one country or culture to another. "One must pay tribute to those nations whose systems permit the largest possible number of the citizens to take part in public life in a climate of genuine freedom."

—*Catechism of the Catholic Church*, 1915 (citing the Second Vatican Council, *Gaudium et spes*, 31)

The social role of the family certainly cannot stop short at procreation and education, even if this constitutes its primary and irreplaceable form of expression.

Families therefore, either singly or in association, can and should devote themselves to manifold social service activities, especially in favor of the poor, or at any rate for the benefit of all people and situations that cannot be reached by the public authorities' welfare organization.

The social contribution of the family has an original character of its own, one that should be given greater recognition and more decisive encouragement, especially as the children grow up, and actually involving all its members as much as possible.

In particular, note must be taken of the ever greater importance in our society of hospitality in all its forms, from opening the door of one's home and still more of one's heart to the pleas of one's brothers and sisters, to concrete efforts to ensure that every family has its own home, as the natural environment that preserves it and makes it grow. In a special way, the Christian family is called upon to listen to the Apostle's recommendation: "Practice hospitality," and therefore, imitating Christ's example and sharing in His love, to welcome the brother or sister in need: "Whoever gives to one of these little ones even a cup of cold water because he is a disciple, truly, I say to you, he shall not lose his reward."

The social role of families is called upon to find expression also in the form of political intervention: families should be the first to take steps to see that the laws and institutions of the State not only do not offend but support and positively defend the rights and duties of the family. Along these lines, families should grow in awareness of being "protagonists" of what is known as "family politics" and assume responsibility for transforming society; otherwise families will be the first victims of the evils that they have done no more than note with indifference. The Second Vatican Council's appeal to go beyond an individualistic ethic therefore also holds good for the family as such.

—John Paul II, *Familiaris consortio,* 44

———— 99 ————
How can families serve together in and outside of their home?

Led by the Spirit, the family circle is not only open to life by generating it within itself, but also by going forth and spreading life by caring for others and seeking their happiness. This openness finds particular expression in hospitality, which the word of God eloquently encourages: "Do not neglect to show hospitality to strangers, for thereby some have entertained angels unawares" (Hb 13:2). When a family is welcoming and reaches out to others, especially the poor and the neglected, it is "a symbol, witness and participant in the Church's motherhood." Social love, as a reflection of the Trinity, is what truly unifies the spiritual meaning of the family and its mission to others, for it makes present the kerygma in all its communal imperatives. The family lives its spirituality precisely by being at one and the same time a domestic church and a vital cell for transforming the world.

—Francis, *Amoris laetitia* 324 (citing John Paul II, *Familiaris consortio*, 49)

Fruitful married love expresses itself in serving life in many ways. Of these ways, begetting and educating children are the most immediate, specific and irreplaceable. In fact, every act of true love towards a human being bears witness to and perfects the spiritual fecundity of the family, since it is an act of obedience to the deep inner dynamism of love as self-giving to others. For everyone this perspective is full of value and commitment, and it can be an inspiration in particular for couples who experience physical sterility.

Christian families, recognizing with faith all human beings as children of the same heavenly Father, will respond generously to the children of other families, giving them support and love not as outsiders but as members of the one family of God's children. Christian parents will thus be able to spread their love beyond the bonds of flesh and blood, nourishing the links that are rooted in the spirit and that develop through concrete service to the children of other families, who are often without even the barest necessities.

—John Paul II, *Familiaris consortio*, 41

Love, too, goes beyond our brothers and sisters of the same faith since "everybody is my brother or sister." In each individual, especially in the poor, the weak, and those who suffer or are unjustly treated, love knows how to discover the face of Christ, and discover a fellow human being to be loved and served.

In order that the family may serve man in a truly evangelical way, the instructions of the Second Vatican Council must be carefully put into practice: "That the exercise of such charity may rise above any deficiencies in fact and even in appearance, certain fundamentals must be observed. Thus, attention is to be paid to the image of God in which our neighbor has been created, and also to Christ the Lord to whom is really offered whatever is given to a needy person."

While building up the Church in love, the Christian family places itself at the service of the human person and the world, really bringing about the "human advancement" whose substance was given in summary form in the Synod's Message to families: "Another task for the family is to form persons in love and also to practice love in all its relationships, so that it does not live closed in on itself, but remains open to the community, moved by a sense of justice and concern for others, as well as by a consciousness of its responsibility towards the whole of society."

> —John Paul II, *Familiaris consortio*, 64 (citing *Apostolicam actuositatem*, 8; and Synod of Bishops' Message to Christian Families, October 24, 1980)

PRAYER AND EVANGELIZATION

—— 100 ——

How is our family a domestic church? Is it something we are already, or do we need to do anything special to become a domestic church?

Here too, we can see another aspect of the family. We know that the New Testament speaks of "churches that meet in homes" (cf. 1 Cor 16:19; Rom 16:5; Col 4:15; Phil 2). A family's living space could turn into a domestic church, a setting for the Eucharist, the presence of Christ seated at its table. We can never forget the image found in the Book of Revelation, where the Lord says: "Behold, I stand at the door and knock; if any one hears my voice and opens the door, I will come in to him and eat with him, and he with me" (Rv 3:20). Here we see a home filled with the presence of God, common prayer and every blessing. This is the meaning of the conclusion of Psalm 128, which we cited above: "Thus shall the man be blessed who fears the Lord. The Lord bless you from Zion!" (Ps 128:4–5).

—Francis, *Amoris laetitia*, 15

The family's communal journey of prayer culminates by sharing together in the Eucharist, especially in the context of the Sunday rest. Jesus knocks on the door of families, to share with them the Eucharistic supper (cf. Rv 3:20). There, spouses can always seal anew the paschal covenant which united them and which ought to reflect the covenant which God sealed with mankind in the cross. The Eucharist is the sacrament of the new covenant, where Christ's redemptive work is carried out (cf. Lk 22:20). The close bond between married life and the Eucharist thus becomes all the more clear. For the food of the Eucharist offers the spouses the strength and incentive needed to live the marriage covenant each day as a "domestic church."

—Francis, *Amoris laetitia*, 318

The family finds in the plan of God the Creator and Redeemer not only its identity, what it is, but also its mission, what it can and should do. The role that God calls the family to perform in history derives from what the family is; its role represents the dynamic and existential development of what it is. Each family finds within itself a summons that cannot be ignored, and that specifies both its dignity and its responsibility: family, become what you are.

—John Paul II, *Familiaris consortio*, 17

In order to understand better the foundations, the contents and the characteristics of this participation, we must examine the many profound bonds linking the Church and the Christian family and establishing the family as a "Church in miniature" (*Ecclesia domestica*), in such a way that in its own way the family is a living image and historical representation of the mystery of the Church....

It is, above all, the Church as Mother that gives birth to, educates and builds up the Christian family, by putting into effect in its regard the saving mission which she has received from her Lord. By proclaiming the word of God, the Church reveals to the Christian family its true identity, what it is and should be according to the Lord's plan; by celebrating the sacraments, the Church enriches and strengthens the Christian family with the grace of Christ for its sanctification to the glory of the Father; by the continuous proclamation of the new commandment of love, the Church encourages and guides the Christian family to the service of love, so that it may imitate and relive the same self-giving and sacrificial love that the Lord Jesus has for the entire human race.

In turn, the Christian family is grafted into the mystery of the Church to such a degree as to become a sharer, in its own way, in the saving mission proper to the Church: by virtue of the sacrament, Christian married couples and parents "in their state and way of life have their own special gift among the People of God." For this reason, they not only receive the love of Christ and become a saved community, but they are also called upon to communicate Christ's love to their brethren, thus becoming a saving community. In this way, while the Christian family is a fruit and sign of the supernatural fecundity of the Church, it stands also as a symbol, witness and participant of the Church's motherhood.

> —John Paul II, *Familiaris consortio*, 49 (citing the Vatican Council, *Lumen gentium*, 11)

———— 101 ————

Should we pray together as a family? How?
What if my kids are crazy, wild toddlers, disaffected teens,
or away at sports and activities all the time?

Family prayer is a special way of expressing and strengthening this paschal faith. A few minutes can be found each day to come together before the living God, to tell him our worries, to ask for the needs of our family, to pray for someone experiencing difficulty, to ask for help in showing love, to give thanks for life and for its blessings, and to ask Our Lady to protect us beneath her maternal mantle. With a few simple words, this moment of prayer can do immense good for our families. The various expressions of popular piety are a treasure of spirituality for many families.

—Francis, *Amoris laetitia*, 318

In the light of God's word, I would like to ask you, dear families: Do you pray together from time to time as a family? Some of you do, I know. But so many people say to me: But how can we? As the tax collector does, it is clear: humbly, before God. Each one, with humility, allowing themselves to be gazed upon by the Lord and imploring his goodness, that he may visit us. But in the family how is this done? After all, prayer seems to be something personal, and besides there is never a good time, a moment of peace.... Yes, all that is true enough, but it is also a matter of humility, of realizing that we need God, like the tax collector! And all families, we need God: all of us! We need his help, his strength, his blessing, his mercy, his forgiveness. And we need simplicity to pray as a family: simplicity is necessary! Praying the Our Father together, around the table, is not something extraordinary: it's easy. And praying the Rosary together, as a family, is very beautiful and a source of great strength! And also praying for one another! The husband for his wife, the wife for her husband, both together for their children, the children for their grandparents ... praying for each other. This is what it means to pray in the family and it is what makes the family strong: prayer.

—Francis, Homily for Holy Mass for the Family Day on the
Occasion of the Year of Faith, October 27, 2013

To hear and accept God's call, to make a home for Jesus, you must be able to rest in the Lord. You must make time each day to rest in the Lord, to pray. To pray is to rest in the Lord. But you may say to me: Holy Father, I know that; I want to pray, but there is so much work to do! I must care for my children; I have chores in the home; I am too tired even to sleep well. I know. This may be true, but if we do not pray, we will not know the most important thing of all: God's will for us. And for all our activity, our busy-ness, without prayer we will accomplish very little.

Resting in prayer is especially important for families. It is in the family that we first learn how to pray. Don't forget: the family that prays together stays together! This is important. There we come to know God, to grow into men and women of faith, to see ourselves as members of God's greater family, the Church. In the family we learn how to love, to forgive, to be generous and open, not closed and selfish. We learn to move beyond our own needs, to encounter others and share our lives with them. That is why it is so important to pray as a family! So important! That is why families are so important in God's plan for the Church! To rest in the Lord is to pray. To pray together as a family.

—Francis, Address to the Meeting of Families in Manila,
January 16, 2015

Family prayer has its own characteristic qualities. It is prayer offered in common, husband and wife together, parents and children together. Communion in prayer is both a consequence of and a requirement for the communion bestowed by the sacraments of Baptism and Matrimony. The words with which the Lord Jesus promises His presence can be applied to the members of the Christian family in a special way: "Again I say to you, if two of you agree on earth about anything they ask, it will be done for them by my Father in heaven. For where two or three are gathered in my name, there am I in the midst of them."

Family prayer has for its very own object family life itself, which in all its varying circumstances is seen as a call from God and lived as a filial response to His call. Joys and sorrows, hopes and disappointments, births and birthday celebrations, wedding anniversaries of the parents, departures, separations and homecomings, important and far-reaching decisions, the death of those who are dear, etc.—all of these mark God's loving intervention in the family's history. They should be seen as suitable moments for thanksgiving, for petition, for trusting abandonment of the family into the hands of their common Father in heaven. The dignity and responsibility of the Christian family as the domestic Church can be achieved only with God's unceasing aid, which will surely be granted if it is humbly and trustingly petitioned in prayer. By reason of their dignity and mission, Christian parents have the specific responsibility of educating their children in prayer, introducing them to gradual discovery of the mystery of God and to personal dialogue with Him: "It is particularly in the Christian family, enriched by the grace and the office of the sacrament of Matrimony, that from the earliest years children should be taught, according to the faith received in Baptism, to have a knowledge of God, to worship Him and to love their neighbor."

The concrete example and living witness of parents is fundamental and irreplaceable in educating their children to pray. Only by praying together with their children can a father and mother—exercising their royal priesthood—penetrate the innermost depths of their children's hearts and leave an impression that the future events in their lives will not be able to efface. Let us again listen to the appeal made by Paul VI to parents: "Mothers, do you teach your children the Christian prayers? Do you prepare them, in conjunction with the priests, for the sacraments that they receive when they are young: Confession, Communion and Confirmation? Do you encourage them when they are sick to think of Christ suffering to invoke the aid of the Blessed Virgin and the saints? Do you say the family rosary together? And you, fathers, do you pray with your children, with the whole domestic community, at least sometimes? Your example of honesty in thought and action, joined to some common prayer, is a lesson for life, an act of worship of singular value. In this way you bring peace to your homes: *Pax huic domui*. Remember, it is thus that you build up the Church."

—John Paul II, *Familiaris consortio*, 59–60 (citing Mt 19:18–20; the Second Vatican Council, *Gravisimum educationis*, 3; and Paul VI, General Audience, August 11, 1976)

——— 102 ———

Does the church officially recommend praying the rosary as a family? Why?

The rosary is a contemplative and Christocentric prayer, inseparable from the meditation of sacred Scripture. It is the prayer of the Christian who advances in the pilgrimage of faith, in the following of Jesus, preceded by Mary. I would like to invite you, dear brothers and sisters, to pray the rosary as a family during this month, and in communities and parishes, for the intentions of the Pope, for the mission of the Church and for peace in the world.

—Benedict XVI, Angelus Message, October 1, 2006

As a prayer for peace, the Rosary is also, and always has been, a prayer of and for the family. At one time this prayer was particularly dear to Christian families, and it certainly brought them closer together. It is important not to lose this precious inheritance. We need to return to the practice of family prayer and prayer for families, continuing to use the Rosary.

In my Apostolic Letter *Novo Millennio Ineunte* I encouraged the celebration of the *Liturgy of the Hours* by the lay faithful in the ordinary life of parish communities and Christian groups; I now wish to do the same for the Rosary. These two paths of Christian contemplation are not mutually exclusive; they complement one another. I would therefore ask those who devote themselves to the pastoral care of families to recommend heartily the recitation of the Rosary.

The family that prays together stays together. The Holy Rosary, by age-old tradition, has shown itself particularly effective as a prayer which brings the family together. Individual family members, in turning their eyes towards Jesus, also regain the ability to look one another in the eye, to communicate, to show solidarity, to forgive one another and to see their covenant of love renewed in the Spirit of God.

Many of the problems facing contemporary families, especially in economically developed societies, result from their increasing difficulty in communicating. Families seldom manage to come together, and the rare occasions when they do are often taken up with watching television. To return to the recitation of the family Rosary means filling daily life with very different images, images of the mystery of salvation: the image of the Redeemer, the image of his most Blessed Mother. The family that recites the Rosary together reproduces something of the atmosphere of the household of Nazareth: its members place Jesus at the center, they share his joys and sorrows, they place their needs and their plans in his hands, they draw from him the hope and the strength to go on.

—John Paul II, *Rosarium virginis mariae*, 41

Among these should be mentioned the recitation of the rosary: "We now desire, as a continuation of the thought of our predecessors, to recommend strongly the recitation of the family rosary.... There is no doubt that ... the rosary should be considered as one of the best and most efficacious prayers in common that the Christian family is invited to recite. We like to think, and sincerely hope, that when the family gathering becomes a time of prayer the rosary is a frequent and favored manner of praying." In this way authentic devotion to Mary, which finds expression in sincere love and generous imitation of the Blessed Virgin's interior spiritual attitude, constitutes a special instrument for nourishing loving communion in the family and for developing conjugal and family spirituality. For she who is the Mother of Christ and of the Church is in a special way the Mother of Christian families, of domestic Churches.

—John Paul II, *Familiaris consortio*, 61 (citing Paul VI, *Marialis cultus* 52, 54)

The recourse we have to Mary in prayer follows upon the office she continuously fills by the side of the throne of God as Mediatrix of Divine grace; being by worthiness and by merit most acceptable to Him, and, therefore, surpassing in power all the angels and saints in Heaven. Now, this merciful office of hers, perhaps, appears in no other form of prayer so manifestly as it does in the Rosary. For in the Rosary all the part that Mary took as our co-Redemptress comes to us, as it were, set forth, and in such wise as though the facts were even then taking place; and this with much profit to our piety, whether in the contemplation of the succeeding sacred mysteries, or in the prayers which we speak and repeat with the lips.

—Leo XIII, *Iucunda semper expectatione*, 2

—— 103 ——

My friend talks about "celebrating the liturgical year" at home with her family. She talks about doing special things on saints' feast days, observing fasting days, and following the liturgical seasons. I'm confused. Isn't that the parish's job?

It is in the Church, in communion with all the baptized, that the Christian fulfills his vocation. From the Church he receives the Word of God containing the teachings of "the law of Christ." From the Church he receives the grace of the sacraments that sustains him on the "way." From the Church he learns the example of holiness and recognizes its model and source in the all-holy Virgin Mary; he discerns it in the authentic witness of those who live it; he discovers it in the spiritual tradition and long history of the saints who have gone before him and whom the liturgy celebrates in the rhythms of the sanctoral cycle.

—*Catechism of the Catholic Church*, 2030

The first precept ("You shall attend Mass on Sundays and holy days of obligation and rest from servile labor") requires the faithful to sanctify the day commemorating the Resurrection of the Lord as well as the principal liturgical feasts honoring the mysteries of the Lord, the Blessed Virgin Mary, and the saints; in the first place, by participating in the Eucharistic celebration, in which the Christian community is gathered, and by resting from those works and activities which could impede such a sanctification of these days.

—*Catechism of the Catholic Church*, 2042

The divine law binds all the Christian faithful to do penance each in his or her own way. In order for all to be united among themselves by some common observance of penance, however, penitential days are prescribed on which the Christian faithful devote themselves in a spe-

cial way to prayer, perform works of piety and charity, and deny themselves by fulfilling their own obligations more faithfully and especially
by observing fast and abstinence, according to the norm of the following canons.

The penitential days and times in the universal Church are every
Friday of the whole year and the season of Lent.

Abstinence from eating meat or some other food according to the
prescripts of the conference of bishops is to be observed on all Fridays,
unless a solemnity should fall on a Friday. Abstinence and fasting are
to be observed on Ash Wednesday and Good Friday. The law of abstinence binds those who have completed their fourteenth year of age.
The law of fasting, however, binds all those who have attained their majority until the beginning of their sixtieth year. Nevertheless, pastors
of souls and parents are to take care that minors not bound by the law
of fast and abstinence are also educated in a genuine sense of penance.

The conference of bishops can determine more precisely the observance of fast and abstinence as well as substitute other forms of penance, especially works of charity and exercises of piety, in whole or in
part, for abstinence and fast.

—*Code of Canon Law*, cc. 1249–53

There exists a deep and vital bond between the prayer of the Church
and the prayer of the individual faithful, as has been clearly reaffirmed
by the Second Vatican Council. An important purpose of the prayer
of the domestic Church is to serve as the natural introduction for the
children to the liturgical prayer of the whole Church, both in the sense
of preparing for it and of extending it into personal, family and social
life. Hence the need for gradual participation by all the members of
the Christian family in the celebration of the Eucharist, especially on
Sundays and feast days, and of the other sacraments, particularly the
sacraments of Christian initiation of the children. The directives of the
Council opened up a new possibility for the Christian family when it

listed the family among those groups to whom it recommends the recitation of the Divine Office in common. Likewise, the Christian family will strive to celebrate at home, and in a way suited to the members, the times and feasts of the liturgical year.

—John Paul II, *Familiaris consortio*, 61

——— 104 ———
What does it mean for a family to evangelize?

In virtue of their baptism, all the members of the People of God have become missionary disciples (cf. Mt 28:19). All the baptized, whatever their position in the Church or their level of instruction in the faith, are agents of evangelization, and it would be insufficient to envisage a plan of evangelization to be carried out by professionals while the rest of the faithful would simply be passive recipients. The new evangelization calls for personal involvement on the part of each of the baptized. Every Christian is challenged, here and now, to be actively engaged in evangelization; indeed, anyone who has truly experienced God's saving love does not need much time or lengthy training to go out and proclaim that love. Every Christian is a missionary to the extent that he or she has encountered the love of God in Christ Jesus: we no longer say that we are "disciples" and "missionaries," but rather that we are always "missionary disciples."

—Francis, *Evangelii gaudium*, 120

The ministry of evangelization carried out by Christian parents is original and irreplaceable. It assumes the characteristics typical of family life itself, which should be interwoven with love, simplicity, practicality and daily witness.

The family must educate the children for life in such a way that each one may fully perform his or her role according to the vocation received from God. Indeed, the family that is open to transcendent values, that serves its brothers and sisters with joy, that fulfills its duties with generous fidelity, and is aware of its daily sharing in the mystery of the glorious Cross of Christ, becomes the primary and most excellent seed-bed of vocations to a life of consecration to the Kingdom of God.

The parents' ministry of evangelization and catechesis ought to play a part in their children's lives also during adolescence and youth, when the children, as often happens, challenge or even reject the Christian faith received in earlier years. Just as in the Church the work of evangelization can never be separated from the sufferings of the apostle, so in the Christian family parents must face with courage and great interior serenity the difficulties that their ministry of evangelization sometimes encounters in their own children.

It should not be forgotten that the service rendered by Christian spouses and parents to the Gospel is essentially an ecclesial service. It has its place within the context of the whole Church as an evangelized and evangelizing community. In so far as the ministry of evangelization and catechesis of the Church of the home is rooted in and derives from the one mission of the Church and is ordained to the upbuilding of the one Body of Christ, it must remain in intimate communion and collaborate responsibly with all the other evangelizing and catechetical activities present and at work in the ecclesial community at the diocesan and parochial levels.

> —John Paul II, *Familiaris consortio*, 52–53 (citing the
> Second Vatican Council, *Lumen gentium*, 35, and
> *Catechesi tradendae*, 68)

One cannot fail to stress the evangelizing action of the family in the evangelizing apostolate of the laity.

At different moments in the Church's history and also in the Second Vatican Council, the family has well deserved the beautiful name of "domestic Church." This means that there should be found in every Christian family the various aspects of the entire Church. Furthermore, the family, like the Church, ought to be a place where the Gospel is transmitted and from which the Gospel radiates.

In a family which is conscious of this mission, all the members evangelize and are evangelized. The parents not only communicate the Gospel to their children, but from their children they can themselves receive the same Gospel as deeply lived by them.

And such a family becomes the evangelizer of many other families, and of the neighborhood of which it forms part. Families resulting from a mixed marriage also have the duty of proclaiming Christ to the children in the fullness of the consequences of a common Baptism; they have moreover the difficult task of becoming builders of unity.

—Paul VI, *Evangelii nuntiandi,* 71

——— 105 ———

How can our family minister to other families?

I encourage the faithful who find themselves in complicated situations to speak confidently with their pastors or with other lay people whose lives are committed to the Lord. They may not always encounter in them a confirmation of their own ideas or desires, but they will surely receive some light to help them better understand their situation and discover a path to personal growth. I also encourage the Church's pastors to listen to them with sensitivity and serenity, with a sincere desire to understand their plight and their point of view, in order to help them live better lives and to recognize their proper place in the Church.

—Francis, *Amoris laetitia,* 312

Families will share their spiritual riches generously with other families too. Thus, the Christian family, which springs from marriage as a reflection of the loving covenant uniting Christ with the Church, and as a participation in that covenant will manifest to all people the Savior's living presence in the world, and the genuine nature of the Church. This the family will do by the mutual love of the spouses, by their generous fruitfulness, their solidarity and faithfulness, and by the loving way in which all the members of the family work together.

—Second Vatican Council, *Gaudium et spes*, 48

CHAPTER 8

The Good News about the Family

As an intimate communion of life and love, the family has a social and missionary role in the church and in society. Families are called to missionary discipleship, showing the face of the Father's mercy to the world through love and service. This sounds good, but what concrete guidance has the church offered?

What is the "Gospel of the Family"?
What is the role of marriage and family
in salvation history?

The Bible is full of families, births, love stories and family crises. This is true from its very first page, with the appearance of Adam and Eve's family with all its burden of violence but also its enduring strength (cf. Gn 4) to its very last page, where we behold the wedding feast of the Bride and the Lamb (Rv 21:2, 21:9). Jesus' description of the two houses, one built on rock and the other on sand (cf. Mt 7:24–27), symbolizes any number of family situations shaped by the exercise of their members' freedom, for, as the poet says, "every home is a lampstand."

> —Francis, *Amoris laetitia*, 8 (citing Jorge Luis Borges, "Calle Desconcida")

On the one hand, it is a particular reflection of that full unity in distinction found in the Trinity. The family is also a sign of Christ. It manifests the closeness of God who is a part of every human life, since he became one with us through his incarnation, death and resurrection. Each spouse becomes "one flesh" with the other as a sign of willingness to share everything with him or her until death. Whereas virginity is an "eschatological" sign of the risen Christ, marriage is a "historical" sign for us living in this world, a sign of the earthly Christ who chose to become one with us and gave himself up for us even to shedding his blood.

> —Francis, *Amoris laetitia*, 161

The Synod Fathers emphasized that Christian families, by the grace of the sacrament of matrimony, are the principal agents of the family apostolate, above all through "their joy-filled witness as domestic churches." Consequently, "it is important that people experience the Gospel of the family as a joy that 'fills hearts and lives,' because in Christ we have been 'set free from sin, sorrow, inner emptiness and loneliness.'"

> —Francis, *Amoris laetitia*, 200 (citing the *Relatio synodi* of the 2014 Synod on the Family, 30; and *Evangelii gaudium*, 1)

From the standpoint of creation, *eros* directs man towards marriage, to a bond which is unique and definitive; thus, and only thus, does it fulfill its deepest purpose. Corresponding to the image of a monotheistic God is monogamous marriage. Marriage based on exclusive and definitive love becomes the icon of the relationship between God and his people and vice versa. God's way of loving becomes the measure of human love. This close connection between *eros* and marriage in the Bible has practically no equivalent in extra-biblical literature.

> —Benedict XVI, *Deus caritas est*, 11

Among these many paths, the family is the first and the most important. It is a path common to all, yet one which is particular, unique and unrepeatable, just as every individual is unrepeatable; it is a path from which man cannot withdraw. Indeed, a person normally comes into the world within a family, and can be said to owe to the family the very fact of his existing as an individual. When he has no family, the person coming into the world develops an anguished sense of pain and loss, one which will subsequently burden his whole life. The Church draws near with loving concern to all who experience situations such as these, for she knows well the fundamental role which the family is called upon to play. Furthermore, she knows that a person goes forth from the family in order to realize in a new family unit his particular vocation in life. Even if someone chooses to remain single, the family continues to be, as it were, his existential horizon, that fundamental community in which the whole network of social relations is grounded, from the closest and most immediate to the most distant. Do we not often speak of the "human family" when referring to all the people living in the world?

The family has its origin in that same love with which the Creator embraces the created world, as was already expressed "in the beginning," in the Book of Genesis (1:1). In the Gospel Jesus offers a supreme confirmation: "God so loved the world that he gave his only Son" (Jn 3:16). The only-begotten Son, of one substance with the Father, "God from God and Light from Light," entered into human history through the family: "For by his incarnation the Son of God united himself in a certain way with every man. He labored with human hands … and loved with a human heart. Born of Mary the Virgin, he truly became one of us and, except for sin, was like us in every respect." If in fact Christ "fully discloses man to himself," he does so beginning with the family in which he chose to be born and to grow up. We know that the Redeemer spent most of his life in the obscurity of Nazareth, "obedient" (Lk 2:51) as the "Son of Man" to Mary his Mother, and to Joseph the carpenter. Is this filial "obedience" of Christ not already the first expression of that obedience to the Father "unto death" (Phil 2:8), whereby he redeemed the world?

The divine mystery of the Incarnation of the Word thus has an intimate connection with the human family. Not only with one family, that of Nazareth, but in some way with every family, analogously to what the Second Vatican Council says about the Son of God, who in the Incarnation "united himself in some sense with every man." Following Christ who "came" into the world "to serve" (Mt 20:28), the Church considers serving the family to be one of her essential duties. In this sense both man and the family constitute "the way of the Church."

—John Paul II, Letter to Families *Gratissimam sane*, 2

―――― 107 ――――

How is marriage and family "good news" for the person and for the church?

The Joy of Love experienced by families is also the joy of the Church. As the Synod Fathers noted, for all the many signs of crisis in the institution of marriage, "the desire to marry and form a family remains vibrant, especially among young people, and this is an inspiration to the Church." As a response to that desire, "the Christian proclamation on the family is good news indeed."

> —Francis, *Amoris laetitia*, 1 (citing the *Relatio synodi* of the 2014 Synod on the Family, 2)

The Church is a family of families, constantly enriched by the lives of all those domestic churches. "In virtue of the sacrament of matrimony, every family becomes, in effect, a good for the Church. From this standpoint, reflecting on the interplay between the family and the Church will prove a precious gift for the Church in our time. The Church is good for the family, and the family is good for the Church. The safeguarding of the Lord's gift in the sacrament of matrimony is a concern not only of individual families but of the entire Christian community." ... The experience of love in families is a perennial source of strength for the life of the Church.

> —Francis, *Amoris laetitia*, 87–88 (citing the Final Report of the 2015 Synod on the Family, 52)

The Christian family is called upon to take part actively and responsibly in the mission of the Church in a way that is original and specific, by placing itself, in what it is and what it does as an "intimate community of life and love," at the service of the Church and of society. Since the Christian family is a community in which the relationships are renewed by Christ through faith and the sacraments, the family's sharing in the

Church's mission should follow a community pattern: the spouses together as a couple, the parents and children as a family, must live their service to the Church and to the world. They must be "of one heart and soul" in faith, through the shared apostolic zeal that animates them, and through their shared commitment to works of service to the ecclesial and civil communities.

The Christian family also builds up the Kingdom of God in history through the everyday realities that concern and distinguish its state of life. It is thus in the love between husband and wife and between the members of the family—a love lived out in all its extraordinary richness of values and demands: totality, oneness, fidelity and fruitfulness that the Christian family's participation in the prophetic, priestly and kingly mission of Jesus Christ and of His Church finds expression and realization. Therefore, love and life constitute the nucleus of the saving mission of the Christian family in the Church and for the Church.

—John Paul II, *Familiaris consortio*, 50

Nor do lesser benefits accrue to human society as a whole. For experience has taught that unassailable stability in matrimony is a fruitful source of virtuous life and of habits of integrity. Where this order of things obtains, the happiness and well-being of the nation is safely guarded; what the families and individuals are, so also is the State, for a body is determined by its parts. Wherefore, both for the private good of husband, wife and children, as likewise for the public good of human society, they indeed deserve well who strenuously defend the inviolable stability of matrimony.

—Pius XI, *Casti connubii*, 38

―――― 108 ――――

What does marriage contribute
to society?

Ecological education can take place in a variety of settings: at school, in families, in the media, in catechesis and elsewhere. Good education plants seeds when we are young, and these continue to bear fruit throughout life. Here, though, I would stress the great importance of the family, which is "the place in which life—the gift of God—can be properly welcomed and protected against the many attacks to which it is exposed, and can develop in accordance with what constitutes authentic human growth. In the face of the so-called culture of death, the family is the heart of the culture of life." In the family we first learn how to show love and respect for life; we are taught the proper use of things, order and cleanliness, respect for the local ecosystem and care for all creatures. In the family we receive an integral education, which enables us to grow harmoniously in personal maturity. In the family we learn to ask without demanding, to say "thank you" as an expression of genuine gratitude for what we have been given, to control our aggressivity and greed, and to ask forgiveness when we have caused harm. These simple gestures of heartfelt courtesy help to create a culture of shared life and respect for our surroundings.

—Francis, *Laudato Si'*, 213 (citing John Paul II, *Centesimus annus*, 39)

The social role of the family certainly cannot stop short at procreation and education, even if this constitutes its primary and irreplaceable form of expression.

Families therefore, either singly or in association, can and should devote themselves to manifold social service activities, especially in favor of the poor, or at any rate for the benefit of all people and situations that cannot be reached by the public authorities' welfare organization.

The social contribution of the family has an original character of its own, one that should be given greater recognition and more decisive encouragement, especially as the children grow up, and actually involving all its members as much as possible.

In particular, note must be taken of the ever greater importance in our society of hospitality in all its forms, from opening the door of one's home and still more of one's heart to the pleas of one's brothers and sisters, to concrete efforts to ensure that every family has its own home, as the natural environment that preserves it and makes it grow. In a special way, the Christian family is called upon to listen to the Apostle's recommendation: "Practice hospitality," and therefore, imitating Christ's example and sharing in His love, to welcome the brother or sister in need: "Whoever gives to one of these little ones even a cup of cold water because he is a disciple, truly, I say to you, he shall not lose his reward."

The social role of families is called upon to find expression also in the form of political intervention: families should be the first to take steps to see that the laws and institutions of the State not only do not offend but support and positively defend the rights and duties of the family. Along these lines, families should grow in awareness of being "protagonists" of what is known as "family politics" and assume responsibility for transforming society; otherwise families will be the first victims of the evils that they have done no more than note with indifference. The Second Vatican Council's appeal to go beyond an individualistic ethic therefore also holds good for the family as such.

—John Paul II, *Familiaris consortio*, 44 (citing Rom 12:13; Mt. 10:42)

The well-being of the individual person and of human and Christian society is intimately linked with the healthy condition of that community produced by marriage and family. Hence Christians and all men who hold this community in high esteem sincerely rejoice in the vari-

ous ways by which men today find help in fostering this community of
love and perfecting its life, and by which parents are assisted in their
lofty calling. Those who rejoice in such aids look for additional benefits
from them and labor to bring them about.

—Second Vatican Council, *Gaudium et spes*, 47

——— 109 ———
What does it mean that my family has a "mission"?

The Synod Fathers emphasized that Christian families, by the grace
of the sacrament of matrimony, are the principal agents of the family apostolate, above all through "their joy-filled witness as domestic
churches." … The Church wishes, with humility and compassion, to
reach out to families and "to help each family to discover the best way
to overcome any obstacles it encounters." It is not enough to show generic concern for the family in pastoral planning. Enabling families to
take up their role as active agents of the family apostolate calls for "an
effort at evangelization and catechesis inside the family."

—Francis, *Amoris laetitia*, 200 (citing the *Relatio synodi* of the 2014
Synod on the Family, 30)

The work of handing on the faith to children, in the sense of facilitat-
ing its expression and growth, helps the whole family in its evangelizing mission. It naturally begins to spread the faith to all around them,
even outside of the family circle. Children who grew up in missionary
families often become missionaries themselves; growing up in warm
and friendly families, they learn to relate to the world in this way,
without giving up their faith or their convictions. We know that Jesus
himself ate and drank with sinners (cf. Mk 2:16; Mt 11:19), conversed
with a Samaritan woman (cf. Jn 4:7–26), received Nicodemus by night
(cf. Jn 3:1–21), allowed his feet to be anointed by a prostitute (cf. Lk

7:36–50) and did not hesitate to lay his hands on those who were sick (cf. Mk 1:40–45; 7:33). The same was true of his apostles, who did not look down on others, or cluster together in small and elite groups, cut off from the life of their people. Although the authorities harassed them, they nonetheless enjoyed the favor "of all the people" (Acts 2:47; cf. 4:21, 4:33; 5:13).

"The family is thus an agent of pastoral activity through its explicit proclamation of the Gospel and its legacy of varied forms of witness, namely solidarity with the poor, openness to a diversity of people, the protection of creation, moral and material solidarity with other families, including those most in need, commitment to the promotion of the common good and the transformation of unjust social structures, beginning in the territory in which the family lives, through the practice of the corporal and spiritual works of mercy." All this is an expression of our profound Christian belief in the love of the Father who guides and sustains us, a love manifested in the total self-gift of Jesus Christ, who even now lives in our midst and enables us to face together the storms of life at every stage. In all families the Good News needs to resound, in good times and in bad, as a source of light along the way. All of us should be able to say, thanks to the experience of our life in the family: "We come to believe in the love that God has for us" (1 Jn 4:16). Only on the basis of this experience will the Church's pastoral care for families enable them to be both domestic churches and a leaven of evangelization in society.

—Francis, *Amoris laetitia*, 289–90 (citing the Final Report of the 2015 Synod on the Family, 93)

For Christian parents the mission to educate, a mission rooted, as we have said, in their participation in God's creating activity, has a new specific source in the sacrament of marriage, which consecrates them for the strictly Christian education of their children: that is to say, it calls upon them to share in the very authority and love of God the Father and Christ the Shepherd, and in the motherly love of the Church, and it enriches them with wisdom, counsel, fortitude and all the other gifts of the Holy Spirit in order to help the children in their growth as human beings and as Christians.

The sacrament of marriage gives to the educational role the dignity and vocation of being really and truly a "ministry" of the Church at the service of the building up of her members. So great and splendid is the educational ministry of Christian parents that Saint Thomas has no hesitation in comparing it with the ministry of priests: "Some only propagate and guard spiritual life by a spiritual ministry: this is the role of the sacrament of Orders; others do this for both corporal and spiritual life, and this is brought about by the sacrament of marriage, by which a man and a woman join in order to beget offspring and bring them up to worship God."

A vivid and attentive awareness of the mission that they have received with the sacrament of marriage will help Christian parents to place themselves at the service of their children's education with great serenity and trustfulness, and also with a sense of responsibility before God, who calls them and gives them the mission of building up the Church in their children. Thus in the case of baptized people, the family, called together by word and sacrament as the Church of the home, is both teacher and mother, the same as the worldwide Church.

—John Paul II, *Familiaris consortio*, 38

This mission—to be the first and vital cell of society—the family has received from God. It will fulfill this mission if it appears as the domestic sanctuary of the Church by reason of the mutual affection of its members and the prayer that they offer to God in common, if the whole family makes itself a part of the liturgical worship of the Church, and if it provides active hospitality and promotes justice and other good works for the service of all the brethren in need. Among the various activities of the family apostolate may be enumerated the follow-

ing: the adoption of abandoned infants, hospitality to strangers, assistance in the operation of schools, helpful advice and material assistance
for adolescents, help to engaged couples in preparing themselves better
for marriage, catechetical work, support of married couples and families involved in material and moral crises, help for the aged not only
by providing them with the necessities of life but also by obtaining for
them a fair share of the benefits of an expanding economy.

At all times and places but particularly in areas where the first seeds
of the Gospel are being sown, or where the Church is just beginning, or
is involved in some serious difficulty, Christian families can give effective testimony to Christ before the world by remaining faithful to the
Gospel and by providing a model of Christian marriage through their
whole way of life.

—Second Vatican Council, *Apostolicam actuositatem*, 11

———— 110 ————

How do marriage and family reveal the Father's mercy?

The couple that loves and begets life is a true, living icon—not an idol
like those of stone or gold prohibited by the Decalogue—capable of
revealing God the Creator and Savior. For this reason, fruitful love becomes a symbol of God's inner life (cf. Gn 1:28; 9:7; 17:2–5, 17:16; 28:3;
35:11; 48:3–4). This is why the Genesis account, following the "priestly
tradition," is interwoven with various genealogical accounts (cf. 4:17–
22, 4:25–26; 5; 10; 11:10–32; 25:1–4, 25:12–17, 25:19–26; 36). The ability
of human couples to beget life is the path along which the history of
salvation progresses. Seen this way, the couple's fruitful relationship becomes an image for understanding and describing the mystery of God
himself, for in the Christian vision of the Trinity, God is contemplated
as Father, Son and Spirit of love. The triune God is a communion of

love, and the family is its living reflection. Saint John Paul II shed light on this when he said, "Our God in his deepest mystery is not solitude, but a family, for he has within himself fatherhood, sonship and the essence of the family, which is love. That love, in the divine family, is the Holy Spirit." The family is thus not unrelated to God's very being.

—Francis, *Amoris laetitia*, 11

And since in God's plan it has been established as an "intimate community of life and love," the family has the mission to become more and more what it is, that is to say, a community of life and love, in an effort that will find fulfillment, as will everything created and redeemed, in the Kingdom of God. Looking at it in such a way as to reach its very roots, we must say that the essence and role of the family are in the final analysis specified by love. Hence the family has the mission to guard, reveal and communicate love, and this is a living reflection of and a real sharing in God's love for humanity and the love of Christ the Lord for the Church His bride.

—John Paul II, *Familiaris consortio*, 17

Resources for Further Reading

While the excerpts from scripture and magisterial documents address the questions in this volume (some directly, some by providing general principles relevant to the issue), they are only excerpts. This section provides a fuller listing of some major documents that articulate the modern magisterium's teaching on marriage and family. Reading these documents will provide a more complete picture of this teaching in its original context. Also included here are additional sources that support this teaching and offer fuller explanations of its meaning than can be conveyed in a format such as this one. This list is not exhaustive—in regard to either documents cited in this volume or secondary sources. The ecclesial documents listed here are those that offer extensive treatments of the issues contained in this volume or because of their import. Secondary sources here listed are chosen for their clarity, substance, or fuller articulation of the church's vision or ideas largely compatible with it.

CHURCH DOCUMENTS (AVAILABLE ON THE VATICAN OR USCCB WEBSITES)

Benedict XVI. Encyclical Letter. *Deus caritas est*. December 25, 2005.
Catechism of the Catholic Church. 2nd ed. August 15, 1997. Esp. 1601–66, 2231–2400.

Congregation for the Doctrine of the Faith. *Persona humana (Declaration on Sexual Ethics)*. December 29, 1975.

———. *Letter to the Bishops of the Catholic Church on the Pastoral Care of Homosexual Persons*. October 1, 1986.

———. *Some Considerations Concerning the Response to Legislative Proposals on the Non-Discrimination of Homosexual Persons*. July 24, 1992.

———. *Considerations Regarding Proposals to Give Legal Recognition to Unions between Homosexual Persons*. July 31, 1993.

Francis. Apostolic Exhortation. *Amoris Laetitia*. April 8, 2016.

John Paul II. Apostolic Exhortation. *Familiaris consortio*. November 22, 1981.

———. Apostolic Letter. *Mulieris dignitatem*. August 15, 1988.

———. Letter to Families. *Gratissimam sane*. February 2, 1994.

———. *Man and Woman He Created Them: A Theology of the Body*. Translation and introduction by Michael Waldstein. Boston: Pauline Books and Media: 2006.

The Order of Celebrating Matrimony. English Translation according to the Second Typical Edition. U.S. Conference of Catholic Bishops. December 30, 2016.

Paul VI. Encyclical Letter. *Humanae vitae*. July 25, 1968.

Pius XI. Encyclical Letter. *Casti connubii*. December 31, 1930.

Pontifical Council for the Family. *The Truth and Meaning of Human Sexuality*. December 8, 1995.

Pontifical Council for Justice and Peace. *Compendium of the Social of the Church*. June 29, 2004.

U.S. Conference of Catholic Bishops. *Marriage: Love and Life in the Divine Plan*. November 17, 2009.

Vatican Council II. *Gaudium et Spes*. December 7, esp. 48–52.

LIGHTS AND SHADOWS

Bransfield, J. Brian. *The Human Person According to John Paul II*. Boston: Pauline Books and Media, 2009.

Chesterton, G. K. *Brave New Family*. Edited by Alvaro de Silva. San Francisco: Ignatius Press, 1990.

Eberstadt, Mary. *Adam and Eve after the Pill: Paradoxes of the Sexual Revolution*. San Francisco: Ignatius Press, 2012.

Freitas, Donna. *Sex and the Soul: Juggling Sexuality, Spirituality, Romance, and Religion on America's College Campuses*. New York: Oxford University, 2008.

———. *The End of Sex: How Hookup Culture Is Leaving a Generation Unhappy, Sexually Unfulfilled, and Confused about Intimacy*. New York: Basic Books, 2012.

Gardella, Peter. *Innocent Ecstasy: How Christianity Gave America an Ethic of Sexual Pleasure*. New York: Oxford, 1986.

DATING AND RELATIONSHIPS

Buono, Anthony. *Would You Date You?* Ann Arbor: Servant, 2012.

Evert, Jason, and Crystalina Evert. *How to Find Your Soulmate without Losing Your Soul*. Lakewood, Colo.: Totus Tuus Press, 2011.

King, Jason. "A Theology of Dating for a Culture of Abuse." In *Leaving and Coming Home: New Wineskins for Catholic Sexual Ethics*, edited by David Cloutier, 29–46. Eugene, Ore.: Wipf and Stock, 2010.

———. *Faith with Benefits: Hookup Culture on Catholic Campuses*. New York: Oxford University, 2017.

Morrow, Thomas. *Christian Courtship in an Oversexed World: A Guide for Catholics*. Huntington, Ind.: Our Sunday Visitor, 2003.

Stimpson, Emily. *The Catholic Girl's Survival Guide for the Single Years: The Nuts and Bolts of Staying Sane and Happy While Waiting for Mr. Right*. Steubenville, Ohio: Emmaus Road, 2012.

Swafford, Sarah. *Emotional Virtue: A Guide to Drama-Free Relationships*. Lakewood, Colo: Totus Tuus Press, 2011.

Zimmerman, Davis, and Kari Shane. "In Control? The Hookup Culture and the Practice of Relationships." In *Leaving and Coming Home: New Wineskins for Catholic Sexual Ethics*, edited by David Cloutier, 47–61. Eugene, Ore.: Wipf and Stock, 2010.

MARRIAGE PREPARATION, WEDDINGS

Calis, Stephanie. *Invited: The Ultimate Catholic Wedding Planner*. Boston: Pauline Books and Media, 2016.

Giandurco, Joseph, and John Bonnici. *Partners in Life and Love: A Preparation Handbook for the Celebration of Catholic Marriage*. New York: Alba House, 2002.

Grabowski, John, and Claire Grabowski. *One Body: A Program of Marriage Formation for the New Evangelization*. Steubenville, Ohio: Emmaus Road, 2018.

Overbeck, T. Jeromem, and Rudy T. Marcozzi. *Preparing Your Catholic Wedding: Practical Considerations*. New York: Alba House, 2002.

Ruhnke, Robert A. CSSR. *For Better and For Ever: A Resource for Couples Preparing for Christian Marriage. Facilitator's Guide.* Rev. ed. San Antonio, Tex.: Marriage Preparation Resources, 2003.

White, Joseph D., and William Cashion III. *Together in God's Love: A Catholic Preparation for Marriage. Facililtator's Guide.* Rev. ed. Huntington, Ind.: Our Sunday Visitor, 2017.

THE THEOLOGY OF THE BODY

Anderson, Carl, and Jose Granados. *Called to Love: Approaching John Paul II's Theology of the Body.* New York: Doubleday, 2009.

Echeverria, Eduardo. *"In the Beginning...": A Theology of the Body.* Eugene, Ore.: Pickwick, 2011.

Healy, Mary. *Men and Women Are from Eden: A Study Guide to John Paul II's Theology of the Body.* Ann Arbor: Servant Books, 2005.

May, William E. *Theology of the Body: Genesis and Growth.* Boston: Pauline Books and Media, 2010.

Petri, Thomas, OP. *Aquinas and the Theology of the Body: The Thomistic Foundations of John Paul II's Anthropology.* Washington, D.C.: The Catholic University of America Press, 2015.

Schmitz, Kenneth. *At the Center of the Human Drama: The Philosophical Anthropology of Karol Wojtyla.* Washington, D.C.: The Catholic University of America Press, 1994.

Shivanandan, Mary. *Crossing the Threshold of Love: A New Vision of Marriage in the Light of John Paul's Anthropology.* Washington, D.C.: The Catholic University of America Press, 1999.

Sri, Edward. *Men, Women and the Mystery of Love: Practical Insights from John Paul II's Love and Responsibility.* Ann Arbor: Servant, 2007.

Stimpson, Emily. *These Beautiful Bones: An Everyday Theology of the Body.* Steubenville, Ohio. Emmaus Road, 2013.

West, Christopher. *Theology of the Body for Beginners: A Basic Introduction to Pope John Paul II's Sexual Revolution.* Rev. ed. West Chester, Pa.: Ascension: 2009.

Windley-Daoust, Susan. *Theology of the Body, Extended: The Spiritual Signs of Birth, Impairment and Dying.* Hobe Sound, Fla: Lectio, 2014.

Wojtyla, Karol. *Love and Responsibility.* Translated by Grzegorz Ignatik. Boston: Pauline Books and Media, 2013. Originally published in 1993.

MARRIAGE: THEOLOGY, LITURGY, LAW

Burke, Cormac. *The Theology of Marriage: Personalism, Doctrine and Canon Law*. Washington, D.C.: The Catholic University of America Press, 2015.

Cahall, Perry. *The Mystery of Marriage: A Theology of the Body and the Sacrament*. Chicago: Hillenbrand, 2016.

Elliot, Peter. *What God Has Joined: The Sacramentality of Marriage*. Eugene, Ore.: Wipf and Stock, 2010. Originally published in 1990.

Hauser, Daniel. *Marriage and Christian Life: A Theology of Christian Marriage*. Lanham, Md.: University Press of America, 2004.

Levering, Matthew, ed. *On Marriage and Family: Classic and Contemporary Texts*. Lanham, Md.: Sheed and Ward: 2005.

Ouellet, Marc. *Mystery and Sacrament of Love: A Theology of Marriage and the Family for the New Evangelization*. Translated by Michelle K. Borras and Adrian J. Walker. Grand Rapids: Eerdmans, 2015.

Schola, Angelo. *The Nuptial Mystery*. Translated by Michelle K. Borras. Ressourcement: Retrieval and Renewal in Catholic Thought. Grand Rapids: Eerdmans, 2005.

Von Hildebrand, Dietrich. *Marriage*. London: Longmans, Green, 1942.

MARRIAGE ENRICHMENT

Alexander, Greg, and Julie Alexander. *Marriage 911: How God Saved Our Marriage (and Can Save Yours, Too!)*. Ann Arbor: Servant, 2011.

Bosio, John. *Happy Together: The Catholic Blueprint for Loving Marriage*. Mystic, Conn.: Twenty-Third Publications, 2008.

———. *Blessed Is Marriage: A Guide to the Beatitudes for Catholic Couples*. New London, Conn.: Twenty-Third Publications, 2012.

Chapman, Gary. *The Five Love Languages: How to Express Heartfelt Commitment to Your Mate*. Chicago: Northfield, 1997.

Hahn, Kimberly. *Chosen and Cherished: Biblical Wisdom for Your Marriage*. Cincinnati: St. Anthony Messenger, 2007.

———. *Beloved and Blessed: Biblical Wisdom for Family Life*. Cincinnati: St. Anthony Messenger, 2010.

Hahn, Scott, and Regis J. Flaherty. *Catholic for a Reason*. Vol. 4, *Scripture and the Mystery of Marriage and Family Life*. Steubenville, Ohio: Emmaus Road, 2007.

Holbock, Ferdinand. *Married Saints and Blesseds through the Centuries*. Translated by Michael J. Miller. San Francisco: Ignatius Press, 2002.

Lenahan, Phil. *7 Steps to Becoming Financially Free: A Catholic Guide to Managing Your Money* (book and workbook). Huntington, Ind.: Our Sunday Visitor, 2006.

Popcak, Gregory. *Holy Sex: A Catholic Guide to Toe-Curling, Mind-Blowing, Infallible Loving.* New York: Crossroad, 2008.

Popcak, Gregory, and Lisa Popcak. *Just Married: The Catholic Guide to Surviving and Thriving in the First Five Years of Marriage.* Notre Dame, Ind.: Ave Maria, 2013.

———. *For Better Forever: A Catholic Guide to Lifelong Marriage.* Rev. ed. Huntington, Ind.: Our Sunday Visitor, 2015.

Smalley, Gary. *For Better or for Best: A Valuable Guide to Knowing, Understanding, and Loving Your Husband.* Grand Rapids: Zondervan, 2012.

Smalley, Gary, Deborah Smalley, and Greg Smalley. *Winning Your Wife Back before It's Too Late.* Nashville: Thomas Nelson, 2004.

Wuerl, Donald. *The Marriage God Wants for You.* Frederick, Md.: The Word Among Us: 2015.

CATHOLIC SEXUAL TEACHING
AND MORAL ISSUES

Abela, Andrew and Joseph Capizzi, eds. *A Catechism for Business: Tough Ethical Questions and Insights from Catholic Teaching.* Washington, D.C.: The Catholic University of America Press, 2014.

Bachiochi, Erika, ed. *Women, Sex, and the Church: A Case for Catholic Teaching.* Boston: Pauline Books and Media, 2010.

Benestad, J. Brian. *Church, State, and Society: An Introduction to Catholic Social Doctrine.* Catholic Moral Thought Series. Washington, D.C.: The Catholic University of America Press, 2011.

Grabowski, John. *Sex and Virtue: An Introduction to Sexual Ethics.* Catholic Moral Thought Series. Washington, D.C.: The Catholic University of America Press, 2003.

Harvey, John F., OFSF. *Homosexuality and the Catholic Church: Clear Answers to Difficult Questions.* West Chester, Pa.: Ascension, 2007.

Lawler, Ronald, OFM Cap., William May, and Joseph Boyle. *Catholic Sexual Ethics: A Summary, Explanation and Defense.* 3rd ed. Huntington, Ind.: Our Sunday Visitor Press, 2011.

Morse, Jennifer Roback. *Smart Sex: Finding Life-Long Love in a Hook-Up World.* Dallas: Spence, 2005.

Santamaria, Carmen, and Angelique Ruhi-Lopez. *The Infertility Companion for Catholics: Spiritual and Practical Support for Couples.* Notre Dame, Ind.: Ave Maria Press, 2012.

Smith, Janet, ed. *Why Humanae Vitae Was Right: A Reader.* San Francisco: Ignatius Press, 1993.

Smith, Janet, and Paul Check, eds. *Living the Truth in Love: Pastoral Approaches to Same-Sex Attraction.* San Francisco: Ignatius Press, 2015.

Therrien, Michel. "The Practice of Responsible Parenthood, NFP, and the Covenantal Unity of Spouses." In *Leaving and Coming Home: New Wineskins for Catholic Sexual Ethics,* edited by David Cloutier, 173–205. Eugene, Ore.: Wipf and Stock, 2010.

Von Hildebrand, Dietrich. *Purity: The Mystery of Christian Sexuality.* Steubenville, Ohio: Franciscan University Press, 1939. (Originally published as *In Defense of Purity* in 1938.)

Wojtyla, Karol. *Love and Responsibility.* Translated by Grzegorz Ignatik. Boston: Pauline Books and Media, 2013.

NFP AND FERTILITY RESOURCES

Couple to Couple League (symptom-thermal methods of fertility awareness). Accessed March 13, 2017. https://ccli.org/.

The Creighton Model Fertility Care System (Creighton model of the Billings method and NaPro Technology resources). Accessed March 13, 2017. http://www.creightonmodel.com/.

Marquette Model of NFP (uses Clearblue Easy Fertility Monitor). Accessed March 13, 2017. http://www.marquette.edu/nursing/natural-family-planning/model.shtml.

Pope Paul VI Institute for the Study of Human Reproduction (therapy for reproductive difficulties consistent with Catholic ethical teaching). Accessed April 26, 2017. http://www.popepaulvi.com/.

U.S. Conference of Catholic Bishops. "Natural Family Planning" (with links and resources). Accessed March 13, 2017. http://www.usccb.org/issues-and-action/marriage-and-family/natural-family-planning/.

FORMATION IN CHASTITY, PARENTING

Bonacci, Mary Beth. *Real Love: Answers to Your Questions on Dating, Marriage and the Real Meaning of Sex.* San Francisco: Ignatius Press, 1996.

Butler, Brian, Jason Evert, and Crystalina Evert. *Theology of the Body for Teens.* Westchester, Pa.: Ascension, 2006.

Dobson, James. *The New Strong-Willed Child*. Carol Stream, Ill.: Tyndale, 2007.

Evert, Jason, and Chris Stefanik. *Raising Pure Teens*. El Cajon, Calif.: Catholic Answers Press, 2010.

Finley, Kathleen. *The Liturgy of Motherhood: Moments of Grace*. Lanham, Md.: Rowman and Littlefield, 2004.

Hahn, Scott. *First Comes Love: Finding Your Family in the Church and the Trinity*. New York: Doubleday, 2002.

Kelly, Matthew. *Building Better Families: A Practical Guide to Raising Amazing Children*. New York: Ballantine, 2008.

Kleponis, Peter. *Integrity Restored: Helping Catholic Families Win the Battle against Pornography*. Steubenville, Ohio: Emmaus Road, 2014.

Lewis, C. S. *The Four Loves*. New York: Harcourt, Brace, Jovanovich, 1960.

Murphy, Ann, and John Murphy. *Sex Education and Successful Parenting*. Boston: Pauline Books and Media, 1996.

Popcak, Gregory, and Lisa Popcak. *Parenting with Grace*. 2nd ed. Huntington, Ind.: Our Sunday Visitor, 2010.

Santos, Manuel, and Karee Santos. *The Four Keys to Everlasting Love: How Your Catholic Marriage Can Bring You Joy for a Lifetime*. Notre Dame, Ind.: Ave Maria Press, 2016.

Sheen, Fulton. *Children and Parents: Wisdom and Guidance for Parents*. New York: IVE Press, 2009.

Wilson, Mercedes Arzû. *Love and Family: Raising a Traditional Family in a Secular World*. San Francisco: Ignatius Press, 1996.

Index

Abortion, 20, 94, 107–8, 113, 116, 121, 217

Adolescence, 45, 127, 233

Adoption, 38, 94, 120–21, 215–16, 248

Agape, 44, 56, 57

Ambrose, St., 163

Augustine, St., 126, 128, 178

Authority: over body of spouse, 101; of the Church, xix, 53, 72, 81, 100, 105; of God, 246; of Jesus Christ, 16; to leave spouse in case of abuse, 183; of parents, 3, 118, 151; public, 18, 106

Baptism: annotated in Church's registers, 96; and call to be missionary disciples, 232; connected to the sacrament of marriage, 21, 31, 40, 64, 201, 225; and disordered desires, 70; and faith formation in the home, 126, 226; and mixed marriage, 51, 55–54, 234; as nuptial mystery, 23

Birth: analogy for baptism, 126; awaited by God with joy, 115; the Church gives birth to its children, 223, 226, 238; and difficulties adjusting to needs of new child, 76, 96; and duty of parents to educate offspring, 128; and family's role in life of its members, 214; and fathers, 118, 136; a mother's spiritual

preparation for, 116; mystery of, 117; spacing births, 99–100, 111–12. *See also* Natural family planning

Birth control, 107. *See also* Contraception

Blessed Virgin Mary: cared for by St. Joseph, 148; example of holiness, 230; as mother of Jesus, 116, 119, 240; and the rosary, 227, 229; sanctification of her holy days, 230, 240; source of consolation for families in difficulty, 8, 182

Breastfeeding, 122, 123

Brothers and sisters, 97, 127, 156, 233

Catechesis, 61, 71, 210, 233, 243; family catechesis, 126, 127, 130, 233, 245

Catholic social doctrine, 17, 216

Charity, 18, 28, 70, 164, 181–82, 194, 106, 202, 221, 231; in marriage 31, 35, 39, 41, 89, 94, 102, 109

Chastity: homosexual persons called to, 206; marital, 41, 100; in marriage preparation, 64; parents educating children for, 131, 134, 172; a training in freedom, 40

Child: a gift from God even when unwanted, 119; a human being of immense worth, 113; in structure of the Christian family, 9, 30, 37, 155, 156, 242; wrongly seen as enemy to adults, 6, 124, 130

*A Catechism for Business: Tough Ethical
Questions and Insights from Catholic Teaching,* 2nd edition
Edited by Andrew V. Abela and Joseph E. Capizzi

Translated into Spanish by Francisco J. Lara as
*Un Catecismo para los Negocios: Respuestas de La Enseñanza
Católica a Los Dilemas Éticos de la Empresa,*
Segunda Edición

*Handbook of Catholic Social Teaching:
A Guide for Christians in the World Today*
Edited by Martin Schlag. Foreword by
Peter K. A. Cardinal Turkson

Called to Holiness: On Love, Vocation, and Formation
Pope Emeritus Benedict XVI. Edited by Pietro Rossotti

The Light of Christ: An Introduction to Catholicism
Thomas Joseph White, OP

*The Business Francis Means: Understanding the
Pope's Message on the Economy*
Martin Schlag

The Quotable Augustine
Saint Augustine. Foreword by James V. Schall, SJ

*Biblical and Theological Foundations of
the Family: The Domestic Church*
Joseph C. Atkinson

*The Theology of Marriage:
Personalism, Doctrine and Canon Law*
Cormac Burke

A Catechism for Family Life: Insights from Catholic Teaching on Love, Marriage, Sex, and Parenting was designed in Arno with Hypatia Sans display type and composed by Kachergis Book Design of Pittsboro, North Carolina. It was printed on 60-pound House Natural Smooth and bound by Sheridan Books of Chelsea, Michigan.